NARRATING TRAUMA

NARRATING TRAUMA

Victorian Novels and Modern Stress Disorders

~

Gretchen Braun

THE OHIO STATE UNIVERSITY PRESS

COLUMBUS

Library of Congress Cataloging-in-Publication Data
Names: Braun, Gretchen, author.
Title: Narrating trauma : Victorian novels and modern stress disorders / Gretchen Braun.
Description: Columbus : The Ohio State University Press, [2022] | Includes bibliographical
    references and index. | Summary: "Examines the pre-history of psychic and somatic
    responses to trauma known as PTSD as they influence canonical and lesser-known
    Victorian novels by Charlotte Brontë, Emily Jolly, Wilkie Collins, George Eliot, Charles
    Dickens, and Thomas Hardy"—Provided by publisher.
Identifiers: LCCN 2021059310 | ISBN 9780814214848 (cloth) | ISBN 0814214843 (cloth) |
    ISBN 9780814282090 (ebook) | ISBN 0814282091 (ebook)
Subjects: LCSH: Brontë, Charlotte, 1816–1855—Criticism and interpretation. | Jolly, Emily—
    Criticism and interpretation. | Collins, Wilkie, 1824–1889—Criticism and interpretation.
    | Eliot, George, 1819–1880—Criticism and interpretation. | Dickens, Charles, 1812–
    1870—Criticism and interpretation. | Hardy, Thomas, 1840–1928—Criticism and
    interpretation. | English fiction—19th century—History and criticism. | Psychic trauma
    in literature. | Narration (Rhetoric)—History—19th century. | BISAC: LITERARY
    CRITICISM / Modern / 19th Century | LITERARY CRITICISM / Gothic & Romance
Classification: LCC PR878.P737 B73 2022 | DDC 823/.8093561—dc23/eng/20220310
LC record available at https://lccn.loc.gov/2021059310
Other identifiers: ISBN 9780814258323 (paper) | ISBN 0814214843 (paper)

Cover design by Jordan Wannemacher
Text design by Juliet Williams
Type set in Adobe Minion Pro

CONTENTS

ACKNOWLEDGMENTS

∼

This book profits from the generosity and insights of many people. I am grateful to Liz Constable, Peter Dale, and Parama Roy for helpful and incisive feedback on early versions of this project. Jennifer Jones also contributed important perspective.

I have benefited tremendously from working among talented colleagues at Furman University. The Department of English has offered invaluable opportunities in teaching Victorian literature and culture that enriched the arc of this project. I am always grateful to my colleagues in the Women's, Gender, and Sexuality Studies Program for our collaborative intellectual exchange. Among Furman colleagues I wish to particularly thank David Bost, Carolyn Day, Mary Alice Kirkpatrick, Ilka Rasch, and especially Lynne Shackelford for steady encouragement of this work. Furman sabbatical leave and a Research and Professional Growth Grant made archival visits possible, and a Furman Humanities Center Book Grant was crucial in the final stages.

My work on this project has coincided with the supervision of several undergraduate research students, and their varied scholarly investigations into gender, sexuality, trauma, and narrative have productively intersected with my own in countless conversations. Thanks to Sam Cannon, Margaret Shelton, and Devin Zhang for sharing the intellectual journey.

This project has benefitted immeasurably from the use of archival materials housed in Rare Books at Cambridge University, the Evanion Collection at the British Library, Special Collections at the University of California at Davis, the Wellcome Collection, and of course Special Collections at Furman University. Particular thanks to Furman University archivist Jeffrey Makala for his support of both student and faculty research.

Earlier versions of some material from chapters 2 and 3 have appeared in *ELH, Pacific Coast Philology,* and *Women's Studies: An Interdisciplinary Journal,* and I appreciate the opportunity to reprint.

My acknowledgments would not be complete without enthusiastic and heartfelt thanks to the Victorians Institute. I have particular gratitude to Keaghan Turner for years of camaraderie and intellectual dialogue.

Finally, of course, I thank my family: Mollie, Charles, Kurt, and Audrey. TJ Banisaukas has done much to make this project possible, and has my endless gratitude for his patience and unflagging support.

Nervous Disorder, Narrative Disorder, and Perspectives from the Margins

How to represent mental pain in culturally legible terms is at once a practical question and an ethical one. This study opens with two interrelated claims. First, our understanding of Victorian literary representations of psychic disorder is enriched through consideration of medico-scientific contexts that shaped the language nineteenth-century people used for their mental pain. Second, Victorian formulations of psychic injury, which foreground diffuse and anticipated harm, can invigorate our current thinking on psychic trauma. The nineteenth century saw the emergence of psychiatry, psychology, and neurology as professional fields and the beginnings of the commercialization and popularization of mental health care that are now familiar. By the fin de siècle, "neurasthenia," an ambiguously psychological and somatic ailment ascribed to nervous dysfunction, was sufficiently common parlance to give A. Mary F. Robinson's poem its title:

I watch the happier people of the house
    Come in and out, and talk, and go their ways;
I sit and gaze at them; I cannot rouse
    My heavy mind to share their busy days.

I watch them glide, like skaters on a stream,
    Across the brilliant surface of the world.

But I am underneath: they do not dream
How deep below the eddying flood is whirl'd.

They cannot come to me, nor I to them;
    But if a mightier arm could reach and save,
Should I forget the tide I had to stem?
    Should I, like these, ignore the abysmal wave?

Yes! in the radiant air how could I know
How black it is, how fast it is, below?

Concerns of perspective and empathy animate this 1888 sonnet: How can "the happier people" possibly grasp the experience of those socially isolated by immovable mental constraints? This new disorder, along with related illnesses such as hysteria and catchall diagnoses like "nervous exhaustion" and "nerves," typified Victorian cultural and scientific anxieties about the strains modern socioeconomic systems placed upon the embodied mind. Modern scholars have read nineteenth-century nervous disorders as precursors to current diagnoses such as depression, post-traumatic stress disorder, and chronic fatigue syndrome, and at least one Victorian disorder, anorexia nervosa, remains relevant in today's psychiatry. These are disorders of the borderline, socially and physically restrictive, but, unlike extreme forms of psychosis, not conducive to total exclusion. Robinson's speaker vividly articulates the sense of bodily as well as mental limitation nervous disorder could engender. The speaker is not irrational or socially disconnected, but she is doomed to remain a peripheral onlooker in the daily life of her household, incapable not only of participating, but also of fully empathizing with the emotional investments of her healthier peers. The metaphor of cold depths beneath the frozen river communicates simultaneously the division, and interdependence, of the sick and the well. The "glittering surface" of the social world where the fortunate "skaters" enjoy mobility and autonomy cannot exist without the "eddying flood" of misery where the neurasthenic is trapped below. The connection is structural. Robinson's poem does not engage the causation of this illness, but physicians ascribed neurasthenia to socioeconomic stressors intensified by the Victorian advent of industrial capitalism and consequent urbanization. The three questions closing the poem articulate the speaker's simultaneous longing for understanding and acknowledgment of the enormous difficulty of bridging the gulf between ailing and healthy, unfortunate and lucky. She is aware that one's position determines what one can see—and feel.

Robinson's fin de siècle sonnet offers a pessimistic assessment of a problem earlier nineteenth-century narrative fiction attempted to mediate: How can literature create meaningful empathy, or at least understanding, between the marginalized and the privileged? As the nineteenth century proceeded, the industrial revolution offered dramatic opportunities for individual socioeconomic advancement, but it also engendered abject poverty and labor unrest. Related urbanization enlivened social life yet intensified its anxieties. Gender roles became increasingly binarized, and even as women gained literary recognition in larger numbers, their economic opportunities outside marriage were limited and their legal autonomy precarious. Fiction increasingly focused on interiority and self-development of characters, with the bildungsroman becoming a dominant literary form. But even as an increasingly literate populace eagerly consumed stories of self-actualization, many individuals whose gender and class limited their agency must surely have struggled to fully identify with the heroes of triumphant fictional accounts of individual success and community integration. How could the stories of people marginalized and damaged by the era's sweeping socioeconomic changes fit within a developmental narrative paradigm?

Advances in the science of the mind offered Victorian novelists a vocabulary and logic for adapting accepted narratives of self-development to accommodate marginalized perspectives. As they did so, these novelists, some quite versed in nascent psychiatry, contributed to scientific debates about cognition and psychic injury and, as Jill Matus has persuasively argued, forwarded understanding of what we now term "psychic trauma." In Robinson's neurasthenic speaker, we see emotional patterns that align with current clinical accounts of post-traumatic stress disorder (PTSD): As the pioneering twentieth- and twenty-first-century trauma researcher Bessel van der Kolk explains, "being traumatized is not just an issue of being stuck in the past; it is just as much a problem of not being fully alive in the present" (223). Victorian diagnoses including "traumatic neurasthenia," "rail spine," and the better-remembered category of "hysteria" represent an earlier clinical mode of defining the physiological experience of being disconnected from social networks, normative emotional responses, and even sensory experience in the wake of a distressing or threatening shock. I do not view Victorian nervous disorders as analogous with our contemporary PTSD (or any other twenty-first-century mental illness)—they are intimately bound to their own cultural location. But I do regard nervous disorders as providing nineteenth-century laypeople, as well as physicians, with language to describe affective, emotional, and physiological experiences of overwhelming loss or threat, and as such, offering contemporary scholars a prehistory of PTSD within Victorian cultural contexts. Nervous disorders not only provided Victorian physicians with medical explanations for ambiguously psychic and somatic suffering, but also generated cultural and literary language for harm materially felt yet difficult to define. The Victorian concept of nervous disorder encompassed both emotional unrest and somatic symptoms, and was ascribed primarily to the influence of environment, rather than any specific material cause or visible wound. Distinctly classed and gendered experiences were often precipitating factors: A genteelly impoverished governess gives way under her daily strain, a maiden lady collapses after years of dutifully nursing a dying parent, an ambitious businessman falls ill when a scheme for profit fails.

A few quick novelistic comparisons point up the way the nervously disordered protagonist challenges developmental mandates of the realist novel. Compare the halting progress and acerbic, evasive narration of Charlotte Brontë's Lucy Snowe in *Villette* to the triumphant upward arc and engaging directness of her earlier *Jane Eyre*; contrast Pip's social isolation and bankruptcy as *Great Expectations* draws to a close with the titular hero David Copperfield's commercial success and bourgeois domestic comfort. Lucy and Pip both display recognizable markers of what Victorian doctors would term nervous disorder, and both, significantly, have vexed relationships with their class and gender roles. Jane, whose inheritance helps facilitate aristocratic marriage, and David, whose professional talent enables reclamation of his gentlemanly social position, actualize progressive narratives. As protagonists and narrators, Lucy and Pip continually revisit a sense of injury that carries with it anger (Lucy), shame (Pip), and a constant awareness of threat and loss. Brontë and Dickens write very different novels when a nervously disordered and socially marginalized protagonist directs the story.

It is no coincidence that while both female and male examples of the nervously disordered protagonist can be found in Victorian novels, women predominate. Medical concern for men's "nerves" was commonplace, despite the prominence of feminine hysteria in our cultural memory. But in the literary imaginary, female characters were noticeably likelier than male to display so-called nervous susceptibility. Similarly, cross-disciplinary feminist scholarship on the nineteenth century has long since demonstrated how frequently "madness" and social disorder were coded feminine in artistic and cultural representations: particularly Sandra Gilbert and Susan Gubar's *The Madwoman in the Attic: The Woman Writer and the Nineteenth Century Literary Imagination* (1979), Elaine Showalter's *The Female Malady: Women, Madness, and English Culture, 1830–1980* (1980), and Lynda Nead's *Myths of Sexuality: Representations of Women in Victorian Britain* (1988). My study departs the path of this foundational work in distinguishing nervous disorder, a border-line ailment between reason and unreason, from the more debilitating forms of psychosis that commonly precipitated institutionalization or required constant familial monitoring. A question arises: If Victorian doctors feared for the nerves of men and women both, why did female protagonists so markedly outstrip male in novelistic representations of nervous illness?

I suggest the answer lies in formal shortcomings of traditional nineteenth-century plot structures to fit the contours of women's development in a self-consciously modernizing era. One of the most common forms for telling women's domestic stories, of course, is the marriage plot, which Elsie B. Michie calls "a mythic structure that articulates modes of thinking characteristic of life in nineteenth-century England" (6). Originating in the mid-eighteenth century when individual choice in matrimony became more typical, it was perfected and popularized around the turn of the nineteenth century by Jane Austen. Critical discourse on the marriage plot has explored symbolic valences that attach to different character positions, interactions, and trajectories within it. Jean Kennard usefully delineated the "two suitors" marriage plot as follows: As she matures, the female protagonist must choose between "the unscrupulous or 'wrong' suitor and the exemplary or 'right' suitor," who respectively embody the values the heroine must reject and those she must accept to demonstrate growth and worthiness of social inclusion (11). Kennard argues that this "structural convention" creates conflict in Victorian novels, as a more complicated understanding of female maturity enters public discourse (10–11). Turning from second-wave accounts centered on women's oppression and resistance, Nancy Armstrong refocused attention on how domestic novels such as *Pamela* and *Emma* centered and normalized autonomous middle-class female subjectivity, thereby developing political discourse. Armstrong claims that "the novel . . . helped to redefine what men were supposed to desire in women and what women, in turn, were supposed to desire to be" (*Desire* 251). More recently, critics have examined the role of eighteenth- and nineteenth-century novels centered on matrimonial choice in documenting and defining kinship structures: marriage as separation from family of origin; alternatively, as solidification of in-group bonds; as outcome and amplifier of amicable bonds between women.[1]

The marriage plot provides a discourse space for negotiation of the balance between individuality and group integration, and facilitates interrogation

---

1. See Ruth Perry, *Novel Relations: The Transformation of Kinship in English Literature and Culture 1748–1818* (2004); Mary Jean Corbett, *Family Likeness: Sex, Marriage, and Incest from Jane Austen to Virginia Woolf* (2008); and Sharon Marcus, *Between Women: Friendship, Desire, and Marriage in Victorian England* (2007).

of the ethical implications of economic choices. Michie has analyzed how the marriage plot structure codes cultural values associated with the use of wealth through contrasting figures of the rich and poor woman: In valorizing the matrimonial choice presented as poor but worthy, the marriage plot promotes and naturalizes altruistic values (3–8). Talia Schaffer further complicates our understanding of what nineteenth-century reading audiences would regard as the "right" choice. Contextualizing the marriage plot within the deeper history of cultural and legal changes to matrimony, Schaffer contends that competing alternatives within the Victorian marriage plot signified not necessarily right or wrong choices, but different visions of selfhood: autonomous and individuated or relational and networked (*Romance's Rival* 23). Schaffer argues that "nineteenth century marriage plots are consumed with the question of what feeling constitutes an appropriate basis for marriage" (68), which may be romantic love, but may instead be mutual esteem and pragmatic interest in securing broader life choices that are safe and satisfying. Marriage plots distill lifelong values into one climactic decision.

In order to do its symbolic work, the marriage plot as written in long-nineteenth-century Great Britain offers a narrowly circumscribed vision of women's experience, focused overwhelmingly on positions of privilege. What counts as being "poor" in a marriage plot novel is, obviously, rather different from what constituted poverty in everyday British society during the period of the genre's greatest popularity. Austen's Dashwood sisters are disinherited by entailment, but they do not engage in exhausting and dispiriting governess work or seamstressing, much less toil in a factory. Of course, beyond those genteel women who lacked financial and social resources for basic marriage marketability, there were working-class and impoverished women for whom marital, care, and sexual relationships were often predicated on practical exigencies; there were colonial subjects excluded from or exploited within British kinship structures. There are also the wide range of experiences that would follow "Reader, I married him": cohabitation, sexuality, childbirth, parenting, aging, the loss of a child or the stigma of infertility.

The common form for stories of men's entry into broader society, the bildungsroman, did not comprehend all life trajectories for Victorian men and was limited by class, but the marriage plot was even more tightly restricted, having no place or language for many common and formative female experiences. In attending to nervously disordered female protagonists, I discuss novels that seek to expand this range: by adapting bildungsroman elements for women characters restricted in their exploration of educational and professional worlds, and by referencing the marriage plot but with significant adjustments, notably, downplaying the centrality of courtship and romantic love. The simultaneous autonomy and social acceptance sought by the psy-chically damaged female characters whose stories compose my study cannot be located within any one romantic or marital relationship. Further, all face practical and especially economic obstacles to the kind of matrimonial union to which an Austen heroine (and even, ultimately, Jane Eyre) aspires. In a Vic-torian context, nervous disorder, understood as the product of environmental and interpersonal stressors, was a plausible consequence of socioeconomic marginality. It is significant that noteworthy examples of nineteenth-century British bildungsroman featuring nervously disordered male protagonists focus on ambitious working-class men: *Great Expectations* and *Jude the Obscure.* Like women of all classes, Victorian working-class men had limited outlets for their aspirations. The ambitious working-class man, like the genteel spin-ster forced to earn her keep, unsettled entrenched socioeconomic and cultural systems. Pip, like Lucy Snowe, does not comfortably fit within standard realist novelistic forms.

The bildungsroman may be broadly understood as the novel of self-development; in its eighteenth- and nineteenth-century British and European manifestations, its focus was the growth and education (intellectual, social, and moral) of a young man as he left the home and explored wider worlds.[2] Peter Brooks aligns its hero's ambition, moving through expanding socioeco-nomic and geographical spaces toward maturity, with the reader's own desire to construct meaning (39). Critical discourse tends to treat the bildungsroman as inextricable from the history of literary realism, although this might be contested. Since Franco Moretti's influential *The Way of the World: The Bil-dungsroman and European Culture* (1987), the traditional European bildungs-roman has widely been understood as the symbolic form of modernity under emergent industrial capitalism: exploring while delimiting the mobility and interiority of a bourgeois youth as he journeys toward mature social integra-tion (3–6). Despite its implied celebration of individualist agency, the tradi-tional nineteenth-century bildungsroman enforces normalcy through social assimilation and polices bodily and behavioral difference (Ehnenn 154–55).

Middle-class women of this era lacked access to the milieu of professional ambition, relative sexual freedom, and ready mobility where Julien Sorel, Wil-helm Meister, and David Copperfield sojourn toward maturity. As Aleksandar Stević writes, "the heroes of the male *bildungsroman* may routinely fail to con-quer the world, but they are at least invited to try" (78). Sara E. Maier explains that "a male *bildungsroman* is a conservative projection of the boy-child into

---

2. For a concise definition, see Fritz Martini, "*Bildungsroman*: Term and Theory," in James Hardin (ed.), *Reflection and Action: Essays on the Bildungsroman, University of South Carolina Press*, 1991, pp. 1–25.

male adulthood, following the necessary steps for education, growth and citizenry. For a [nineteenth-century] girl-child to take that same path would, in fact, be extraordinarily progressive, and be an invitation to personal development beyond social accomplishments and wifehood" (319). In practice, the self-assertion and independence characteristic of the bildungsroman hero were discouraged in Victorian girls, who were trained instead in the passivity deemed appropriate for marriage (Maier 319). Nineteenth-century novels centered on female protagonists have certainly been read within or in dialogue with the bildungsroman tradition, including some, such as *Pride and Prejudice* and *Jane Eyre*, that critics typically or occasionally align with the marriage plot. But as Maier argues, "a female novel of development" in this era "cannot possibly be linear"; it tracks its protagonist's self-reflective negotiation with and against social forces that limit, rather than encourage, her impulse toward creative expression (333). Even a Victorian female character situated within comparative privilege cannot readily claim the traditional bildungsroman protagonist's characteristic forward momentum and cohesive self-development.

While the nineteenth-century bildungsroman and marriage plot place limitations on the range of stories that can be told about any man or woman, their focus on goal-directed forward motion, orderly resolution, and social integration present particular impediments to communicating the experience of a psychically damaged and economically marginalized individual. An author who selects a socially marginalized character as a central protagonist of a Victorian novel faces a complex negotiation. How might an unconventional heroine fit into the narrative situations available to female characters in the nineteenth century? What resolutions are possible for a hero whose ambitions defy societal standards? How might the development of a disruptive, rather than a socially normative, psyche be made sympathetic and appealing to a broad audience?

The novels my study comprises attempt to do so by integrating their modernity's prototypical malady, nervous disorder, with elements of its most powerful narrative of self-assertion, the bildungsroman. Nervous disorder speaks to inevitable hazards attendant on modernization. This malady produces fragility and extreme emotionality, qualities Victorians coded feminine. In contrast, the bildungsroman expresses the modern potential for self-definition. It is linked to disciplined vitality and the spirit of exploration, which Victorians coded masculine. The protagonist I term "the traumatized and transgressive heroine" is prevented from direct self-assertion not only by the emotionally shattering force of her loss or threat, but also by her socially peripheral position. Therefore, unlike more conventional protagonists, she cannot follow an even path toward maturity. She must instead take a circu-itous, halting route toward social participation and psychic unity. She seeks an empathetic interlocutor (both within the novel's imagined world and in the reader) to provide social validation for her emotional life. Yet she recoils from scrutiny, aware that her social marginality might become total exclusion if her negative emotions (such as grief and anger) become too disruptive of commu-nity standards. As a result, the story of her developing psyche cannot follow the steady progression toward satisfying closure that typifies both the mar-riage plot and the nineteenth-century bildungsroman. Her narrative is instead characterized by the repetitions, omissions, and evasions common to psychic trauma. The related male plot I discuss as the story of the "self-unmade man" results when masculine ambition, the driving force of the traditional bildungs-roman, is pathologized and turns back on itself. In the mid-to-late Victorian articulation of neurasthenia, excessive masculine ambition was feared to degenerate into its opposite, feminized submission and indecision. A neuras-thenic male protagonist produces a narrative that, rather than building toward mature social integration, loops back to its origins without meaningful psy-chological or economic progress.

The social boundary crossing of the traumatized and transgressive hero-ine and the self-unmade man is not necessarily intentional or adaptive. I do not argue that the defiance of gender norms exhibited by these characters rep-resents a conscious or successful strategy of feminist empowerment or gender neutrality, either for the character in the novel's imagined world or on the part of the author navigating a professional relationship with readers and publish-ers. Rather, I posit that masculinized behaviors such as Lucy Snowe's acerbic criticism and Gwendolen Harleth's imperious bullying are best understood within the broader pattern of a coping strategy in response to gendered and classed experiences of overwhelming threat or loss: a behavioral and physi-ological response that also includes Lucy's and Gwendolen's intermittent hys-teric outbursts and cautious returns to relationships of emotional intimacy. In modern clinical parlance, these patterns are described as a trauma response; in a Victorian context, they would be understood through the medical lens of nervous disorder. Allowing such characters to direct the narrative and shape how readers see the novel's imagined world, Victorian authors train their readership to perceive and critique the gendered experiences of struc-tural oppression that incite these patterns, such as Lucy's genteel poverty and Gwendolen's economic disempowerment as stepdaughter then wife without settlement. Of course, we should take under advisement Suzanne Keen's cau-tions that empathy may be more readily developed through fiction precisely because novels make no demand upon readers' action, and "the ongoingness of a fictional situation (never really over because never really occurring)" is in part why fiction lends itself to empathetic identification (*Empathy* 4, 79). I do not argue that novels featuring a nervously disordered, marginalized protagonist necessarily materially improved the lives of similarly circumstanced individuals; rather, I make the more modest claim that such novels facilitated mainstream discourse on those experiences and perspectives.

Beyond the symptomology of nervous disorder, the common thread uniting these disparate fictions is that each features a protagonist whose life experiences are in some way culturally unspeakable, and who therefore exists on the margins of Victorian social legibility. A rape victim (Jolly's Lady Ana), an abused aristocratic wife (Eliot's Gwendolen Harleth), an illegitimate daughter (Collins's Magdalen Vanstone)—these individuals, like the genteel spinster-governess and the ambitious working-class man, are defined (against their will) by a subject position that inherently threatens the bourgeois domesticity Victorian culture normalized. Economic circumstances and class position intersect with gender to make the character socially peripheral: For example, a wife's loss of legal personhood and control of property obliges Gwendolen to tolerate Grandcourt's sexual and psychic torment. To be clear, I recognize in the Victorian era a far wider range of psychically harmful experiences related to structural disempowerment, particularly connected to poverty and colonization, than this study attempts to survey. In order to accommodate breadth of time frame and fictional genre, and address both feminine and masculine experiences, I tighten my focus on characters adjacent to, but not comfortably situated within, conventional middle-class economic and cultural privilege. Although diagnosed across class levels, nineteenth-century nervous disorder was associated with stressors and ambitions of middle-class lifestyles, so characters struggling to maintain or establish middle-class identity present an apt ground to explore its cultural meanings. I am particularly interested in the position of nervously disordered protagonists, as opposed to minor characters or antagonists, and in how the content and form of fiction evolve as an author centers this character's experience and perceptions.

Restoring the medical context that would be obvious to Victorian readers allows us better to appreciate nuances of these novelistic critiques and define how their plots revise standard narratives of self-development. Eighteenth- and nineteenth-century medicine is rife with accounts of nervous disorders, frequently feminized (not necessarily female) ailments. Within the Victorian era, the broad category of "functional nervous disorders" or "neuroses" encompassed a range of ailments ascribed to failures of the nervous system not structurally identified, although assumed to have physiological basis (Oppenheim 8). According to historian Janet Oppenheim, "nervous" in

Victorian medical parlance "referred only to the structure and activities of the nerves, but the popular meaning dealt with personality traits and conveyed edginess, agitation, and irritability" (9). The discourse of nervous disorder presented an ideal vehicle for Victorian novelists seeking to explore the perspective of the marginalized subject in an empathetic way. The nervous sufferer was at odds with his or her social and material environment, and registered, in illness, its harmful effects. Yet unlike the diagnosed maniac or lunatic, the nervous sufferer was not branded dangerous or even, necessarily, irrational. In contrast with those confined to asylums for mania or delusions, most nervous sufferers could take part, at least peripherally, in community life: like the speaker of Robinson's poem, who witnesses activity with which they cannot emotionally connect. The nervous sufferer is inherently liminal, poised between normative and pathologized, socially involved and excluded. In efforts to make meaningful social contact with a damaging world, the nervous sufferer produces a vacillating narrative that fragments more traditional novelistic patterns. Whereas late-twentieth- and twenty-first-century discourse on psychic trauma has often foregrounded the catastrophic (genocide, war, terrorism), Victorian formulations of nervous disorder offer a model of psychic injury that highlights the impact of more diffuse social and material threats to the psyche, calling to our attention the insidious traumas at the charged conjunction of gender and class marginality.

While I affirm fundamental consistency in the narrative patterns characteristic of trauma, including fragmentation, repetition, and gaps, this book does not view clinical PTSD or related psychiatric disorders as static transhistorical phenomena. Rather, it accepts historian Joan Jacobs Brumberg's assertion that "even when illness is organic, being sick is a social act" (8). The experience and expression of psychic and even physical pain is inevitably mediated and channeled by cultural forms, particular to gender, class, age, and ethnicity; not only the physician's, but also the patient's perception of the illness is influenced by nonorganic and nonobjective factors (Brumberg 8). Given that interplay between biological and social factors in traumatic stress response is now widely acknowledged in the medical community, it is even more important for scholars to recognize historical and cultural variations in discussions of PTSD than in retrospective studies of more strictly biological illnesses. As neuroscientist-turned-literary-critic Laura Otis argues, "whether or not emotions involve more than physiology, and whether or not people experience them as enduring selves, emotions are social phenomena" (13). Undoubtedly, the condition we term PTSD and its diagnostic precursors entail both emotional (not just prediscursively affective) experiences and assessable bodily symptoms (for instance, elevated heart rate).

It is doubtless the case that some historically distant diagnostic categories were not only inaccurate from a physiological standpoint, but were also mobilized to support oppressive regimes with regard to gender, sexuality, and race. While less stigmatizing than other mental disorders, nervous diagnoses could be used not only to disparage certain populations, but sometimes to warehouse individuals whose families found them economically or socially inconvenient, in the absence of discernable psychiatric symptoms, let alone mental distress severe enough to warrant institutionalization.[3] However, social control is not the only purpose these diagnoses served. They were also employed to describe genuine experiences of felt pain and distress. Historians and sociologists trace an arc of meaningful connection, as well as change, between nineteenth-century and contemporary descriptions of psychological injury. Attending to the different ways laypeople and physicians have described psychological injury over time offers insight into shifting cultural values and material life circumstances.

We may regard variation in medical descriptions of trauma response across eras not necessarily as misdiagnosis or malingering, but as genuine changes in how overwhelming threat affects human physiology and psychology and becomes culturally visible. For instance, with regard to the combat trauma that was the predecessor of our contemporary PTSD diagnosis, we find different symptomology in soldiers seeking medical treatment during the First and Second World Wars. As sociologist Allan V. Horwitz reports, combatants in the Great War diagnosed with "shell shock" suffered apparently psychosomatic symptoms such as "hysterical deafness, muteness, blindness, paralysis of limbs, and violent tremors" in addition to memory loss and sleep disruption (53–54). Materially inexplicable somatic symptoms and memory problems were aspects of hysteria, a familiar, though feminized ailment for the young men who fought in the trenches at the beginning of the twentieth century. Their mental distress presented in a manner legible within Edwardian culture, influenced by the prevalence of hysteria in Victorian popular and medical discourse. Nearing mid-century, classic hysteria had been diagnostically eclipsed by other forms of psychiatric illness, and lacked the cultural familiarity it once commanded. Psychiatric combat casualties of the Second World War, Horwitz outlines, displayed an "almost complete absence of the hysterical symptoms that had marked so many soldiers during the previous world war" (69), instead presenting "anxious and depressive symptoms" similar to what

---

3. In her analysis of asylum records, *Lost Souls: Women, Religion and Mental Illness in the Victorian Asylum* (2020), Diana Peschier documents the use of hysteria and other psychiatric diagnoses to justify admission of working-class women whose ailments were clearly physical, such as cancer.

clinicians commonly observed in civilian culture of that period (69–70). The experience of psychic trauma, as a clinical phenomenon, is shaped by cultural factors, even more so than are strictly biological illnesses such as influenza or cancer.

This is not to deny empirical evidence that trauma response produces physiological symptoms and measurable changes in the brain, as late-twentieth- and twenty-first-century neuroscience has shown.[4] However, a discussion of psychic trauma within a particular historical period and cultural location should recognize that experiences individuals find overwhelming, intolerable, or threatening to self-identity are defined by contemporary social norms. I am inclined to accord with Horwitz's claim that "even if PTSD has a neurological basis, history shows that any biological substructure must have an interpretive superstructure that shapes the manifest presentations of the constantly changing symptoms of this condition" (183). The physical changes and affective/emotional patterns we now classify as post-traumatic stress disorder are always experienced, and described, through language available to the sufferer by cultural background. A subject's interpretation of his or her symptoms will be further guided and delimited by professional structures and trends of contemporaneous medicine (for example, the neuroscientific bent of psychiatry from the 1980s onward) and by economic factors that encourage or discourage the public acknowledgment of suffering (such as the newfound possibility of securing compensation for British rail accident victims in the 1860s, in contrast with the lack of pension for psychiatric casualties of the US Civil War).

Recognizing the variability of traumatic experience (or mental illness more broadly) across cultures and historical periods does not mean discounting the validity of claims to mental suffering or their connection to material changes in brain function. As medical historian Jonathan Sadowsky affirms, "culture-bound illnesses are as real as any other" (18). *Narrating Trauma* situates psychic injuries within relevant social contexts for the purpose of analysis. Central to this project is an acknowledgment that although nineteenth-century discourse of nervous disorder offers a medical and cultural prehistory of PTSD (among other forms of mental and physical illness), it cannot be regarded as identical to our contemporary PTSD symptomology or cultural meanings. I do not seek to validate "nervous disorder" as a legitimate diagnostic category (which would exceed the scope of this book's expertise). Rather, I explore the language nineteenth-century people used to describe ambiguously

---

4. For an accessible recent account of the neurobiology of trauma, see van der Kolk's *The Body Keeps the Score*, especially chapters 3 and 4. Current psychiatric research on PTSD is discussed at greater length in my first chapter.

psychic and somatic experiences of pain precipitated by threat and loss, and the patterns that attend narration of those experiences.

In placing Victorian fiction within a trauma studies frame, *Narrating Trauma* stands adjacent to several fields—narrative theory, which informs my framing of the plot trajectories of the traumatized and transgressive heroine and self-unmade man; disability studies; and mad studies—and intersects with medical humanities, a cross-disciplinary field focused upon medical practice and education. The question arises why trauma studies, rather than either disability studies or mad studies, as a frame for my analysis, given that all three focus on psychosocial construction of a subject deemed non-normative by prevailing cultural standards. The most straightforward answer, although not a complete one, is that the characters under discussion in this book likely would not have been considered mad or disabled by Victorian readers, but would instead have been understood as experiencing overwhelming loss, threat, or shock affecting their overall well-being: in our terminology, traumatized. I will briefly distinguish trauma studies from mad studies and disability studies, then outline why trauma studies best fits my goals.

Mad studies emerged as an offshoot of disability studies but retains points of intersection. Both fields have activist roots in the rejection of stigmatizing and diminishing meanings written onto bodies and minds deemed outside the norm. Mad studies contests "the illness model of mental difference and the hegemony of psychiatry" (Brewer 14), embracing the nonmedicalized resonance of "madness" as an identity descriptor. The mad studies community employs the phrasing "consumer/survivor/ex-patient" to describe an individual's relationship to the psychiatric establishment, rather than assigning them "mental illness," which, Margaret Price outlines, "introduces a discourse of wellness/unwellness into the notion of madness; its complement is *mental health,* the term of choice of the medical community as well as the insurance companies" (12). There is acknowledged overlap and some strategic alliance with disability studies, given that mental illness is covered under the Americans with Disabilities Act (ADA), but as Elizabeth Brewer, who like Price positions her scholarship within both fields, explains, "psychiatric survivors who view themselves as mentally different and celebrate their uniqueness might reject the label of disability or impairment and its implied pathology to explain their experience" (15).

Trauma studies scholarship can be skeptical toward the therapeutic project and critical of mental health care systems. But trauma studies values psychiatric and psychological research, as well as psychoanalytic theory, and typically regards contemporary mental health care as one possible avenue to relieve suffering (while not a substitute for addressing structural conditions that cause mental harm). Trauma studies engages biomedical models in conjunction with psychosocial and cultural components of human response to overwhelming experience. Indeed, cross-disciplinary dialogues among therapists, psychiatric researchers, and humanist scholars were pivotal to establishing trauma studies as a field. In addition to taking a different position in relation to the psychiatric establishment, trauma studies is distinguished from mad studies in its tighter focus on those disruptions to psychic life ascribed to external forces rather than innate to the subject. Trauma is a pattern of experience and response that may or may not shape an individual or group's long-term identity.

This brings us to several distinctions between a trauma studies approach and a disability studies approach. Disability, while varied in meaning across sociocultural contexts, has stability in the sense that it can be construed as an identity (and potential source of community) through which the subject relates to the world. Lennard Davis, whose work has been foundational to disability studies, suggests the variety of physical and mental conditions covered under the ADA ensures no individual can be "representative," and due to its "porous" nature, disability elides efforts to essentialize it, to which identity categories such as race or gender have been subject (321–22). Michael Bérubé posits that "disability is . . . always already a social relation, involving beliefs and social practices that structure the apprehension of disability—and of putative social 'norms'" (25). Bérubé argues convincingly that disability can motivate narrative in ways that reveal readerly expectations for narrative form and human "normalcy," but stresses that narratives motivated by disability do not develop into predictable structural patterns (48–58). Trauma, in contrast, is not an identity category in itself, but does entail distinct patterns the subject or narrative moves within; trauma narratives share core formal components including fragmentation, gaps, repetition, and misdirection. Traumatic experience may be disabling physically (losing a limb in a train wreck) or mentally (walking away from a train wreck physically unharmed but psychically wounded in ways that limit or modify social participation). This presents overlap between the experience of trauma and the identity category of disability.

Disrupting the able/disabled binary is the more recently introduced third term "debility." Jasbir Puar argues that "three vectors, capacity, debility, and disability, exist in a mutually enforcing constellation" (xv). Debility, impairment construed as bio-power, entails the wearing down of structurally disempowered populations by imperialist and capitalist forces: "To whatever extent living is, can be, has been, or continues to be a maximal output of energy and capacity with a minimal set of resources, many populations are engaged at

some moment, if not continuously, with their slow deaths" (Puar 30). Puar
outlines how limited access to health care, in conjunction with environmental
toxins, risky laboring conditions, and military action, render certain populations, particularly in the contemporary "global south," at far greater chance
of debilitation (xvi–xvii). She posits the profitability of debilitation (which
produces debt and creates consumers of medical treatment) as part of why it
is "endemic to disenfranchised communities" worldwide (16–18). This theorization of debility offers intriguing connections with forms of gradual impairment prevalent in working-class and colonized populations under Victorian
industrial capitalism, and could also provide a useful framework to read
broader effects of urbanization and reified patriarchy within the period.

Ultimately, however, it is trauma studies that best speaks to the combined interests of this project. Trauma studies unites consideration of clinical
effects, cultural formations, and narrative structures that develop in response
to experiences of overwhelming threat and loss. Trauma studies can therefore
elucidate meaningful connections among superficially incongruous elements
in fiction: for example, an atypical narrative structure, a character's culturally discordant affect and self-expression, and material conditions depicted
in the storyworld. The trauma studies lens brings into focus how these atypical novels of self-development critique their contemporary socioeconomic
structures.

A related word about terminology. I sometimes employ the broad term
"mental illness" and specific contemporary category of PTSD, and when discussing how nineteenth-century people understood and defined their experience, I use their now outmoded diagnostic category "nervous disorder" and its
subsets, including nervous exhaustion, hysteria, neurasthenia, and rail shock.
Sometimes I find the phrase "psychic disorder" most apt, as it captures experiences of mental distress, disruption, or disarray that may or may not fit within
either contemporary or historical medical frames.

Across the rapidly evolving and conflicted field of nineteenth-century
mental science, several trends emerge as influential to my project: the location
of a category of mental dysfunction, nervous disorder, on a continuum with
normative mental function; the recognition of interplay between environmental factors and inborn predisposition or personal choice; and the discovery
of a model of psychic injury, resultant from accident or other sudden shock,
that disrupts memory or perception and transforms personality. My first chapter brings these trends into relation with our contemporary formulations of
psychic trauma. It reviews late-twentieth- and twenty-first-century medico-
scientific understandings of PTSD and traces parallel debates within trauma
studies in the humanities, suggesting how attentiveness to nineteenth-century

formulations of psychic injury might invigorate twenty-first-century trauma studies. This discussion lays the groundwork for analysis of how Victorian novelists mine their contemporary scientific discourse for models of psychic injury and dialogue back to both the medical establishment and elements of Victorian culture.

My analysis of literary texts opens with a fundamental shift in plot structure: how nervous disorder reconfigures women's narratives away from questions of courtship. My second chapter outlines how a traumatized and transgressive heroine's narrative can evolve in dialogue with, but distinct from, the marriage plot (contrasting life options presented by potential suitors), employing elements of the bildungsroman (centering work and education), but driven by conflicting impulses toward self-concealment and self-disclosure. My analysis of Charlotte Brontë's *Villette* argues that a complex understanding of trauma allows us to read Lucy Snowe's silences, repetitions, and evasions as a means to communication rather than either an indication of oppression or a means to empowerment. Lucy's omissions and evasions within the story and discourse, which follow alternating impulses to withhold and share her experience of pain and longing, generate a narrative framework that, without open invective, communicates the pain of not only her personal loss, but her marginalized position, which alienates her from her own experience of grief. By anchoring Lucy's search for a witness in the recognizable narrative pattern of the search for a husband, *Villette* assimilates Lucy's marginal story into a familiar mode of novelistic discourse. Brontë's construction of Lucy's interiority deploys and manipulates Victorian theories of mental function, specifically competing phrenological and neurological models, to achieve these narrative effects.

Chapter 3 explores fiction that tracks women's self-development in relation to experiences within marriage. I consider two novellas by Emily Jolly, a now out-of-print protégé of Charles Dickens, that interrogate the premise of the marriage plot by exploring the consequences of, rather than the journey toward, matrimony. Jolly's oeuvre is notable for sustained interest in women's artistic avocations, and her protagonists' negotiations between their work and domestic lives. In both the sentimentally inflected *A Wife's Story* and the gothic *Witch-Hampton Hall,* a young woman who has suffered loss marries with a guilty secret and consequently endures worsening psychic turmoil. Both protagonists' psyches are shaped by events excluded from the discourse: in *A Wife's Story,* death of family, and in *Witch-Hampton Hall,* rape and resultant pregnancy. Following a pattern that echoes vacillations of the courtship plot, each protagonist hesitates between sharing her emotional life with her partner or concealing it from him. The divergent fates of Annie and Lady Ana are tied to the traditionally patriarchal values of one husband and the more reciprocal vision of marital responsibility embraced by the other. Rather than openly challenging medical discourse connecting women's mental suffering to reproductive function, Jolly works within it to suggest that socioeconomic and cultural structures of patriarchy, not female biology, make sexuality and maternity risky to women's mental development.

Having established two modes for the traumatized and transgressive heroine's narrative—transposing the search for an empathetic witness onto the more culturally legible journey toward matrimony, and following self-development within marriage rather than leading up to it—I transition to exploring technological, cultural, and economic changes that increased pressures on the Victorian psyche and accordingly, fragmented novelistic form. Focusing on the era of sensation (roughly, the 1860s), I read Wilkie Collins's *No Name* (1864) and George Eliot's *Daniel Deronda* (1876) through contemporaneous medical discourse on psychic shock, embodied operations of memory, and the related physiological strain of anticipated harm. These novels work to ally readers with the female protagonist's increasingly disordered perspective, and portray her not as inherently pathological, but rather as an extreme example of the nervous sensitivity characteristic of life under modern industrial capitalism.

Chapter 5 turns from the question of narrating female experience to related anxieties about male nervous disorder that intensified as the Victorian era progressed. It considers how the traditional bildungsroman turns back on itself when male ambition, its driving energy, is pathologized. Nervous exhaustion or neurasthenia was ascribed to the depletion of natural vitality through emotional, intellectual, or physical strain. Gender-neutral or coded masculine, it typified the human cost of economic advancement. Such forces constrain the narrative trajectory in Charles Dickens's *Great Expectations* and Thomas Hardy's *Jude the Obscure*. Each features a male protagonist who suffers nervous breakdown when his working-class origins block his desire for high culture. When the hero's erotic desires and public aspirations are infused with modernity's pathologized elements as well its potential, the bildungsroman becomes the story of the self-unmade man. Both novels are characterized by repetitions without forward progress; their ambivalent conclusions show that the bildungsroman's goal of meaningful transformation is in fact unattainable for many Britons.

My selection of fictional texts is deliberately broad in generic affiliation. Although most novels I focus on are generally considered realist, all of these may be viewed as pushing boundaries of realist representation (*Daniel Deronda, Jude the Obscure*) or including elements associated with another genre (*Villette* and gothic, *Great Expectations* and sensation). I also engage fiction best classified as sentimental, gothic, or sensation (*A Wife's Story, Witch-Hampton Hall,* and *No Name*). I focus on how each text manipulates narrative technique and scientific discourse to tell a difficult story of psychic harm, one that may not be readily palatable to its reading publics. This study attends to the ways psychic experience may be unfolded in nineteenth-century fiction beyond the boundaries of what we understand as a traditional realist representation of interiority. Elaine Freedgood has recently traced how the dominance of realism in theoretical discourse on the Victorian novel was not solidified until the 1980s. She argues that subsequent critical accounts of Victorian fiction privileging formal cohesion and realist representation not only obscure wider formal variation within nineteenth-century British and French novels, but also impose this constructed "Western" ideal upon other national literatures (*Worlds* x–xii, 136–39). In charting the ways novels in this study diverge from readerly expectations of genre, I think in terms of strategic departures rather than formal flaws.

Narrating Trauma traces renovations to novelistic modes of depicting self-development in relation to shifting scientific understandings of the embodied mind. As they maneuver socially peripheral and psychically disordered protagonists into central narrative positions, these novels reimagine their contemporary modes of storytelling.

The overall arc of this analysis suggests plasticity within traditional gender roles and conventional narrative forms, and relatedly, reveals public ambivalence about whether the dominant organically based explanations for psychic dysfunction can tell the full story. As they depict characters assaulted as much by diffuse environmental stressors as by discrete instances of loss, these novels capitalize on the nascent psychiatric field's theorization of a consciousness shaped by its socioeconomic and material environment. Victorian depictions of psychic damage provide our contemporary trauma studies an archive documenting multifaceted, diffuse, and unpredictable threats to coherent selfhood, a view of psychic trauma that feels particularly relevant in our pandemic or post-pandemic landscape. The fictional accounts I explore convey varying degrees of skepticism toward medical solutions for mental pain. They seek interpersonal, cultural, and economic remedies for the marginalization and even alienation their nervous sufferers experience. A key goal of my project is to restore the liminal figure of the Victorian nervous sufferer to full visibility as an embodied consciousness shaped and constrained by economic and cultural inequalities.

CHAPTER 1

~

Contemporary Trauma Studies and Nineteenth-Century Nerves

T he capaciousness of psychic trauma as a concept makes it a valuable analytical tool connecting a range of human experiences and cultural productions, but the fluidity of what is meant by "trauma" across disciplines and historical time frames can be a source of confusion and imprecision. The strength of trauma as an interpretive paradigm is that it links disparate modes of knowledge production: medico-scientific, cultural, and artistic. By crossing disciplinary boundaries, trauma studies provides comprehensive inquiry into what happens to human identity in the face of overwhelming threat and loss. However, this cross-disciplinarity can also lead to confusion about the nature of the claims trauma theory makes. Introducing their recent interdisciplinary collection, Eric Boynton and Peter Capretto reflect that "given the many conflicts among . . . disciplines and their methods, the very idea of trauma is becoming increasingly unclear" (1) as "one discipline's careful analysis is another's theoretical violence" (4).

Before bringing theories of psychic injury to bear upon the study of literature, I review key movements in contemporary trauma studies and illustrate their relation to nineteenth-century concepts of mental function and dysfunction. I will first outline characteristics of post-traumatic stress disorder in modern medico-therapeutic contexts, then explore its migration into humanities theoretical discourse, where it has become closely intertwined both with the experience of modernity and with explicitly or implicitly Freudian models of psychic life. Next, I will reconstruct a nineteenth-century scientific perspective on the residual physiological and emotional consequences of psychic injury by surveying the evolving diagnostic category of nervous disorder. *Narrating Trauma* also incorporates dialogue with nineteenth-century scientific sources, in tandem with literary analysis, throughout subsequent chapters; the review here of broad developments in Victorian mental science is intended to provide a general contextual frame for more focused investigations to come.

I wish to illuminate several points through this chapter's discussion. First, twentieth- and twenty-first-century humanities trauma theory has focused significantly on psychic injury resulting from a victim's interaction with a unitary aggressor. This theoretical focus is a logical response to the types of psychic trauma most visible in the twentieth century and turn of the millennium (genocide, mechanized and nuclear warfare, terrorism), but it can inadvertently obscure the claims of individuals and texts that manifest more diffuse forms of psychic strain. Second, key movements in nineteenth-century mental science show that prior to the Freudian shift and devastating effects of modern mechanized warfare, there was instead a significant, even dominant, conception of psychic injury as the result of decentralized environmental and cultural factors. In this period, psychic injury was most commonly understood as a maladaptive but not unexpected somatic, affective, and intellectual reaction to socioeconomic changes and technological advancements attendant on modern capitalism. The way Victorian novels represent the interiority of individuals who suffer psychic injury invites us to read for diffuse forms of trauma, which appear increasingly germane in the second decade of the twenty-first century, as we emerge hesitantly from pandemic lockdowns to grieve a staggering loss of life that occurred without violence.

PSYCHIC TRAUMA AS
CONTEMPORARY CLINICAL PHENOMENON

The clinical history and prehistory of post-traumatic stress disorder stretching back through the nineteenth century is varied and contentious, but several characteristics remain reasonably consistent in descriptions of psychic trauma from the industrial revolution onward. Personality changes that negatively influence socioeconomic integration, as well as an ongoing or recurrent sense of threat, provide a common thread between Victorian sufferers of "rail spine," shell-shocked Great War troops, Vietnam veterans agitating for medical recognition in the 1970s, and rape and incest survivors whose domestic traumas second-wave feminism brought to public and psychiatric attention

in the 1980s. With developments in brain imaging technology in the 1980s
and 1990s, psychiatrists attained the ability to measure material changes correlated with these maladaptive cognitive and emotional processes. Van der
Kolk, one of the pioneers of neuroimaging the traumatized brain, explains
that "when something reminds traumatized people of the past, their right
brain reacts as if the trauma were happening in the present," while the left
brain, the center of language processing that enables us to "organize experience into logical sequences," shows decreased activity (45). Such physiological data seems to validate long-standing beliefs that the traumatized cannot
differentiate between their dangerous past and more secure present, or effectively verbalize their painful memories or present strife.

    Mental health professionals in the late twentieth and twenty-first century
affirm that disconnection from reciprocal social relations, and absence of
unified selfhood with agency, are central to trauma response as it is clinically defined. In her landmark text *Trauma and Recovery: The Aftermath of
Violence from Domestic Abuse to Political Terror* (1992), psychiatrist Judith
Herman declares that "traumatic events call into question basic human
relationships" (51). These events "shatter the construction of the self that is
formed and sustained in relation to others" and "destroy the victim's fundamental assumptions about the safety of the world, the positive value of
the self, and the meaningful order of creation" (Herman 51). Herman also
reports traumatized patients possess diminished capacity to anticipate future
events and plan accordingly (46–47). Clinicians have found that such damage to the coherent social self can result from a series of dangers or losses
in the context of economic precarity or belonging to a nondominant and
stigmatized group, rather than from one overwhelming event that defies the
victim's schema of the world. Arguing for a vision of PTSD encompassing
everyday dangers of poverty, misogyny, and homophobia as well as the catastrophic threats of the battlefield, psychologist Laura Brown observes that
"social context, and the individual's personal history within that social context, can lend traumatic meaning to events that may only be sad or troubling
in another time and place" (110). Clinicians and researchers increasingly recognized that the triggers and symptomology of PTSD vary across individuals
and social groups.

    In the twenty-first century, developing knowledge of the human genome
and refinement of neuroimaging techniques advanced medical understanding of the biology correlated to behavioral changes and affective experiences
of post-traumatic stress. Many twenty-first-century studies emphasize the
interdependence of biological and social factors in the development of and
recovery from acute and chronic post-traumatic symptoms. For instance, in

a 2006 paper, epidemiologist Sandro Galea and his colleagues argue "there is ample theoretical and empirical evidence to suggest that social context is an important determinant of PTSD and that it may influence the relationship between specific genetic and molecular factors and the risk of PTSD" (239). Three years later, psychiatrists Rachel Yehuda and Linda Bierer would propose that epigenetic modifications (stable alterations in gene function, but not structure, in response to environmental stressors) can explain why trauma exposure causes persistent, rather than transient, behavioral transformation in some individuals (427–28) and may elucidate why trauma exposure can affect individuals differentially based upon maternal trauma history, developmental timing, and whether exposure is repeated or limited to one event (431–32).

In the twenty-first century, epigenetics dovetails with cultural approaches to trauma in addressing cross-generational forms of psychic harm. Social work researcher and practitioner Maria Yellow Horse Brave Heart pioneered the concept of historical trauma, "the collective, cumulative psychological wounds of massive, repeated, transgenerational group trauma," in the late 1990s (185). Recently, she led a team piloting clinical trials of group interpersonal psychotherapy that "demonstrated promise for reducing depressive symptoms, trauma, and grief responses within American Indian populations" through culturally sensitive and community-engaged approaches (Brave Heart et al. 194). Brave Heart's interventions focus primarily on clinically significant depression and PTSD. In the wake of the Black Lives Matter and Me Too movements, mental health practitioners have entered popular discourse to describe how trauma travels through bodies and shapes social interactions even in the absence of diagnosable PTSD. Therapist Alex Iantaffi theorizes our rigid gender binary as deeply imbricated in culturally normalizing practices of settler colonialism, making gender a source of historical trauma affecting people of all genders and backgrounds (albeit differentially) (22–27). In his 2017 *New York Times* best seller, *My Grandmother's Hands: Racialized Trauma and the Pathway to Mending Our Hearts and Bodies,* therapist Resmaa Menakem calls on Americans to recognize and confront the embodied nature of racialized trauma as necessary groundwork for political and structural change. Writing for a broad audience and anchoring his claims in epigenetics, Menakem argues that toxic cultural patterns and family dynamics can often be understood as "traumatic retention that has lost its context over time" (39). These contemporary perspectives illustrate how clinical mental health research, practice, and outreach develop in dynamic relation to cultural change: both driving social transformation and responding to needs exposed by activist movements.

Genetics is not the only research methodology to explore interrelated social and biological factors that cause variation in trauma response. In their 2015 text aimed at clinicians, psychiatrist Ruth Lanius and psychologist Paul Frewen employ neurophenomenology, which "integrates the study of an individual's first-person experience with objective neurophysiological measures" (xxiv). Lanius and Frewen propose a model of post-traumatic stress accounting for four dimensions of consciousness: disruptions to sense of time (flashbacks, intrusive recall), thought processes (disjointed experience of consciousness, negative self-referential thoughts), connection with the body (experiencing it as foreign or feeling sensations of partial disembodiment), and emotion (increased and/or decreased arousal, compartmentalized experience of emotion) (28–32, 38–41). Stressing the influence of social experience on biological processes, they argue that chronic childhood trauma exposure, particularly within attachment relationships, influences neurodevelopment (35). In a 2018 literature review and meta-analysis published in the journal *Genes, Brain, and Behavior,* psychiatrists Jennifer Stevens and Tanja Jovanovic likewise find much to confirm the relevance of social environment to PTSD risk and resilience, and to suggest how PTSD negatively influences brain functions that enable social interaction. Stevens and Jovanovic study social cognition, defined as "the wide variety of processes that link the perception of social information with a behavioral response, including perception, attention, decision-making, memory and emotion" (2). They find a wide range of studies linking PTSD "numbing symptoms (feeling distant from others)" to poor social cognition, particularly "deficits in emotion recognition tasks" (5). Reviewing neuroimaging studies of PTSD-affected adults and controls, Stevens and Jovanovic suggest that social deficits of PTSD sufferers may result from heightened response to social threat cues, which interferes with the capacity to perceive and reason about another person's emotional state (6). The current direction of medical research stresses the interaction of biological and social factors in PTSD development and recovery.

Surveying key trends in contemporary mental health from the first appearance of PTSD in the DSM-III (1980) to the present, we find important parallels with pre-Freudian nineteenth-century psychiatric formulations of what was termed nervous disorder, nervous exhaustion, and nervous shock: (1) acknowledgment that the disorder impairs individual agency and relationship-building, (2) recognition of the interrelation of hereditary predisposition and social environment in risk and resilience, (3) affirmation that psychological response to potentially traumatizing experiences can vary markedly between individuals, and (4) an expectation that the emotional and cognitive changes associated with the disorder have material traces that the right scientific equipment or technique could detect. Before turning in detail to the Victorian prehistory of the clinical phenomenon we now term PTSD, I will first outline briefly the migration of trauma theory from the sciences to the humanities from the 1990s onward and explore its implications.

TRAUMA STUDIES IN THE HUMANITIES

The late twentieth century's burgeoning interest in psychic trauma stems from an interrelation of historical factors and medical developments, notably the mental health aftermath of America's war in Vietnam, the memory work associated with Holocaust and broader Second World War commemoration, and the second-wave feminist activism uncovering the private traumas of sexual assault and domestic abuse. In the early '90s, Herman's influential *Trauma and Recovery,* which gained readership outside the psychiatric community, shifted the discourse around PTSD to include "a spectrum of traumatic disorders, ranging from the effects of a single overwhelming event to the more complicated effects of prolonged or repeated abuse" (2–3). In public imagination as well as clinical discourse, the site of possible trauma spread from the battlefield to the living room, expanding the cultural relevance of the concept.

Literary theorist Cathy Caruth, in conjunction with psychiatrist Dori Laub and literary critic Shoshanna Felman, popularized the discourse of psychic trauma within the humanities in the 1990s. Caruth's approach is influenced by de Manian deconstruction, a model of bearing witness based in Holocaust studies, and by the hypothesis, put forward by psychiatrists and neuroscience researchers such as Bessel van der Kolk, that traumatic memories are, on a material level, engraved and stored differently in the brain. Her influential collection *Trauma: Explorations in Memory* (1995) synthesizes perspectives from practicing psychotherapists and physicians as well as literary critics. Her monograph *Unclaimed Experience: Trauma, Narrative, and History* (1996), productively extends these analyses through literary and filmic texts, similarly engaging Freud's theories of trauma. Caruth's foundational work offers a nuanced and compelling view of trauma's narrative effects, but tends to collapse differences between historical moments and types of traumatic experience, and elide its pre-Freudian medical history.

Caruth casts psychic trauma as a phenomenon that tests the limits of medicine's explanatory powers. She observes that therapists are often struck by the literality—the unprocessed nature—of traumatic dreams and flashbacks, which signal the patient's "delay or incompletion in knowing, or even in seeing, an overwhelming occurrence that then remains, in its insistent return, absolutely *true* to the event" (*Trauma* 5). In her most recent monograph, *Literature in the Ashes of History* (2013), Caruth suggests "traumatic memory . . . totters between memory and erasure, producing a history that is, in its very events, a kind of inscription of the past; but also a history constituted by the erasure of its traces" (78–79). Her conception of psychic trauma posits the traumatized subject as a vessel for unspeakable history that resists cohesive and deliberate narrativization, a history that defies integration within meaningful psychic and social frameworks.

Several subsequent perspectives on trauma challenge and complicate Caruth's skepticism toward the feasibility of representing traumatic experience in socially productive ways. Historian Dominick LaCapra, in *Writing History, Writing Trauma* (2001), advocates that secondary witnesses to trauma (such as those born after the Holocaust) develop "an affective relation, rapport, or bond with the other recognized and respected as other" (212–13). He advocates the value of mourning practices as "ways of coming to terms with losses as well as other significant transitions . . . in social life" (214). Similarly emphasizing socially and politically productive possibilities in communication of traumatic experience, literary and cultural critic Ann Cvetkovich, in *An Archive of Feelings* (2003), documents how "affective experience can provide the basis for new cultures" (7). For Cvetkovich, the very "unspeakable and unrepresentable" nature of traumatic experience catalyzes innovations in communication and commemoration, "giving rise to new genres of expression, such as testimony, and new forms of monuments, rituals, and performances that can call into being collective witnesses and publics" (7). She explores "how affect, including the affects associated with trauma, serves as the foundation for the formation of public cultures" (10), notably, AIDS activism. Shifting the question of representation from individual interpersonal to the public sphere, both LaCapra and Cvetkovich envision productive cultural consequences of actively working through loss.

Relatedly, the socially oriented psychoanalytic philosophy of Kelly Oliver, particularly *Witnessing: Beyond Recognition* (2001) and *The Colonization of Psychic Space: A Psychoanalytic Theory of Social Oppression* (2004), suggestively explores both the challenges and social and ethical value of "bearing witness," in "the double sense" (*Witnessing* 18) of testifying to what one has seen and also to what one cannot ever fully comprehend—such as religious faith or the experience of another. Oliver explores how economic and cultural injustice become inscribed in the psyches of oppressed individuals, as through racism, sexism, homophobia, colonialism, or classism. Articulating a psychoanalytic theory of social oppression, she delineates how "domination infects those oppressed with the punishing superego that excludes and abjects them"

(*Colonization* 105). Unlike traditional Freudian melancholy, "the internalization of a lost love," the social melancholy attendant on oppression is caused by "the loss of the self as an active agent and positive force in the world" (*Colonization* 121). Oliver's work outlines both the obstacles to bearing witness to the trauma of socially othered people, and the potential personal and societal benefits of witnessing.

Some twenty-first-century perspectives on psychic injury directly confront shifting economic, political, and technological conditions that have transformed how people navigate selfhood and experience crisis. In *Disappear Here: Violence after Generation X* (2015), Naomi Mandel reflects upon how violence is experienced and represented by the generation that came of age in the 1980s and 1990s. Lacking "a definitive vast and violent event, a generational trauma like World War II or Vietnam, or a defining cultural moment like 1968," Gen Xers, she argues, "experienced violence as paralysis (the 1980s were ushered in with the Iran hostage crisis), menace (Reagan's play on the looming specter of the Evil Empire) and complicity, wherein violence is battled—or not—with the pocketbook" (15). Even Xers experiencing direct personal harm and threat, she suggests, are without the central organizing dynamic of a unitary opponent culturally figured as evil (Mandel 19). "*Violence is real*"—indeed, Mandel explores literary responses to 9/11 at length—but "reality, for Xers, is mobile, appropriable, subject to revision, rewriting, rewiring, and reworking in the digital age" (26). Mandel's analysis places weight upon an affect not typically associated with trauma studies, but characteristic, even stereotypical, of Gen X: disaffection.

While not directly a theory of trauma, Lauren Berlant's influential *Cruel Optimism* (2011) seeks to articulate the origins of disaffection that permeates particularly American, but broadly liberal-capitalist, contemporary societies. Berlant's key contention is that "cruel optimism" structures the modern subject: "a relation of attachment to compromised conditions of possibility whose realization is discovered to be impossible, sheer fantasy, or *too* possible, and toxic" (24). Cruelty lies in the necessity of maintaining the *form* of the attachment in order for the subject to sustain a sense of possibility and promise in life, even as the *content* of the attachment actually disappoints or harms (Berlant 24). Berlant's emphasis on how affective perception, structured through such attachments, precedes other forms of comprehension has implications for how trauma is conceptualized in the twenty-first century. Situating affective attachments in relation to historical events, and engaging Caruth directly, they argue that "literature on the traumatic event has been dominated by a consensus that trauma detaches the subject from the historical, sentencing its subjects to a terrifying suffusion of the past into something stuck in the

subject that stands out ahistorically from the ordinary" (Berlant 80). Berlant alternatively proposes "crisis ordinariness" (82) as the "modes, habits, or
genres of being" (82) that emerge in relation to unfolding conditions of crisis, juxtaposing this concept with Caruth's model of the discrete retrospective
traumatic event that produces definable if not universal effects. Berlant's analysis emphasizes ongoing adaptation of the subject to destabilizing conditions.

Work such as Berlant's challenges twenty-first-century trauma studies
further to expand its formulation of psychic harm beyond the retrospective temporality of the singular event model. Thinkers such as LaCapra,
Cvetkovich, and Oliver have already modeled how we might examine psychic trauma as a sociocultural and philosophical problem, beyond medico-
scientific frameworks. In so doing, they help us recognize how interpersonal
relationships and cultural formations that develop around experiences of profound loss or threat can sometimes be socially productive rather than exclusively pathological. Nonetheless, Caruth's insistence on the unrepresentability
of traumatic experience, which is influenced by the therapeutic tradition it
mistrusts, offers a compelling perspective on the narrative effects that follow
from traumatic experience. Central to Caruth's formulation is the assertion
that it is not the nature of a particular event, but the pattern of reception it
produces in the individual, that defines the traumatic. The subject's inability
to assimilate the unexpectedness, enormity, or obscenity of a given instance
of loss or threat produces a pattern of unwilled repetitions, in which the
survivor is haunted by her own memory (*Unclaimed Experience* 4). Moving
past the event temporally would imply comprehension and even acceptance
that the trauma survivor cannot endure. Texts that document trauma, she
argues, demonstrate an "oscillation between a *crisis of death* and a *crisis of life*:
between the story of the unbearable nature of the event and the story of the
unbearable nature of its survival" (*Unclaimed Experience* 7). Invaluable for its
delineation of the formal properties of trauma narrative, Caruth's work tends
to efface the historical specificity of its source material, particularly Freud's
fin de siècle bourgeois milieu. As a result, psychic trauma is implicitly represented as a transhistorical phenomenon.

Arguably the most important critique of Caruth's theorization of trauma
is Ruth Leys's *Trauma: A Genealogy* (2000). Leys, seeking to restore the intellectual history of psychic trauma, traces medical engagement with the concept
from case studies of hysteria at the turn of the twentieth century, through
shell-shock victims of both world wars, up to the neurobiology of van der
Kolk and its influence on Caruth's theory. Leys points out the confluence
between the practice of hypnosis and the rise of trauma studies, suggesting
that the latter is more indebted to the former than either medical practitio-

ners or theorists acknowledge (8). By emphasizing the role of hypnosis, primarily though not exclusively a late-Victorian and twentieth-century medical practice in the treatment of nervous disorders or shell shock, Leys excludes an older and more varied history of medical attention to psychic shock and nervous disorder in which hypnosis plays only a minor treatment role, outstripped in popularity by drugs, rest, exercise, and electrotherapy.

Central to Leys's argument is the idea that trauma studies itself oscillates between what she terms mimetic and antimimetic theories in its attempt to account for the behaviors and thought processes of trauma patients. According to the mimetic theory of traumatic experience, the victim, like a hypnotized subject in a trance state, dissociates from himself and unconsciously identifies with the aggressor (Leys 8). The competing antimimetic theory views trauma instead as "a purely external event coming to a sovereign if passive victim" (Leys 10). Leys regards the irresolvable oscillation between these mutually exclusive positions as endemic to trauma studies, and does not foresee any theoretical means of bridging the impasse (307).

Caruth and Leys understand the nature of traumatic experience and our capacity to define it in radically different ways. Whereas Caruth treats trauma as a cross-disciplinary phenomenon with stable, arguably transhistorical characteristics, Leys regards psychic trauma as an inherently unstable theoretical concept that oscillates between mimetic and antimimetic poles depending upon historical and situational context. What I find particularly instructive is that on one crucial point, their positions seem to coincide. Both Caruth and Leys—Caruth implicitly, Leys quite explicitly—read psychic injury in terms of an at times mobile aggressor/victim dichotomy. As Mandel observes, Leys critiques Caruth with regard to "the danger that the distinction of perpetrator from victim may be blurred" (160), mobilizing a broader ethical imperative in cultural dialogues around trauma to distinguish "victim from nonvictim and, by extension, victim from perpetrator" (161). The aggressor/victim dichotomy is a logical and useful model for discussion of the psychic trauma related to warfare and genocide that comprises the majority of twentieth- and early-twenty-first-century trauma studies: the Nazi Holocaust, the US bombing of Hiroshima, the Rwandan genocide, and 9/11. Likewise, such a model is helpful for discussion of traumas such as rape, incest, and other instances of interpersonal violence. But an aggressor/victim dichotomy cannot fully capture the nuances of psychic injury that accrues gradually, particularly without intentionality or direct violence.

Contemporary trauma studies might therefore benefit from attention to older models of psychic injury. Victorian physicians studying and treating what they called "nervous disorder" were particularly attentive to the poten-

tial for damage in the multitudinous stimuli of life under modern urban capitalism, what Walter Benjamin identifies as "the inhospitable, blinding age of
big-scale industrialism" (157), the "shock" that results from "contact with the
metropolitan masses" (165). The Victorian medical establishment saw risk in
the lifestyles and social arrangements engendered by industrial capitalism.
Their efforts to understand that risk lack the technological advantages modern
psychiatrists and neurologists enjoy, and remain imbricated with nineteenth-
century biases, but they nonetheless productively foreground diffuse forms of
suffering that result from ongoing threat. In our era, attuned to the psychological and physical detriments of structural inequality, and freshly attentive
to lurking, unpredictable threats like contagion and cyberattack, Victorian
mental science offers timely insights into the effects of dispersed, ongoing
stressors and anticipated harm.

NINETEENTH-CENTURY NERVES TO
TWENTIETH-CENTURY TRAUMA

Explaining what nervous disorder meant to nineteenth-century people begins
with outlining what it did not mean. While the boundaries of nervous disorder diagnosis were porous, distinctions were drawn, medically and culturally,
between the nervous sufferer and others experiencing mental distress or physical ailments. First, in recorded experience and fiction, nervous disorder typically is not, excepting extreme cases, the defining identity of any individual.
This distinguishes nervous disorder from invalidism as theorized by Maria
Frawley, which "subsumed other determinants of identity" (12) and signified
"lingering, stasis, and inertia" (13). In literature, nervously disordered protagonists collapse in illness (Pip) or hysterics (Gwendolen Harleth), or are subject
to gossip like Annie Aston, whose neighbors snidely call her a "mad wife"
(153) during her most unstable period. But these situations pass; the characters are defined socially through other roles, for instance parents, workers,
and lovers. They are not medically marked off from the normative Victorian
body. Relatedly, nervous disorder was not regarded as a physical disability;
indeed, the medical diagnosis of functional nervous disorder was reserved
for cases where no lesion, injury, or structural anomaly could be found. One
of its defining characteristics was unpredictable and sudden reversibility. It is
also distinct from, although related to, the cultural category of madness and
Victorian psychiatric diagnoses like lunacy and mania, understood to entail
loss of reason and deeply stigmatizing. In severe cases, the Victorian nervous
sufferer and his doctor would fear the slide into madness, but the fact a transi-

tion was feared indicates a line to be crossed. In fictional texts, nervous disorder can be slippery to read for precisely because the nervous sufferer, unlike the invalid, the physically disabled character, or the so-called madwoman, was not regarded as medically or socially atypical, but instead as representative of modern trends.

From the late eighteenth century onward, pre-Freudian medical thought posited a class of ailments wherein the individual embodied psyche retained and expressed residue of the material and social stressors of life under industrial capitalism. The eighteenth century brought medical consensus that consciousness resided in the brain and nervous system (Micale 21). In the early decades of the nineteenth century, neurophysiological research developed a medical understanding of nervous system localization and reflex action, and by the 1830s, according to historian Roger Smith, "scientists discussed inhibition as a function within the nervous system" (*Inhibition* 8–9). Therefore, from the early Victorian period onward, questions of nervous disorder were broadly understood as questions of agency: whether an individual consciousness could produce, moderate, control, and direct impulses toward bodily action and speech; whether, alternatively, that consciousness would be overwhelmed and dysregulated by external stressors.

The notion that consciousness and affect were intimately bound in physicality through the nervous system gave physicians, novelists, and social critics a uniquely powerful indicator of Britain's cultural health. As Peter Melville Logan contends, "the distinguishing feature of the nervous body, the one that made it particularly useful for social criticism, was that it was highly responsive to cultural conditions" (6). Concerns about nerves began with the aristocracy in the eighteenth century and gradually worked downward through the class structure. By the late eighteenth century, doctors identified the rapidly expanding middle class as susceptible to nervous ailments, brought about by class-specific social habits such as continuous urban residency, concern with acquisition (male merchants and speculators), and a culturally enforced sedentary lifestyle (their wives and daughters) (Logan 1). Scientific understanding of nervous disorder was imbricated in the social construction of classed identities.

Early-nineteenth-century physicians understood "neurosis" as a dysfunction of the nervous fibers' ability to transmit sense perceptions to, or motor impulses from, the brain (Logan 18). Overstimulated nerves, unlike healthy ones, were believed to retain a material record of the sense impressions that passed through them, eventually reaching a saturation point that triggers nervous attack (Logan 28). In marked contrast with twentieth-century trauma theory, which tends to differentiate normative and pathological, theories of the nervous body viewed nervous disorders on a continuum with regular nerve function. Every body was a potential nervous body, contingent on cultural and socioeconomic influences. Logan argues that the defining aspect of the nervous temperament is "that it destroys the body's assumed ability to resist the ill-effects of impressions," creating "an overly inscribable body, one that is too easily written upon by the stimulus of its day-to-day experience" (28). Such a paradigm of nervous disorder is strikingly similar to modern theory's figuration of the traumatizing event as that which enters the psyche without proper mediation because it is too overwhelming to be processed as it occurs. But it also aligns nervous disorder with an inability to manage information in a systematic fashion and to regulate the body's inherent permeability. Given long-standing traditions of Western philosophy and culture that code irrationality and bodily excess as feminine, we might say this etiology implicitly feminizes the nervous sufferer. Loss of masculine-coded vitality and decision was constructed as the risk of progress.

As the Victorian period began, two significant theoretical developments occurred regarding mental function: J. Marshall Hall's reflex arc theory and James Cowles Prichard's concept of moral insanity. Hall's investigation of nervous system physiology had far-ranging implications for both medical and philosophical discussions of human behavior. Through laboratory experiments on animals and case studies of ill or injured human patients, Hall, founder of the British Medical Association, concluded that contrary to previous theories, the brain did not control all nervous function; rather, the body had two nervous systems, one controlled by the brain, and the other by the spine (Logan 167–68). Hall's influential articles, published as a series beginning in 1833 and in collected form as *Memoirs on the Nervous System* in 1837, suggested that the cerebral system controlled judgment and voluntary actions, while mechanistic functions and automatic actions were governed by a separate spinal system (Logan 167). This theory had implications for how physiological responses to fear or surprise were interpreted: For example, he claimed that "the arm which is totally paralyzed to volition or voluntary motion, in hemiplegia [a weakness of one side of the body ascribed to brain injury], is strongly agitated by surprise and other emotions. The seat of these emotions is, therefore, placed *lower* down in the nervous system, than the seat of volition and of the disease" (Hall 95). Hall's theory of "a unique spinal cord subsystem, the excito-motory, anatomically and functionally distinct from the rest of the nervous system," has now been disproven, but his explanation of nervous action and reflex through material anatomy was a crucial advancement in the study of physiology (Clarke and Jacyna 123–24). Setting forth what would much later become a key premise of trauma studies, Hall argued that behaviors that appear purposeful might in fact be triggered, organically, on a level of function other than deliberate decision.

The reflex arc theory complicated how conscious control over somatic responses was understood across the population; the notion of moral insanity, in contrast, posited an absence of self-regulation regarding emotional life within a pathologized subset of the population. In 1835, James Cowles Prichard, an English psychiatrist who subsequently became the commissioner of lunacy, defined moral insanity as a "disorder of the moral affections and propensities without any illusion or erroneous conviction impressed upon the understanding" (841). No intellectual deficiency corresponded with a moral insanity diagnosis (Prichard 839). As Elaine Showalter observes, "this definition could be stretched to take in almost any kind of behavior regarded as abnormal or disruptive by community standards" (29). Indeed, Prichard himself seems aware (though uncritical) of the role cultural standards play in designating moral insanity, blaming the condition for "certain perversions of natural inclination which excite the greatest disgust and abhorrence" (841). Moral insanity involved no loss of reason, only emotional and moral dysregulation. Without delusions or hallucinations, moral insanity, Prichard claims, entails "a want of self-government" and excessive, often angry emotion, which may issue in violence (840). Here it is crucial to note that moral insanity was *not* classed as a nervous disorder, and unlike nervous disorders, it was a diagnosis more associated with the asylum than the drawing room.

Meanwhile, outside asylum walls, people worried they might be incapacitated should their "nerve force" be run down by the pace of modern life. By the mid-nineteenth century, scientists broadly accepted electricity as the medium of nerve impulse, and both the medical establishment and general public believed that if one's finite quantity of nerve force were depleted, individual consciousness, like a spent battery, would cease to operate (Oppenheim 81). Bodily rest and social seclusion were popular treatments for functional nervous disorders, particularly in the second half of the century, as the "rest cure" popularized by American physician Silas Weir Mitchell (Shorter 129–30). Drugs and electrotherapy were also widely accepted treatments for nervous complaints, with the former being especially common among the working and lower middle classes, who could not afford an extended spa visit.[1] An advertisement for "Smith's Phosphorous, Quinine, and Iron Pills, a Specific for Neuralgia" typifies claims made for such patent medicines, promising "Food

---

1. See Oppenheim 110–39 on Victorian treatment regimens for nervous disorder, including nerve tonics, opiates, exercise, and change of climate.

for the brain, nerves, and muscles!" in bold capital letters. The manufacturer offers relief from a dizzying array of symptoms:

> loss of memory and nerve power, lassitude, anoemia, hysteria, female irregu-
> larities, wasting diseases, ague, low fever, and when recovering from fevers
> of any kind, or small pox, diseases of the brain and spinal cord, lumbago,
> sciatica, indigestion, nervousness, depressed spirits, trembling, inaptitude
> for work, melancholia, pains in the back, impotence, excesses of all kinds,
> epileptic fits, and all affections of the brain, nerves, and muscles.[2]

Quinine in particular is praised for its "great success with all maladies of the nervous system," "giving power and tone to the most shattered and broken down constitution." In contrast, an advertisement for the "nerve tonic" called "Muracum" scolds makers of "countless quack remedies now-a-days so extensively advertised" that "profess to cure every disease the flesh is heir to" and also criticizes opiates, a popular physician's prescription, as "afford[ing] temporary relief, by merely deadening the nerves." The advertised product instead promises targeted relief from nervous maladies, "attacking the disorder in its very stronghold." Such marketing demonstrates that not only medical professionals, but the general public, were at once conscious of the wide psychic and somatic scope ascribed to nervous dysfunction, and increasingly skeptical of this lack of definition.

Advertising for nervous remedies demonstrates how widespread and relatively nonstigmatizing these complaints were throughout the Victorian era. For example, the Baldwin company advertises on a single page a pill for digestive problems, an herb tobacco to relieve "shortness of breath," a lozenge for "throat or bronchial irritation," and "Baldwin's Celebrated Nervous Pills," which profess to cure psychological symptoms including "lowness of spirits" and "bad dreams" as well as strictly physical ones such as "toothache" and the ambivalently mental or bodily discomfort of "nervousness." Nervous dysfunction is treated as one of a variety of troubling but ordinary medical problems. It is easy to see how in fiction, characters coded as nervously disordered might seem ordinary and sympathetic to Victorian readers more readily than would characters displaying behaviors or thought processes their contemporary mental science coded as, for example, moral insanity or monomania. In Wilkie Collins's *The Woman in White*, Frederick Fairlie is an unattractive caricature of the male nervous sufferer, but the novel's three central protago-

---

2. All advertisements referenced here are located in the Evanion Collection of Victorian Ephemera, British Library.

nists, Walter Hartright, his eventual bride Laura Fairlie, and her admirable half-sister Marian Holcombe, all display symptoms of nervous dysfunction under stressful conditions.

Men and women alike were deemed susceptible to nervous illness, but the medical belief that women were more nervously excitable persisted. Thomas Laycock, like Hall a prominent neurologist interested in reflex function, published his influential *A Treatise on the Nervous Diseases of Women; Comprising an Inquiry into the Nature, Causes, and Treatment of Spinal and Hysterical Disorders* in 1840 (Oppenheim 28–29). Laycock was typical of Victorian medical men who believed the female nervous system, by virtue of its interaction with the ovaries and uterus, was less stable than the male, particularly in connection with puberty and menopause (Oppenheim 187). A firm believer in biological roots of psychic gender difference, Laycock argued that "it is by no means certain that all sexual differences depend upon the sexual organs: on the contrary, it is highly probable that there is organization and development of the primitive tissues to which these are subservient" (13). For Laycock, sexual difference pervaded one's entire physiology, not only reproductive structures.

Laycock was nonetheless conscious of the role the social and material environment played in precipitating women's nervous dysfunction. Of adolescent ladies, he argues, "mere delicacy of system . . . is not the sole general predisposing cause of hysteric affections" (139). Laycock acknowledges the role of heredity, especially in severe manifestations of mental dysfunction (139), but expresses serious concern about the effects of lifestyle. Among harmful factors Laycock lists sedentary habits and absence of outdoor exercise (140), "severe application" in pursuit of musical skill (140–41), and unnaturally constraining modes of dress (142). He particularly faults the social environment of the upper-class Victorian girl. Of the marriage market, he writes,

> The excitement and competition of social life, excited love, ungratified desire, disappointed vanity as well as affection, late hours, long and late indulgence in sleep, and the excessive use of stimulants, as wines, liqueurs, coffee, tea, and c., all act with more or less of a combined energy upon the unfortunate young lady in fashionable life. (142)

Laycock depicts a socioeconomic system that not only encourages but *requires* emotional excess and immoderate indulgence from young women he deems physiologically vulnerable. Victorian medicine evinced awareness that culture was complicit in developing the character traits and forms of bodily illness that it most lamented in women.

Pressures of the socioeconomic environment were also implicated in the causation of neurasthenia, a gender-neutral or masculinized category of nervous disorder that the American medical community codified in the 1860s. By mid-century, the emerging psychiatric establishment sought to modernize terminology for functional nervous disorders; eighteenth-century diagnoses of hysteria, hypochondria, and nerves were imprecise (Shorter 129). In 1869, American physician George Beard outlined characteristics of "neurasthenia," a disorder that historian Edward Shorter calls "a bridge between supposedly organic causes and symptoms involving mood and cognition" (129–30). Socioeconomic and cultural changes as well as innovations in technology and communication contributed to rapid modernization physicians judged hazardous to the nervous system. Despite capacious and potentially contradictory symptomology, the causation of neurasthenia was, Beard claimed, consistent. He envisioned modernity as a constant drain upon reserves of nervous energy, and the individual who succumbed to its pressures, he posited, had "a narrow margin of nerve-force," such that "a slight mental disturbance, unwonted toil or exposure, anything out of and beyond his usual routine, even a sleepless night" (Beard 9, 10), could trigger debilitating physical symptoms coupled with mental despair, irritability, or anxiety. Neurasthenia provided late-Victorian physicians a theoretical frame for diffuse forms of psychic injury engendered by a world rapidly modernizing in its technology, financial systems, and social arrangements.

The material nature of mind, which implicitly threatened some religious and philosophical conceptions of soul, was a point of investigation and contention in this period. In the Victorian era, disciplines of psychology, psychiatry, neurology, and anatomy overlapped with one another and with philosophy (Stiles, "Victorian Literature" 2). As a result, scholars of very different formal and informal preparation found themselves in dialogue. George Henry Lewes, distinguished as a philosopher and literary critic as well as a serious amateur physiologist, and William Benjamin Carpenter, a physician and physiologist, both sought to outline the material basis of mental life. Lewes was substantially influenced by continental and particularly German science and psychological theory, and maintained throughout his evolving philosophy "the belief that the real basis of human thought and action lies in our subrational, or animal, nature" (Dale 68, 73). While he viewed the human mind, embodied in the brain, as responsive to environment, Lewes insisted that "the mind is not a passive recipient of external impressions, but an active cooperant" (91). He posited that inscriptions of past experience interact with sensory input of new ones, so that history guides the perception of and reaction to current stimulus (Lewes 91). Carpenter similarly saw interplay between personal history and present intention guiding action; he argued that "exercise of Will, . . . if habitually exerted in certain directions, will tend to form the Character, by establishing a set of *acquired habitudes*" (97). Thinkers such as Lewes and Carpenter further complicated questions of intention in action, materially accounting for the development of character over time.

The influential Henry Maudsley explored interaction between environment and predisposition, but set an increasingly pessimistic tone for British psychiatry moving into the close of the century. Not only Darwin's *On the Origin of Species* (1859) and *The Descent of Man* (1871), but also vivisection experiments in cerebral localization from the 1860s onward, revealed connections between the minds of human and nonhuman animals that many found unsettling (Stiles, *Popular Fiction* 12–13). In keeping with Darwinian currents, Maudsley's initial interest in environmental influences on the embodied mind shifted toward greater emphasis on heredity later in the century. *The Physiology and Pathology of the Mind* (1867) stressed that all psychic and somatic function results from "reciprocal action of an individual organism and external forces" (Maudsley 199). Maudsley posited mental health or disorder as the product of interaction between inherited qualities and environment (particularly occupation) (*Physiology* 205–6). He dealt with the imprecision of Prichard's account of interrelations between physical and moral factors simply by acknowledging ambiguity: "It is custom to treat the causes of insanity as physical and moral, though it is not possible thus to discriminate them with exactness" (*Physiology* 198). He regarded degeneration, including and especially mental deterioration, as an inevitable corollary of advanced civilization (*Physiology* 201), a mindset that deepened as his career progressed.

Similar attitudes developed abroad. French neurologist Jean-Martin Charcot, whom Mark Micale calls "the most important medical figure in the history of nineteenth-century hysteria," regarded the disease he studied from the 1870s to the 1890s as a confluence of hereditary predisposition and environmental influence (often physical or emotional shock) (24–25). While Charcot treated some male patients exhibiting neurological malfunction, he believed certain symptoms, such as "ars hysteria," were grounded in female anatomy, despite conceding the absence of clear data supporting this theory in "pathological anatomy" (269). Hysteria was for Charcot a neurological defect without any effective cure (Micale 25). But in the late nineteenth century, psychiatrists and neurologists positing organic causes for mental illness repeatedly, like Charcot, fell short in their search for anatomical proof. By the end of Charcot's lifetime, the degenerationist model was losing sway in the medical community (Micale 26). When Charcot's former student Sigmund Freud entered the field with very different theories about hysteria, he found an intellectual community ready for a fresh perspective.

Despite the prevalence of Darwinian-inflected perspectives from the 1860s through the fin de siècle, the period saw increasing attention to one mental disorder triggered by external influence: psychic shock. As railroads proliferated, so did railway accidents. Train wrecks motivated physicians to study psychic injury intensively; indeed, historian Ralph Harrington suggests that "systematic medical theorization about psychological trauma in the modern West commenced with the responses of mid-Victorian medical practitioners to the so-called railway spine condition" (32). Passengers who walked away from train accidents without evident bodily injury, but suffered psychic shock, presented a challenge to physicians trying to verify victims' claims and define the nature of their injury (Matus, "Trauma" 415). As I shall discuss in detail in chapter 4, in 1861, the *Lancet* focused medical attention on health risks associated with rail travel in an eight-article series. In the section on "Secondary Effects of Railway Accidents," the authors demonstrate awareness of mental as well as physical aftereffects of railway disaster that may manifest in individuals who initially appear unharmed. Citing evidence from court cases related to rail catastrophes, the *Lancet* reports that immediately observable injuries do not offer a reliable indicator of "insidious results" that may appear at a later period (112). Along with physiological symptoms of numbness and partial paralysis, the *Lancet* includes "slowly ensuing intellectual derangement" as a possible delayed consequence to "severe cerebral concussion" from train accidents (112). The *Lancet* authors seek an explanation for *mental* symptoms in *physical* stress along the cerebral-spinal axis. Victorian medical practitioners acknowledged the possibility of a belated mental health impact of severe physical and emotional shock, more than a century before our contemporary model of PTSD.

In 1866, British surgeon John Erichsen published the first detailed medical account of "rail spine" or "rail shock," *On Railway and Other Injuries of the Nervous System,* which garnered both public and medical attention due to Erichsen's professional stature and the topic's relevance to lay readers (Harrington 43–44). Erichsen initially ascribed the emotional symptoms following a rail accident to the effects of spinal compression (Horwitz 28). Finding no empirical evidence of physical injury, he maintained an ambivalent position regarding the material versus psychological basis of the shock that precipitated disorder (Harrington 44–45). Erichsen posited that although these shocks "commonly arose from railway collisions, they were not peculiar to them, but might be the consequence of the more ordinary accidents of civil life" (preface). By the 1880s, he affirmed that symptoms associated with "nervous shock" were in some cases prompted by "mental and moral" causes related to "fear" (Erichsen 91). In addition to physiological symptoms modern readers would associate with material spinal injury, Erichsen ascribes to nervous shocks such as those attendant on railway collisions mental symptoms including "defect of memory," disrupted thought process and difficulty focusing upon a task, loss of "business aptitude," and changes of "temper" (75). Physicians responding to rail accidents discovered that somatic as well as psychic symptoms could manifest in previously healthy and mentally stable individuals as a result of sudden overwhelming fear.

Victorian doctors sought observable physical injuries in rail shock victims, but acknowledged emotional, cognitive, and somatic changes unconnected to any specific wound. In *Medical Evidence in Railway Accidents* (1868), John Charles Hall, who consulted for both plaintiffs and rail companies, professes no desire "to establish a pet theory" but instead "only to state facts," as "a practising physician of thirty years' standing" (preface). He documents one case of an "elderly gentleman" who lost consciousness in an accident and subsequently displayed an array of psychic and bodily symptoms. After the collision, the man was confused, had no memory of the accident, complained of pain where no bruise or wound was visible, and reported difficulty sleeping and reading (28). A friend of the victim indicated that following a previous rail accident in which he was physically injured, the man was "for a long time unable to attend business" and as a result displayed "a disposition to look gloomily on the future" (28). For several days following the most recent accident, the victim exhibited "exalted sensibility of the whole nervous system" (28) and was extremely sensitive to medical examinations of his back and eye, where no injury could be detected (29). The present-day reader will recognize parallels with our diagnostic criteria for PTSD: disruptions to memory and heightened arousal. Hall prescribed several months of "perfect rest, abstaining from business and all mental exertion"; the victim received an out-of-court settlement of five hundred pounds plus costs and eventually made a full recovery (29). Hall's case study, like Erichsen's widely read textbook and subsequent lectures, discerns the capacity for emotional shock and fear to act upon the brain and nervous system in material ways, long before modern neuroscience and biochemistry provided diagnostic tools to explain how it does so. Such cases demonstrate physicians' developing awareness of the interrelation of emotional and physical shock and represent a countercurrent to Darwinian-based theories of mental dysfunction.

By the fin de siècle, physicians had defined a subset of neurasthenia called "traumatic neurasthenia," giving shape to a diagnostic category that bears obvious similarity to our modern concept of PTSD. Traumatic neurasthenia developed in relation to overwhelming shock, including but not limited to rail accident. In an 1899 essay describing the disorder, Victor Horsley, a surgeon attached to University College Hospital, specifies that it typically manifests not immediately following the event but rather after a latency period of about a week (166). Horsley lists alterations in memory and emotion (167), shaking or trembling (171), and changes to vision (168), sensation (169), and reflexes (173) among common psychic and somatic symptoms. While optimistic about treatment through medication and rest cure, Horsley cautions, "the lasting effect of an injury on the patient's nervous system must be recognized" (176). Here, we see striking parallels with late-twentieth-century accounts of combat-related PTSD, particularly the recognition that onset may be delayed and effects persistent. Notably, the anthology in which Horsley's essay appears, *A System of Medicine by Many Writers*, classifies traumatic neurasthenia, along with neurasthenia and hysteria, as "diseases of the nervous system" rather than "mental diseases." Moving into the twentieth century and the Great War, physicians were still inclined to cordon off nervous disorders from more socially disruptive forms of psychic distress.

My study draws upon this medical prehistory of PTSD to reconstruct the scientific language of psychic injury available to Victorian novelists and identify its cultural associations. The intersecting discourses of hysteria, neurasthenia, and psychic shock, all situated within a broader understanding of a nervous economy subject to external forces, provided nineteenth-century authors with tools to describe the influence of the socioeconomic and material environment upon the development of an individual consciousness. Rail shock notwithstanding, Victorian medicine's overall privileging of diffuse and insidious forces over catastrophic or singular events differs in emphasis from twentieth-century theories of PTSD—while presenting parallels to our contemporary twenty-first-century moment. I now turn to a key early-Victorian fictional depiction of the wounded mind, Charlotte Brontë's final novel *Villette,* to illustrate how nineteenth-century formulations of psychic injury can enrich our perspective on trauma studies as well as our reading of the Victorian novel.

CHAPTER 2

⌁

"Dim as a Wheel Fast Spun"

Repetition and Instability of Memory in Charlotte Brontë's *Villette*

"To be homesick, one must have a home, which I have not" (363): Lucy Snowe's poignant assertion of her personal dilemma touches *Villette*'s core artistic problem, as well as Lucy's social and psychic one. The extremity of Lucy's loss—family, property, and accordingly social standing—prevents her from describing it in terms that might gain real sympathy within her social milieu, not only because the intensity of her grief renders her inarticulate, but because her losses have diminished her social and economic worth almost to the point of invisibility. Any effort she might make to communicate her experience and gain empathy is severely compromised by her position as a penniless redundant woman, at the bare edge of (though not entirely excluded from) Victorian social intelligibility and empathetic range. We find, emerging from a culture enthralled with, and perhaps in thrall to, domesticity, a novel whose female narrator-protagonist's entire family is dead as the main action of the story begins; who lacks the means, in terms of inheritance, to establish a new family through marriage; and who cannot even lay claim to the most basic requirement for a home, namely, a stable habitation. This novel whose title is an imagined place is, at its elusive center, a narrative of psychic and social placelessness and dislocation. We experience *Villette* within the narrator-protagonist's "homeless, anchorless, unsupported mind" (51). Readers of Victorian novels are well acquainted with orphans seeking to make their way in the world, with young ladies looking to marry, and even with characters who unite these two categories in one protagonist. Lucy's story differs from those of literary peers like Gaskell's Margaret in *North and South,* Dickens's *David Copperfield* and *Oliver Twist,* and Brontë's own earlier *Jane Eyre* is that the protagonist remains friendless and obscure at the novel's close. *Villette* provides no validating closure to the attention it has lavished on Lucy Snowe for five hundred pages, at least not in the terms novel readers have learned to expect: no wedding, no substantial inheritance, no significant public achievement. In *Villette,* Lucy's social and psychic dilemma is one and the same with Charlotte Brontë's artistic one. How can a novelist construct a meaningful narrative for a woman whose life falls outside the socially accepted boundaries of a story worth telling? How might the protagonist or narrator of such a story explain, validate, and respond to a loss whose parameters are hard to define?

Modern theories of narrative structure related to trauma and witnessing, in conjunction with Victorian theories of the materiality of the mind and its capacity for memory, can illuminate the significance of *Villette's* departures from more typical narrative forms and productively contextualize its narrator-protagonist's acerbity and evasions. Narrative structures attendant on traumatic experience provide a model for understanding Lucy Snowe's silences, repetitions, and obfuscations (both as narrator and as protagonist) as more than either an indication of oppression or a strategy for empowerment. *Villette's* gaps and dodges both represent and enact a model of communication that seeks to render accessible experiences and perspectives generally considered "nonnarratable" within both Brontë's contemporary culture and the traditional realist novel.[1]

As previously outlined, I define trauma as an overwhelming threat to bodily integrity and/or to the coherent, socially viable selfhood that enables psychic and cultural agency, and that produces variable but definable psychic, narrative, and cultural patterns resulting from the tension between the desire to tell and the desire to conceal the threat or psychic wound. In Lucy's case, there is both catastrophic trauma—the unnamed disasters that result in the death of her entire family and her financial ruin—and insidious trauma, the subsequent daily strain faced by a fortuneless single woman attempting to keep body and mind together in a society that provides her few social or professional opportunities. Lucy's story entails both a catastrophic

---

1. Here I employ D. A. Miller's term, which he defines thus: "the 'narratable': the instances of disequilibrium, suspense, and general insufficiency from which a given narrative appears to arise. . . . [I]t is thus opposed to the 'nonnarratable' state of quiescence assumed by a novel before the beginning and supposedly recovered by it at the end" (ix).

event that produces particular narrative effects, and circumstances of—and, from the author's perspective, a way into discussion of—insidious trauma. *Villette* reveals how contradictory directives of Victorian femininity threaten the formation of a coherent, socially accepted female self, potentially generating what we might consider insidious trauma. It attends particularly to the ways these pressures are exacerbated in women who have a nominal claim to gentility and must act the "lady" but lack economic privilege—indeed, in Lucy's case, lack basic economic stability. Psychological pain and socioeconomic constraint converge in what Lucy calls her "system of feeling" (175) dictating resistance to self-disclosure. By investing narrative control in a traumatized consciousness, *Villette* achieves a shift in perspective that redefines whose voices and stories matter in the mainstream novel, and addresses, through the indirect and circuitous route of trauma narrative, concerns that could be deemed either too trivial or too inflammatory if tackled directly, such as women's legal and cultural handicaps in the labor market and the related plight of redundant women. By bringing the familiar marriage plot into contact with both the educational and labor concerns of the bildungsroman, and the repetitions and delays of trauma narrative, Brontë places a marginalized social perspective into the center of literary discourse.

First, I will consider Lucy's omissions and evasions within story and discourse, which follow from her alternating impulses to withhold and share her experience of pain and longing. I trace their generation of a narrative framework that, without open invective, communicates to the reader the pain not only of her personal loss, but of the marginalized position that alienates her even from her own experience of grief. Next, I outline how Brontë's construction of Lucy's interiority, through the deployment and manipulation of Victorian theories of mental function, enables this plot structure. From competing scientific discourses of mental function—forward-looking phrenology and the memory-driven discourse of nerves—Brontë creates different models of novelistic interiority. By braiding them together, she produces the narrative effects we now associate with trauma, particularly the simultaneous excision and return of the past. I close with analysis of the recurrent image of the shipwreck, which both emblematizes Lucy's trauma and masks its specific details, exploring what this symbol reveals about the nature of traumatic experience. I diverge from readings that position Lucy's omissions and evasions as indicators either of oppression or empowerment, and instead consider how these patterns of speech and narration communicate kinds of experience difficult to address directly within Victorian society and traditional realist narrative.

PSYCHIC FRAGMENTATION TO SOCIAL INTEGRATION:
SEEKING A WITNESS

Critical attention to the tension between withholding and disclosure in *Villette* often regards Lucy's reticence and social invisibility as either symptoms of oppression, clandestine means of empowerment, or some fusion of the two. Mary Jacobus's influential reading recognizes both the external socioeconomic factors that engender this pose and its strategic uses, calling Lucy's invisibility both "a calculated deception—a blank screen onto which others project their view of her" (44) and "an aspect of her oppression" (45). Important early feminist readings focused on the relation of Lucy's silence to her socioeconomic subjugation and resultant stifled emotions.[2] Other critics shifted attention from the pain of Lucy's self-suppression to its affective, social, or narrative value.[3] Positing Lucy's self-suppression as a sign of social oppression or a means to power, these critics tended to treat the cause of her reticence as either self-evident or unfathomable. Recent analyses align Lucy's narrative misdirection with her complex sociological position as a foreign worker in a non-Anglophone country.[4] The very plausibility of competing arguments regarding the import of Lucy's stifled desires and narrative withholding suggests the novel's characteristic ambivalence, and points to the value of considering silence, either voluntary or socially mandated, not only as an indication of disempowerment or a strategy for the exercise of power, but also, as Foucault has proposed, a part of the discourse, rather than the marker of its limit.[5]

---

2. Helene Moglen (*Charlotte Brontë: The Self-Conceived*) as well as Sandra Gilbert and Susan Gubar (*The Madwoman in the Attic*) connect Lucy's socioeconomically mandated self-suppression with the stunting of a possible and desirable fullness of identity.

3. John Kucich suggests the "repressive solitude" of Brontë's narrator-protagonists, including Lucy, enables the author to explore "heightened inwardness" of interiority (77). Such repression of desire also empowers protagonists within the novels' imagined worlds, allowing them to "convert self-negating impulses into self-containing ones," facilitating maintenance of a cohesive self (78). Karen Lawrence argues that Lucy's invisibility within the novel's imagined world affords privileged access to the lives of others, empowering her to develop skill as observer and interpreter (449–51). Ivan Kreilkamp proposes that "Lucy acquires value by refusing to narrate" (145).

4. See Siobhan Carroll, "'Play You Must': *Villette* and the Nineteenth-Century Board Game" (2017) and Talia Schaffer, "Why Lucy Doesn't Care: Migration and Emotional Labor in *Villette*" (2019).

5. Foucault argues "silence itself—the things one declines to say, or is forbidden to name, the discretion that is required between different speakers—is less the absolute limit of discourse, the other side from which it is separated by a strict boundary, than an element that functions alongside the things said, with them and in relation to them within over-all strategies" (27).

Lucy's alternating impulses to divulge and conceal emerge from the traumatic nature of her experience and related affective response. As early in the critical dialogue as 1979, before PTSD had entered the DSM, much less trauma studies the academy, Gilbert and Gubar observed that "the horror of [Lucy's] life . . . is the horror of repetition," a painful "fragmentation within" that returns unbidden (412). The dynamics of trauma narrative offer insight into the logic of Lucy's repetitions, both their agonizing psychic effects and their confusing and unsettling narrative ones. Originary trauma dictates not only the events of *Villette* (as in many Victorian novels), but also its aesthetic form.

Some Victorian novels employ psychically disordered characters as antagonists or minor characters, who are described by first-person narrators that seek to position themselves, contrastingly, as rational, for instance Brontë's own earlier *Jane Eyre*, Collins's *The Woman in White*, or Dickens's *David Copperfield*. *Villette*, in contrast, places the disordered consciousness in the narrator's role. Here the psychically disordered character shapes not only the way we see her, but the way we see other characters, and how the story is told. Through the eyes of desiring and self-denying Lucy Snowe, Brontë presents a world vividly attuned to the ideology of Victorian femininity: denial of appetite, with regard to food, love, lust, and knowledge, is the mark of a lady. Within this moral landscape, the impoverished and unattached Lucy seeks to gratify her desires for both professional self-advancement and affection without losing her genteel self-identity and social status. Not only, as with the previous novel, the events, but here also the structure of the narrator-protagonist's quest is complicated by a prior loss, whose consequences ripple through her narrative like the aftershocks of an impact. Whereas *Jane Eyre* traces a steady, mythologized progression of personal development, *Villette*'s plot, along with Lucy's emotions and fortunes, oscillates and repeats, always circling back to the earlier tragedy whose details the narrator will not share. *Villette* draws upon established narrative forms: the marriage plot, wherein the process of a young lady's education closes with the mature choice of marriage to a chosen suitor, and the male ambition plot, wherein the worthy but penniless young man establishes himself as a gentleman through ingenuity and diligence. Yet it disappoints readers who expect the steady progression and satisfying closure common to these models. This sense of uncertainty depends as much on the evasive, circular, and at times seemingly exaggerated narration as it does on the events of the story. The instability of Lucy's consciousness renders her mundane surroundings fantastical. Jane relates gothic horrors in a steady tone and domesticates her eerie dreams with folklore interpretations; in Lucy's narration it can be difficult to pinpoint where real events end and symbolic hallucinations begin. (Her waking vision of dormitory beds as haunting "spectres" in the midst of a bout of depression [160] and her opium-addled perceptions of the fête in the public park are prime examples.) Further, manipulative and evasive, Lucy reports and critiques the actions and feelings of others to convey her own history and desires (the opening interlude with Polly at Bretton, for instance),[6] while concealing from both the reader and other characters the source of the grief that triggers her periodic outbursts and fuels her latent hostility. The resulting narrative is, to borrow a phrase Paul Emmanuel applies to Lucy herself, "at once mournful and mutinous" (232). Why might Brontë employ such an unsympathetic narrator and protagonist, whose convoluted storytelling and seemingly passive behavior result in what has been criticized as a strangely wandering and actionless plot? And why does Lucy, so similar to Jane in outward circumstances, prove so different a narrator?

Villette's narrative style reflects and mediates the central narrative problem of the novel: Lucy's inability to square psychic experience with material reality. The disjunction between her powerful desires and emotions and her socially limited means to act upon or express them provides narrative tension and shapes the novel's uneven and repetitive plot. The narrator-protagonist's marked divide between psychic and social/material realms originates in her mysterious bereavement that, prior to the novel's main action, separates her from her only source of both affection and social standing, her family, leaving her active and ardent mind, devoid of social outlets, to turn on itself. Initially, Lucy owns herself content to endure an austere and unsatisfying social and material existence so long as her psychic life may flourish undisturbed. The story gains traction when she attempts to bring the two realms into meaningful relation through a human connection. Contrasting her intense and painful emotional experience with her mundane social and material one, Lucy explains that she "seemed to hold two lives—the life of thought, and that of reality; and, provided the former was nourished with a sufficiency of the strange necromantic joys of fancy, the privileges of the latter might remain limited to daily bread, hourly work, and a roof of shelter" (77). The strict dichotomy will not endure at Rue Fosette, however; only the most complete retirement—as available at Miss Marchmont's—allows her to police this artificially imposed line. Immediately after the preceding declaration, Lucy is thrust into a social interaction that obliges her to call on her utmost emotional and intellectual resources to negotiate the social and material world: Madame Beck asks her to stand in for the suddenly absent English teacher, thus to assert authority and convey knowledge to rebellious pupils, employing a foreign language. Private sorcery of the imagination will not do; Lucy's

---

6. Moglen, *Charlotte Brontë* 197–99.

mental powers must focus on an immediate interpersonal goal. She discovers maintaining order, respect, and productivity in daily public interactions with numerous students and colleagues obliges her to bring the psychic and the social realms into contact far more than did tending to the needs of an invalid or several young children. As she masters French and her professional life develops, she grows more eager for a social connection that would allow her not only selectively to draw upon her psychic life, but to validate it fully.

Yet interactions with students and fellow teachers do not alleviate Lucy's core dilemma of the inarticulable nature of her loss. When, during a school vacation, she finds herself alone and without an intellectually challenging task, she concedes, "My spirits had been gradually sinking; now that the prop of employment was withdrawn, they went down fast" (156). Brontë's scientifically informed delineation of Lucy's mental and physical breakdown is an issue to which I will later return. For my present line of inquiry, it is key to observe that Lucy's collapse is triggered not simply by an episode of relative solitude and intellectual dormancy—both circumstances to which she has been long accustomed—but by the combination of those circumstances with knowledge that other teachers and students have a home to return to, whereas she has none. Collapsing ill, beset by hallucinatory visions and an excruciating nightmare about the dead, the Protestant Lucy finally, without any deliberate plan that she shares with the reader, seeks relief in a Catholic confessional. She reflects only that "to take this step could not make me more wretched than I was; it might soothe me" (161). This action begins the process by which Lucy attempts to bring psychic reality into meaningful relation with her social and material world through communication with a sympathetic interlocutor. While Lucy herself does not initially understand what she is trying to do, only that the internal pressure of her psychic life has become unbearable, Brontë structures the novel around the vacillating movement this impulse entails. The dialectic between the compulsion to tell and the need to conceal directs the novel's movement. Its plot traces Lucy's halting yet persistent attempts to form a relationship of affective reciprocity, which correlate not only with a desire to articulate and move beyond her painful history, but also with her efforts to forge a social identity that commands respect and enables active social participation. *Villette*'s striking differences from superficially similar Victorian novels stem from the fact that Lucy Snowe seeks more than just a husband. She searches for a witness whose empathetic affirmation of her perspective might help her to recover the unified sense of self that would enable psychic and social agency.

At this juncture it is necessary to consider in more depth what witnessing entails. Kelly Oliver's model posits witnessing—an interaction with the other

defined by responsibility and "response-ability" rather than subordination—
as the means by which agency can be recuperated for victims of oppression
and domination, who have undergone the traumatic experience of extreme
objectification. Oliver regards this type of interpersonal interaction as crucial to establishing individual agency (*Witnessing* 87). Paradoxically, however,
even as the performance of giving testimony affirms the victim as a subject,
the constative element of that testimony, which is the story of oppression,
reinscribes the victim's objectification, producing pain and shame (98–99).
And for those victims who are members of groups oppressed and othered
by the dominant culture, there is the additional problem of credibility; their
testimony is always considered suspect (99–100). Nonetheless, Oliver insists,
"bearing witness works-through the trauma of objectification by reinstituting
subjective agency as the ability to respond or address oneself" (105). What is
at stake here is not just the possibility of telling a story of traumatic experience, or even of asserting one's needs and opinions, but the very capacity to
maintain and validate one's own perspective and thus a coherent individual
identity.

There is no direct link between Lucy's catastrophic trauma (loss of family
and fortune) and any extreme or systemic form of oppression. But the financially, socially, and professionally limited position of a single woman without
fortune in nineteenth-century Europe intensifies Lucy's grief and contributes
to what we might call the insidious trauma that afflicts her, making her way
as a foreigner through a world not friendly to "redundant" women. Isolated
by her anomalous social status, Lucy seems gradually to intuit that forging
a meaningful affective bond with another person is a crucial step toward
recouping her sense of coherent self and agency. *Villette*'s central plot follows
Lucy's cautious advances toward and painful reverses from men who might
serve as her witness and help bridge the psychic and social divide, with the
more conventional love stories of the rivals Ginevra and Paulina (neither of
whom comprehend themselves to be Lucy's rivals) integrated for comparison
as auxiliary plots. One cannot overstate the significance of the way these bright
beauties are made foils to plain, poor Lucy, whereas Lucy herself is the center
of the novel's discourse and the reader's emotional investments although not
the story's imagined world. A few comparisons intensify our shock at this
reversal: It is as if Emma exists to deepen our understanding of Miss Bates and
Jane Fairfax, or Elizabeth Bennet to heighten the pathos of Charlotte Lucas.
By shifting the focus of narration from a search for a husband to a search for
a witness, Brontë allows a woman distinguished neither by wealth, beauty,
illustrious heritage, nor sparkling wit to make her perspective as central in art
as it is peripheral in society. The novel is Lucy's story of her attempts to tell

her story, and her discovery that it is far easier to relate a conventional story of love than to communicate her own experience of loss. There are two layers to Lucy's task of witnessing: her actions and words as a character within her own narrative, seeking an empathetic connection, and her choices as a narrator, attempting to convey her experience to readers.

It is worth considering at length why Lucy repeatedly seeks a male interlocutor, when it might seem a woman would better understand the nuances of her social position. Lucy's antagonism of other women would be regarded as markedly atypical and culpable within Brontë's contemporary culture. Sharon Marcus posits female friendship as central to the construction of normative Victorian femininity and suggests that by cultivating traits such as self-effacement, altruism, and sweetness, it reinforced qualities valued in wives (59) even as it provided women a relationship in which they could assert agency, compete, and show affection in ways they could not around men (107). Noting the dismay with which contemporary reviewers received Lucy Snowe's hostility toward other women (106), Marcus further suggests that Lucy's inability to form female friendships contributes to her failure to marry in a novelistic milieu in which the one rapport frequently provided narrative impetus for the other (108). Indeed, in contrast with Jane Eyre, who learns the self-regulation and capacity for affection she needs for marriage through formative female friendships, Lucy Snowe expresses varying degrees of scorn and mistrust for all her female peers.

Yet the difference lies not entirely in Lucy's perception. In the later novel, Brontë constructs a novelistic universe devoid of any nurturing and considerate Bessie, Helen Burns, Miss Temple, or Rivers sisters. Lucy's stay with Miss Marchmont sets up the pattern, which repeats throughout *Villette*, wherein women are so absorbed in their own emotional lives and/or socioeconomic interests that they are either unable to perceive or unwilling to respond sympathetically to one another's troubles. Madame Beck, of course, monitors Lucy's character and emotional state in a purely instrumental way, to determine how useful or hazardous Lucy might be to her own plans, but even Lucy's apparent friends among the novel's female characters display an insensitivity to her sadness and the awkwardness of her social position that is at times startling. Both Ginevra and Paulina revel in their romantic good fortune—clearly enabled, in both instances, by their socioeconomic status—in confidential conversations with this lonely woman who has lost her fortune and chances of a respectable marriage along with her entire family. Louisa Bretton, Lucy's godmother, is just as absorbed in her own happiness as are the young girls. The only female character we meet whose position is analogous to Lucy's—she is genteel yet fortuneless—is Zélie St. Pierre, her aggressive competitor for Paul's attention.

And of course, Lucy herself demonstrates little sympathy for other women and girls, not only behaving with cold reserve or sardonic, even caustic verbal aggression toward them much of the time, but also manipulating their lives in her narration to communicate her own emotional state to the reader. All female interactions in *Villette* are governed by pragmatic considerations: How is she useful to me, and how is she a threat? Repudiating the dominant ethos of female amity, *Villette* suggests that under its contemporary socioeconomic system, a thinking woman cannot view her peers as other than rivals, and thus cannot share with them a genuinely disinterested, respectful sympathy. Given this context, it is not surprising that *Villette*'s one attempt at witnessing between women goes badly awry.

The episode in which the crippled spinster Miss Marchmont tells Lucy of the tragic romance that arrested her youthful potential establishes both the attraction of and the hazard posed by an attempt to unburden the injured psyche. One evening Lucy, serving as Miss Marchmont's paid companion, notices her employer is feeling strangely revived. Miss Marchmont then makes Lucy the confidant of her youthful hopes, the tragedy that destroyed them, and her reckoning with God's inscrutable ways. Feeling improved in health and spirits, Miss Marchmont goes to bed resolving to be a better woman and implies that one of her good deeds will be writing the penniless Lucy into her will. Then Miss Marchmont dies. Were it not for this dénoument, Miss Marchmont's testimony to both her youthful trauma and its impact on her life and character would seem to demonstrate only the positive, healing power of sharing an experience of pain and loss with a patient and supportive interlocutor. Yet in depicting both the vivid yet momentary relief of such an interaction, and its mortal consequences—Lucy implies that Miss Marchmont's heightened awareness and excitement are linked to the fit that kills her—Brontë demonstrates the paradox of witnessing, acknowledging both its urgency and its potential danger.

Reliving her brief happy courtship produces evanescent euphoria for Miss Marchmont, but reliving the horror of seeing her lover mortally wounded and reflecting on the intervening years of meaningless pain produces a more substantial and damaging self-knowledge. Miss Marchmont concedes that she has not turned her grief to any useful or noble end; rather, she has "only been a woe-struck and selfish woman" (41). Lucy's subsequent attempt to affirm that her employer's philanthropy has indeed done good falls flat. Miss Marchmont's new resolution to be worthy of her dead Frank does not assuage her painful conviction that her efforts thus far have been futile, just as her heroic efforts to aid the dying lover were futile. Witnessing is transformative, but that self-transformation can end in total self-negation. Miss Marchmont's fragile identity cracks under the weight of self-examination and self-assertion, as emblematized in the final breakdown of her worn body. And Lucy, inheritor of this experience, is left simultaneously tempted by the relief, albeit temporary, such unburdening offers, and repelled by its potential link to self-annihilation. Even as she moves toward dialogue and away from solipsism, Lucy's ambivalence about affective connections is persistently registered in her tendency to maintain close relationships characterized by either overt combativeness within the story (as with Paul and Ginevra) or covert sarcasm within the discourse (as with Graham and Paulina). She prefers a few intimate friends to a crowd of casual companions, but the more intense the bond, the more she maintains a sort of affective buffer through her own rancor.

In spite of her ambivalence about the efficacy of sharing a story of loss, as Lucy's self-enforced dividing line between the psychic and social begins to blur, she seeks external social validation for her internal affective life. Significantly, the first two potential witnesses to whom Lucy turns, but whom she finally rejects as unsuitable, are a priest and a doctor, who in Foucault's understanding of confession serve as ministers of surveillance and control. As Cvetkovich suggests, "the audience for the story is crucial to its effects, and some stories serve the interests of their listeners at the expense of the teller" (*Archive of Feelings* 93). As I analyze in succession the three potential witnesses Lucy approaches, I will consider how the expectations and cultural or personal investments of each influence both the kind of story Lucy can tell and her affective response to sharing some portion of her traumatic experience. Lucy's confession to the priest (whom she later identifies as Père Silas, Paul's old tutor) is the first attempt to speak the truth of her experience that she relates to the reader. Both the hierarchical, formalized nature of the confession ritual and Lucy's double sense of her own foreignness in this environment, and of the priest's foreignness from her perspective, hinder the development of any empathetic rapport. As discussed, Lucy's confession to the priest is precipitated by her depression when the exodus of teachers and students returning to their families over vacation plunges her back into the solitude of her painful memories, under circumstances that necessarily remind her of what she has lost. In expressing her psychological distress at economic deprivation and social isolation through a religious framework, Brontë's narrator-protagonist echoes the discourse of actual Victorian women, who drew upon culturally familiar scriptural language when medical terminology fell short.[7] Given her resolute Protestantism and open scorn for the

---

7. In her recent study of Victorian asylum records, Diana Peschier finds that absent suitably precise medico-psychological language, female Victorian inmates "frequently described their symptoms in religious terminology," which was broadly accessible across educational

Catholic church, Lucy's willingness to seek sympathetic dialogue in a priest's confessional indicates the extremity of her desperation. Yet readers expecting a climatic revelation will be disappointed; the priest solves nothing, and the reader learns little.

The first point to consider is that Lucy's confession is actually spoken in French, a language in which she never feels comfortable with her powers of articulation. So, in addition to the obstacles to communication inherent in the relation of traumatic experience, there is an added layer of difficulty. In her English rendition, her confession, such as the reader gets of it, and the priest's response, are as follows:

> I said, I was perishing for a word of advice or an accent of comfort. I had been living for some weeks quite alone; I had been ill; I had a pressure of affliction on my mind of which it would hardly any longer endure the weight.
> "Was it a sin, a crime?" he inquired, somewhat startled.
> I reassured him on this point, and, as well as I could, I showed him the mere outline of my experience.
> He looked thoughtful, surprised, puzzled. "You take me unawares," said he. "I have not had such a case as yours before: ordinarily we know our routine and are prepared, but this makes a great break in the common course of confession. I am hardly furnished with counsel fitting the circumstances."
> (161–62)

The diction that opens Lucy's confession—"perishing for"—suggests starvation, want of emotional nourishment. However, these words, like the rest of what Lucy relates that she spoke to the priest in the course of her confession, are not in quotation marks, whereas his responses are. In her narration of the event, Lucy paraphrases her actual words spoken at the time. What the reader receives not only contains gaping factual omissions, but is offered in a mediated form. In this mediated or diluted manner, Lucy relates to the reader those brief sections of her confession that address what precipitated her current crisis and how it makes her feel, but not the nature and certainly not the details of her grief, loss, or transgression. Even her response to the priest's question of whether the source of her pain is a crime or a sin—"I reassured him on this point"—does not conclusively specify whether she answered in the positive or the negative, though it does suggest the latter. Lucy employs the priest's

---

levels and central to women's social lives in the lower and middle classes (58). Peschier's survey supports the oft-repeated dictum that the unique strains of genteel-poor teachers and governesses such as Lucy Snowe made them particularly susceptible to the mental breakdowns that sent women to asylums (56–58).

responses—given in quotation marks to signal exactitude—to manipulate the reader's understanding. On a concrete level, the priest's response demonstrates that the circumstances of Lucy's pain are unique. One can assume that an elderly priest has heard a wide range of human experience and spiritual trouble narrated; in order for her story to present a fresh problem, it must be truly beyond the pale. One suspects, based on her reference to memories of the "well-loved dead" (160) as she begins her spiral into depression, that the missing story within the narrative concerns the tragedy of Lucy's early life, and perhaps also some intimation of her hopeless infatuation with Dr. John. There is, however, no conclusive evidence in the text. Such omissions serve to deepen mystery. But beyond simply establishing the seriousness of her plight and building readerly anticipation for a revelation she ultimately never makes, what does Lucy's rhetorical obfuscation in the above-quoted passage accomplish? Why might Lucy seek out a priest to whom to confess her innermost pain, and why might she then decline to share with the reader what she related to him?

Some answer can be found in the complex nature of traumatic experience. Explaining the resistance of survivors who hesitate to speak of the traumatic event, Caruth states that "beyond the loss of precision, there is another, more profound, disappearance: the loss, precisely, of the event's essential incomprehensibility, the force of its *affront to understanding*" (*Trauma* 154). By reducing the ethically and emotionally obscene event—the event so totally unacceptable that it cannot be assimilated—to a comprehensible narrative, the survivor feels he or she is conceding something, giving in to the trauma. Taken in this light, Lucy's narrative evasion can be seen not as unnecessary coyness, but as the manifestation of unbearable psychic pain. Moreover, the priest, while sympathetic, must necessarily fail as a witness for trauma because he cannot allow himself to be changed by Lucy's testimony; it is his duty to convert her to his worldview, not to validate and empathize with hers. By telling her story to a Catholic priest, Lucy succeeds only in inadvertently demonstrating the inadequacy of her Protestant theology for helping her cope with grief. The effective witness must be alive to the uniqueness of an individual's experience and able to respond to its particular significance. Lucy's confession to the priest ultimately has no healing power—a fact Brontë underlines by having her heroine collapse with physical illness shortly after leaving the church. Lucy has rehearsed the story of her personal loss and concomitant social marginalization in a context that can only lead to institutional judgment, not social validation. Having experienced the renewed pain of this failed attempt at relief, Lucy avoids repeating the failure by not relating it to the reader, and thus indicates the total unacceptability of her suffering.

At first glance, Dr. John Graham Bretton seems a more promising potential witness for Lucy. Their shared youthful history and shared culture ensure
she will experience none of the formality and distrust inherent to any attempt
this fiercely Protestant Englishwoman might make to speak her truth in a
foreign Catholic confessional. Further, due to family connections, Graham
must surely already know at least the outline of Lucy's experience of loss,
which should smooth the way for their communication. In a limited way
and for brief periods, Graham's company brings relief from her loneliness.
Lucy longs for communication with Graham and cherishes the breezy visits
and letters that, however sparingly, nourish her affectively "famished" (244)
consciousness, so long deprived of substantive sympathy. Nonetheless, she is
canny enough to discern that this favorite son of fortune diffuses his good
nature as unthinkingly "as the ripe fruit rewards with sweetness the rifling
bee" (362). The comfortable Graham lacks both motive and the requisite
humility to enter into the feelings of a less advantaged person. His response
to Lucy's sorrow, most significantly when summoned to attend her collapse
following a sighting of the ghostly nun, is to listen, assess, and advise—sympathetically, but as a superior immune to or removed from the pressures
that afflict his patient and kinswoman. Lucy insists that in this instance Graham's conduct in soothing her fears is nothing short of "heroic" (247). Yet
the similes she employs to convey its effect reveal her consciousness that his
kindness can be only of a passive sort, careless of its object and without reciprocity. She claims that he was "as good to me as the well is to the parched
wayfarer—as the sun to the shivering jay-bird" (247). Such language shows
an inherent emotional inequality to the relationship: It is a crucial life-source
to Lucy, yet a passive, casual, unsought contact for Graham. The individual
who can serve as a witness to trauma must be willing to be transformed by
the survivor's testimony, and both receptive and perceptive enough to help
her recuperate an image of herself as an active agent, while still acknowledging the severity of the psychic wound that has damaged her sense of agency.
Graham is so carelessly unperceptive that he fails to notice the woman he
fondly dismisses as "quiet Lucy Snowe" (317), whom he makes the audience
of his love conquests and seeks to employ as a go-between, has been hope-
lessly smitten with him since childhood. However much she wishes it to be
otherwise, Lucy knows better than to share more intelligence of her suffering
with Graham than he, in his professional capacity, requests in order to evalu-
ate and treat her. As a provider of temporary relief, Graham is far more helpful than the priest, yet again the impossibility of affective reciprocity prevents
the relationship from meeting Lucy's need. For Lucy, the communication and
need must go both ways.

Lucy at last finds affective reciprocity in her relationship with Paul Emanuel. Paul has two key points of connection with her experience: He has suffered a tragic loss, and he is her professional colleague. Yet unlike the women with whom she shares similar connections, he is not her direct competitor. A male professor, better paid and enjoying more public cachet than a female teacher, will never be Lucy's rival as is her fellow fortuneless but genteel schoolteacher, Zélie St. Pierre, with whom she competes for employment as well as romantic attention. Because they are neither considered to be on the same intellectual level nor eligible for the same professional positions, Lucy and Paul are never in direct social or economic competition, however much they verbally spar. Because they work side by side, however, Paul both understands her professional life and appreciates (and cultivates) her growing competence. It has been noted that *Villette* opens with its heroine's entry into the labor market rather than the novelistic convention of entry into the marriage market (Newton 93). As professionalism is crucial to Lucy's growing capacity for self-assertion, the importance of this connection with Paul should not be underestimated.

The still more crucial link is shared experience of loss and grief. Many at the pensionnat perceive Lucy's unhappiness, but only Paul treats her suffering with respectful concern. Throughout the novel it is Paul who, out of inclination rather than, like Graham, professional duty, or, like Madame Beck, self-interest, looks after Lucy's physical health and intellectual development. In contrast with Graham, Paul takes an active interest in her well-being. He quite literally feeds the pining and slender Lucy as well as nourishes her intellect with books, lessons, and conversation. Upon finding her in tears, midway through the narrative, Paul attempts to draw out her grief with the carefully phrased question, "Tell me the truth—you grieve at being parted from friends—is it not so?" He waits patiently for Lucy to share her story, but she sends him away, because, she insists, "The insinuating softness was not more acceptable than inquisitorial curiosity," and she finds that she "*could* not talk." She then sits alone and weeps, and, she states, "These tears proved a relief" (233). Much later we learn, through the Madame Walravens episode, that Paul's sensitivity toward Lucy's suffering originates in his direct empathy with her situation; he, too, lost the hopes of his youth when his fiancée, forbidden to marry him by her wealthy parents, faded into an early death during her novitiate at a convent.

Paul is able to help Lucy recover her sense of agency without denying the weight of her grief, and further, he shows willingness to be changed by her experience rather than simply expecting her to adjust her perceptions to his. Paul's interpretation of Lucy's temperament and behavior is perhaps no more accurate than Graham's, but the key difference is that Paul's misin-

terpretations ascribe activity, competence, and self-assertion to her. She may
not really be learned or intellectually ambitious, and she certainly does not
play the coquette to Graham Bretton, but by reacting to Lucy as if she were
in a position of power, Paul helps her imagine herself in a position of power.
Paul's unique perception of Lucy's capacity for passion and assertion is figured metaphorically as his sensitivity to the flames beneath her icy demeanor.
Lucy insists that she "had feelings: passive as I lived, little as I spoke, cold as
I looked, when I thought of past days, I *could* feel" (109). Of all her acquaintance, only the "fiery" (154) Paul Emmanuel correctly interprets the warmth
of both love and rage in Lucy's grief, saying, "I see on your cheek two tears
which I know are hot as two sparks, and salt as two crystals of the sea" (232).
His language echoes the sea and shipwreck metaphors Lucy herself employs
to describe her pain, further underscoring their connection. Over the course
of their relationship, we see the positive effect of Paul's affirmation of Lucy's
capacity for agency. She is increasingly assertive, saving money to start her
own school and taking Paul into her confidence in this plan, and standing
up to the wheedling of Pere Silas and bullying of Madame Beck when they
oppose her interest in him. Why, then, does Lucy persist in concealing the
details of her pain from Paul, even after she has developed her capacity for
self-assertion, and even when he is her fiancé? Why is he, even as her chosen
and accepted suitor, not quite a suitable witness?

It is tempting to argue that simple ingrained habits of misogynist culture
are the primary obstructions to communication. Although Paul declares to
Lucy that "we are alike" (367), it is unclear if he can ever understand her intellect as anything other than what he calls, in an outburst, a "Lusus naturæ, a
luckless accident, a thing for which there was neither place nor use in creation, wanted neither as wife nor worker" (354). There are some aspects of
Lucy's experience that she gradually learns to share with Paul, but she makes
clear that he never quite appreciates the dilemma of a woman who rejects supporting or decorative roles and seeks to define herself as an autonomous individual. Moreover, his participation in Madame Beck's system of surveillance
aligns him with the forces of intrusion and control that are antithetical to
Lucy's desire to direct the narrative of her own life. However, I would ascribe
the ultimate impasse in communication to a difference in their experience of
loss occasioned by the intersection of class and gender. No degree of personal
sensitivity on Paul's part could alter the fact that Lucy's bereavement involves
socioeconomic consequences that his does not. Paul manages to overcome the
financial straits caused by his father's business failure through industry and
professional achievement, eventually becoming affluent enough to charitably
support his dead fiancée's mother and grandmother when they fall into ruin

and disgrace. Lucy, left destitute as well as bereaved at the loss of her family, likewise hopes to earn both social respect and financial security through work. But the employments open to a genteel woman—lady's maid, lady companion, governess, or schoolteacher—command neither social status nor significant financial reward. The marriage market, which requires bartering of the beauty, fortune, and connections that Lucy does not have, remains the most respectable way for a woman to provide for herself. Even the measure of security she attains as the director of her own school at the novel's close owes more to Miss Marchmont's bequest than to Lucy's work, in spite of her diligence and skill; it is a reward parceled out by the author, not the society.

Paul appears to believe, not unreasonably, that his loss is like Lucy's, and he therefore can comprehend her grief. But his loss, however painful, does not impede and indeed enables his gaining respect for the industry with which he earns his way through the world and the chivalrous charity he bestows on his would-have-been mother-in-law. As Brenda Silver notes, "nowhere, perhaps, are the effects of Lucy's solitude more evident than in the loss of social status that accompanies her loss of family, a clear indication of the interconnected role of class and gender in determining a person's development—and worth" (95–96). Lucy's loss of family, like that of any fortuneless woman, affords her, if anything, the kind of pity rooted in fear of the object's social stigma. What Paul cannot comprehend, Brontë implies, is the shame of being considered a burden to society that, for so many of her contemporary women, deepens the pain of loss. As Brontë wrote to her friend W. S. Williams in 1849, "Your daughters—no more than your sons—should be a burden on your hands: your daughters—as much as your sons—should aim at making their way honorably through life. . . . Believe me—teachers may be hard-worked, ill-paid and despised—but the girl who stays home doing nothing is worse than the hardest-wrought and worst-paid drudge of a school" (Barker 241). For Brontë, no degradation and penury of humble employment could surpass the pain of being a "burden" to others, but she well knew, writing *Villette* after years of schoolteaching followed by her more satisfying, but equally gendered, experience of authorship, a woman's aspirations in the public sphere were, to her contemporary society, dubious at best. Lucy's ambitions, unlike Paul's, will never be celebrated, at best tolerated, and as a penniless, bereaved woman, she cannot be the charitable hero, like him, only the object of charity, like Justine Marie's mother.

Lucy's work offers subsistence wages and distraction from psychic pain, but it is not a path toward public reward or personal healing. In a reading focused on Lucy's status as migrant laborer, Talia Schaffer observes that *Villette* disappoints those expecting a protagonist's self-development through meaningful employment: "Readers are used to a *bildungsroman,* in which a young person grows to discover ideal work; but in migrant literature, the work comes first: uninteresting labor painfully, inexorably, remakes a person" ("Why" 93). In contrast with Paul, who after personal and economic catastrophe finds redemption through his career, Lucy attains only survival, not flourishing, from often dreary and sometimes combative workplace interactions that fill her days at Pensionnat Beck. Lucy's fiancé can connect with her lingering sadness at the deaths of loved ones, and remember the shock and humiliation of suddenly lost financial stability, but her ongoing psychic distress inheres in the gendered socioeconomic conditions that constrain her social outlets for processing grief. That experience is inaccessible to him. While Lucy herself appears to believe that if her fiancé lived, the perfect communion would have been achieved, Brontë, in snatching him away, implies that the socially imposed inequality of their suffering precludes genuine affective reciprocity.

THE MATERIAL AND NARRATIVE FORMS OF PSYCHIC LIFE

The narrative vacillations that signal traumatic experience are grounded in fluctuations of Lucy's embodied mental life. As Aleksandar Stević observes, "the psychological crisis of Lucy Snowe [extends] into a crisis of narrative authority and, finally, of novelistic form" (96). Other recent readings similarly emphasize the disunity of her narrating consciousness.[8] By the mid-nineteenth century, the practice of phrenology had widely disseminated an idea of selfhood as divided among discrete mental capacities. Just as important, the developing science of neurology localized physiological control of distinct bodily functions within specific points in the brain, whose overall importance as an active organ within the nervous system was gradually recognized in medical circles.[9] Reflective of contemporaneous scientific discourses that figured normative consciousness as characterized by multi-

---

8. Elisha Cohn reads *Villette* as "divided" between "the developmental plot, which is explicitly embraced even though its promises are not borne out," and "the suspended mood of lyric" (31). Highlighting Brontë's use of phrenological models of the mind, Anna Gibson argues that "Lucy Snowe experiences and narrates herself as fragmented, heterogeneous, and processual rather than unified and stable" (208). In a formalist analysis, Ezra Dan Feldman takes the more extreme position that the novel's narration is depersonalized, not reflective of any stable human consciousness (79).

9. On the transformations of nineteenth-century neurological thought as Victorian novelists would have understood them, see Rachel Malane's *Sex in Mind,* especially 27–33.

plicity, *Villette* presents Lucy (as both protagonist and narrator) as an espe-cially fragmented psyche.

Even so, within the novel's active plot, Lucy as protagonist is increasingly motivated to seek harmony if not unity among disparate aspects of her self-hood and between self and social world. In tracing the narrator-protagonist's attempts to reintegrate her fractured psyche through social interactions, Brontë draws upon contemporary models for the materiality of the mind and cultural modes of relating corporeal form to moral character. This is not to say the author, or her narrator-protagonist, endorses the veracity of any one medico-scientific system for mental function. I accord with Alexandra Lewis's assessment that "Lucy struggles to articulate the truth of her experience, in a medical language frustratingly ill-equipped to capture its reality" (91), and *Villette* "challenges theories which reduce mind to body" (92). Rather than align the experience of psychic trauma with one diagnosis, or indeed, one system for describing mental function, Brontë integrates the competing discourses of neurology and phrenology to negotiate the temporality of Lucy's desire: backward pull of embodied memory and forward momentum of aspiration. Scientific discourse enables the author to interrogate links among Lucy's intellectual, emotional, and physical deprivation. By opposing phrenology and neurology as models of mental function, *Villette* juxtaposes categorical potential against individual history. Brontë employs these alternative theories of cognition to create, in Lucy's narration, the oscillating plot structure and narrative gaps I have previously linked to traumatic experience.

The most gripping action of *Villette* occurs inside its protagonist's mind. Both disciplines that provide terminology for that action claimed a scientific basis and enjoyed widespread cultural relevance in Brontë's lifetime; although neurology was the medical establishment's privileged discourse for material-ity of the mind, phrenology had not been conclusively discredited.[10] Brontë knew both neurological and phrenological models of the mental function through direct personal experience: She consulted medical doctors regard-ing her nervous symptoms and also received a "reading" from a professional phrenologist.[11] Lucy Snowe is similarly diagnosed, by Graham in his capac-ity as physician, with a loosely defined ailment "of the nerves" (249) and, of

---

10. On the liminal position of phrenology in the early Victorian period, see Dames, *Amne-siac Selves* 80–81.

11. Sally Shuttleworth and Nicholas Dames both discuss Brontë's 1851 phrenological read-ing, which she considered an accurate assessment. See Shuttleworth's *Charlotte Brontë and Victorian Psychology* 57, and Dames's more substantial engagement in *Amnesiac Selves: Nostal-gia, Forgetting, and British Fiction, 1810–1870*, 76–78. Athena Vrettos notes Brontë's exposure to theories of neurosis via her own medical consultations in "From Neurosis to Narrative: The Private Life of Nerves in *Villette* and *Daniel Deronda*" 560.

course, subjected to a phrenological reading by her other love interest, M. Paul (66–67). Before discussing Brontë's manipulation of these scientific modes of knowledge within characterization and narration, it will be useful to review their main precepts as understood by her contemporary society.

Phrenology and neurology shared an understanding of human consciousness as materially based, and there is overlap between their histories: Franz Joseph Gall, the Viennese physician, figures significantly in both. While the practice of phrenology or neurology was socially compatible with theological positions ranging from evangelical Christianity to atheism, as systems of thought they presented an obvious challenge to long-standing and persistent philosophical commitments to the division between mind and body.

Phrenology evolved following tenets of brain physiology established in Europe by Gall in the late eighteenth century and imported for the British lecture circuit in the early nineteenth century by his acquisitive and entrepreneurial former student, Johann Gaspar Spurzheim.[12] Key components of Gall's system, including the ideas of cerebral localization and innate rather than acquired faculties, were culled from other contemporaneous medical thinkers; Gall's original contribution was in arranging these theories in a diagnostic method that utilized physiognomy to predict character and intellectual capacity (van Wyhe 15). Spurzheim's modifications included hierarchical organization of faculties, with those shared by humans and nonhuman animals at the base and those judged unique to "man" highest (van Wyhe 33–34). Phrenology understood the brain as the materialization of the mind, composed of distinct and innate "faculties" located in separate "organs," by whose shape and size, as determined by examination of the skull, the trained phrenologist could predict a given human subject's inclinations and capabilities (van Wyhe vi). British phrenology derived popularity from its promise to reveal scientifically credible information about the character of others to any layperson that studied its system (van Wyhe 58). By the time of *Villette*'s publication in 1853, Edinburgh phrenologist George Combe's *The Constitution of Man Considered in Relation to External Objects* (1828), a work of natural philosophy, was in its eighth edition, with over seventy-five thousand copies in circulation in the United Kingdom (van Wyhe 129). One notable aspect of the phrenological model, as Nicholas Dames observes, was its excision of memory, to which it did not assign an "organ" (78).[13] Also of particular significance to

---

12. van Wyhe v–vi; Combe. The reprint of Combe's book I am using draws its text from the eighth edition of his original 1828 publication.

13. We see Brontë's disinclination to subscribe wholeheartedly to the phrenological model in the way both Miss Marchmont and Lucy personify "Memory" as an influential tenant of the mind (39, 165).

Brontë's engagement with phrenological theory, as Sally Shuttleworth posits, is its insistence on the "segmented basis of the mind," which threatened "ideas of psychic unity and integration," and its simultaneous, seemingly contradictory exhortation "for ever greater self-command and faculty development" in the face of internal conflict (69). While wildly inaccurate, phrenology was important to the development of scientific thought in that, as historian Roger Smith observes, it "emphatically focused both popular and medical attention on the brain" (*Inhibition* 36). During Brontë's lifetime, Victorians from all walks of life turned to phrenology for a logical way to read and understand human character.

It should be noted that the phrenology popularized in Britain by Spurzheim and his Scottish disciple Combe was, unlike Gall's original system, laced with moral implications. As phrenology supposedly derived its insights about human abilities directly from nature, to defy its edicts was to self-destructively violate the natural order (van Wyhe 34). Such claims, if credited, allowed the trained practitioner to both assert absolute knowledge of a human subject's character through noninvasive visual observation, and issue pronouncements regarding normative behavior from an unassailable position of authority. In his best-selling *The Constitution of Man,* Combe confidently declares that through phrenology, "the organs of the mind can be seen and felt, and their size estimated,—and the mental manifestations also that accompany them can be observed" (56). A key difference of emphasis, if not doctrine, between Combe and his European predecessors was his focus on the improvability of specific faculties through their judicious and regular application (Shuttleworth 63). Phrenology viewed each individual's character as a collection of innate capacities that could be cultivated by exercise and brought into harmony through regulation. But it also implied predetermined limitations and susceptibilities.

Neurology, on the contrary, was by the 1830s positing a decentralized, concealed, and changeable model of the human consciousness, which, far from excising memory as phrenology did, understood the body to retain and transmit a record of its social and physical influences. In the end of the eighteenth through the first half of the nineteenth century, developing understandings of the nervous system undermined aspirations to unitary mental control. A body ruled or misruled by its nerves, in this era, was a body sensitive to cultural influences and to healthful or stifling lifestyles; further, one of the medically identified characteristics of nervous disorder was the sufferer's impulsion to speak of their body's pain and its history (Logan 2). Within Brontë's lifetime, the conceptualization of nerve function and hence the stories the nervous body could tell underwent a critical change. While eighteenth-century medicine envisioned the nervous system as entirely centralized, with the nerves serving as mere pathways to convey sensations to the brain and transmit motor impulses back to the muscles, between 1800 and 1840 new scientific data radically revised this model, dispersing control between semiautonomous nerve centers along the cerebrospinal axis (Logan 166–67). Galen's notion of the brain as the singular organizing force of the nervous system was discredited; new theories emphasized the importance of the spinal cord (Clarke and Jacyna 55). Physiologist Marshall Hall posited the spinal cord contained "marrow" that possessed nerve force, and was therefore not just a passive conductor (Clarke and Jacyna 120). Unlike his German contemporary neurophysiologist Johannes Müller, who understood the nervous system as integrated, the British Hall differentiated structurally as well as functionally between volitional and mechanistic nervous system activity (Smith, *Inhibition* 68). Peter Melville Logan argues that Hall's research provided a medical framework to explain how a sane individual might, without deliberate deception, take actions that defied stated intentions or conscious control (167–68). Significantly, moral and religious notions of personal restraint and biological understandings of self-regulation were not yet clearly differentiated. In the 1830s and 1840s, Smith argues, "the language of higher and lower was simultaneously, and without contradiction, physiological and moral" (*Inhibition* 40) in describing a nervous system understood as both hierarchical and segmented.

In contrast with the knowable body and readable character posited by phrenologists, the nervous body as charted by physicians was assumed to possess hidden, multiple, and fluid meanings not always accessible even to the trained practitioner. Graham's insistence, during one of Lucy's nervous episodes, that "I look on you from a professional point of view, and I read, perhaps, all you would conceal" (248) seems more indicative of his patriarchal overconfidence, which Lucy elsewhere chides, than the state of medical opinion during the period. The medical establishment resisted the reassuring absoluteness that characterized phrenological theory and instead recognized ambiguities in diagnosis.

Sir Benjamin Collins Brodie, fellow and president of the Royal College of Surgeons and a prominent medical figure in the first half of the century, demonstrates typical attitudes. He acknowledges phrenology's valid insight in its impulse to localize functions in specific parts of the brain, but critiques its failure to account for anatomical parallels and distinctions between humans and nonhuman animals, and ultimately deems the phrenological distribution of faculties artificial and forced (*Psychological Inquiries* 221–26). He emphasizes interconnections among lifestyle, bodily well-being, and moral character, including having "nervous energies exhausted by excessive labor," and stresses the changeability of personality over time (*Psychological Inquiries* 236–39).

Brodie associates the direction of higher mental function and emotion with the brain and "animal" functions with the spinal cord, but observes that "perceptions and thoughts, admit of being excited and acted upon through the medium of the nervous system," whose influence is dispersed throughout the body (*Psychological Inquiries* 112). Addressing colleagues in 1837 on the subject of "nervous affections" (i.e., hysterical symptoms) that mime the symptomology of non-nervous ailments, he explains that even a skilled practitioner might misread not only the patient's body, but her character. Brodie relates to the professional audience his "great perplexity" when unsuccessfully treating patients suffering observable physical symptoms of joint degeneration or sprain neither responsive to conventional treatments nor progressive in the anticipated manner. He subsequently suspected the pathology to be nervous in nature, hence requiring different treatment. Brodie similarly counsels that just as physicians should not jump to conclusions about the origins of a potentially nervous affliction, neither should they assume that they can read the patient's character in her disruptive and deceptive bodily symptoms: "We must not adopt . . . the harsh conclusion, that these symptoms exist only in those who are of a fanciful or wayward character. Young women of the highest moral qualities, and of the strongest understanding, are not exempt from these maladies" ("Local Nervous Affections" 862). Further, Brodie stresses that *hysterical symptoms frequently disappear at once, without any manifest cause for their disappearance . . . . It still more frequently happens that recovery . . . immediately follows a forcible impression of any kind made on the nervous system*" ("Local Nervous Affections" 864). Here we have a model of a body whose observable characteristics possess multiple meanings that have no necessary correspondence with the individual's character, an embodied consciousness subject to sudden and unpredictable modification, either from unknown internal causes or as a result of external stimuli, that is, lived experience. In contrast with the phrenological body, whose potentialities were predetermined and whose visible qualities possessed a one-to-one correspondence with character and capabilities, the nervous body was not entirely knowable through observation. It was capable of dynamic change and improvement, influenced by its environment. Critically, for the novelist's purposes as well as the physician's, the nervous body offered no reliable outward record of inward character.

Brontë's use of both phrenological and neurological accounts of psychic life and its bodily markers has been well documented.[14] My particular con-

---

14. See particularly Athena Vrettos's "From Neurosis to Narrative: The Private Life of Nerves in *Villette* and *Daniel Deronda*"; Sally Shuttleworth's *Charlotte Brontë and Victorian Psychology*; Nicholas Dames's *Amnesiac Selves: Nostalgia, Forgetting, and British Fiction, 1810–1870*; Rachel Malane's *Sex in Mind: The Gendered Brain in Nineteenth-Century Literature and Mental*

cern is how scientific discourse provides Brontë competing but not mutually exclusive languages of, respectively, forward-looking and memory-bound mental functioning. By manipulating phrenological and neurological discourse within *Villette*, Brontë employs the psychological terminology of her contemporary society to construct, in narrator-protagonist Lucy Snowe, a self at once consciously directed toward maximizing the potential for future achievement (which engenders a new plot) and involuntarily impelled back into its own history (which compels narration). This juxtaposition within the narrator-protagonist's consciousness generates a nineteenth-century psychiatric framework for the narrative patterns we now characterize as typical of traumatic experience. I concur with Dames's assertion that phrenology encoded "an ethic of progressiveness, of future-oriented activity, that excludes memory altogether—as if in the act of *surfacing* the personality, of making it completely legible," the capacity for memory that contemporary readers associate with interiority is erased (86). I likewise agree with his claim that in Brontë's novels, "memory is never comfortably integrated into a larger consciousness," and that phrenological discourse and practice figures prominently in Lucy's gradual and empowering transfer of desire from people and places rich in memory of loss or inadequacy (particularly Graham Bretton) to those divorced from her youthful memories (notably M. Paul) (93, 113–16). But, I would argue, it is crucial to read the phrenological discourse within *Villette*, which constructs character based on present potentialities with an eye toward future achievement, alongside the neurological discourse, which posits an embodied consciousness unable to escape the reverberations of its history. It is true, as Dames observes, that as the story progresses Lucy frees herself from the weight of her history through emphasis on future potential, connected to the rhetoric of phrenology. But *Villette* is equally rich in the language of the nerves, which, following its contemporary scientific milieu, it associates with the inevitable bodily return of past experience. The juxtaposition of these competing psychic forces underpins the novel's narrative vacillations.

Medical rhetoric of nervous disorder describes Lucy's breakdowns, which are implicitly or explicitly associated either with her memories of the dead or with her related anxiety about the growth of new affections. In spite of Lucy's conscious endorsement of the forward-looking ideals of self-control, self-regulation, and acceptance of one's given lot, all watchwords of phrenology, her psyche and bodily frame are periodically riven by the affective and physical

Sciences; Elisha Cohn's *Still Life: Suspended Development in the Victorian Novel*; and Alexandra Lewis's "Being Human: De-Gendering Mental Anxiety; or Hysteria, Hypochondriosis, and Traumatic Memory in Charlotte Brontë's *Villette*."

consequences of disordered nerves, which, in Brontë's contemporary society, were understood to carry and communicate the material inscription of their history. As she sinks into despondency when left alone during the long vacation, the future-oriented rhetoric of self-improvement through self-regulation deserts Lucy: "Even to look forward was not to hope: the dumb future spoke no comfort, offered no promise, gave no inducement to bear present evil in reliance of future good" (156). Severe storms, which Lucy metaphorically connects with her sense of loss, then trigger a reaction both psychic and bodily: "My nervous system could hardly support what it had for many days and nights to undergo in that huge, empty house. How I used to pray to Heaven for consolation and support!" (157). When she becomes so physically ill that she takes to bed with "a strange fever of the nerves and blood" (159) that entails a nightmare and waking hallucinations, "the worst" of her mental torments consists of a vision of her dead loved ones: "Methought the well-loved dead, who had loved *me* well in life, met me elsewhere, alienated: galled was my inmost spirit with an unutterable sense of despair about the future" (160). In this formulation, the nervous body thrusts the loss the individual would rather put aside before her unwilling consciousness, and future potential is negated by a history of pain.

Unlike phrenology, which located the mind fully within the brain, neurology proposed a dispersed form of psychic regulation, only partially under conscious control and extended throughout the body. Lucy's breakdown during the long vacation is informed by the neurological model of a body that materially inscribes and transmits its experience rather than the phrenological model of a mind that has no place for memory. Similar moments of unwilled blockage—an inability to move forward—occur with decreasing severity when Lucy loses her letter from Graham (245–50) and declines to see Paul when she clearly suspects he might propose (384–85). Both episodes include mention of the term "nerve" or its variations. Brontë implies the nervous body's record of past pain can, against an individual's conscious wishes, block future potential, in Lucy's case, preventing her from imagining an independent life without her dead loved ones and triggering self-destructive, paralyzing anxiety around newly developing affective bonds. The forward movement of Lucy's desire is arrested, at key points, by a corporeal trace of loss that turns her energies backward and inward. But another key characteristic of the nervous body is its capacity for transformation: At the final turning point in her emotional life, Lucy is not ossified with morbid terror but instead cries out, "My heart will break!" (481) when she thinks Paul is leaving her, enabling the understanding that leads to his marriage proposal. The discourse of nerves helps Brontë structure the narrator-protagonist's response to mental pain, but the novel resists reducing Lucy to a case study. Reading *Villette* against contemporaneous medico-scientific discourse, Lewis observes that Brontë's depiction of Lucy's memory "mediates between and moves beyond . . . distinct conceptions of the ill and healthy mind in calamity" (91). The novel is informed by scientific discourse of mental wounding, and by self-help discourse of mental wellness, but it declines to affix distinct nervous psychopathology on its narrator-protagonist or portray Lucy's limitations as static. She is materially influenced by her past yet not unalterably trapped within its patterns.

In employing the language of nerves, *Villette* not only invokes memory, but portrays social isolation as a deprivation felt in body as much as mind. Of the tragedian Vashti, Lucy observes, "To her, what hurts becomes immediately embodied" (258); the same might be said of Lucy, who admires and identifies with the actress. Repeatedly, Lucy's narration metaphorically links social contact and affection to nourishment. For instance, the academic study she pursues to distract herself from Graham's absence is described "as if I had gnawed a file to satisfy hunger, or drunk brine to quench thirst" (267).[15] Lucy employs a commonly felt and widely understood need—adequate food—to explain to more fortunate readers, accustomed to habitual social inclusion, the suffering of being denied empathetic social interaction. The novel also moves beyond analogy, ascribing Lucy's materially depleted nervous system to her present loneliness and remembered loss. As Graham turns his attention to Paulina and neglects his god-sister, Lucy describes how while awaiting letters, the "solitary" individual finds that "his nerves ache from long expectancy" (267). She then likens herself to a man "going mad from solitary confinement," whose "nerves first inflamed, underwent nameless agony, then sunk into palsy" (273). Significantly, Lucy's narration masculinizes and generalizes these experiences, presenting them as standard medical cases showing the effect of social isolation on the nervous system, without reference to feminine physiology or her personal circumstances.

Villette employs phrenological discourse, in contrast, to code self-improvement and signal potential, as well as excise memory. Lucy describes her challenging promotion from nursery governess to English teacher, which directs her thoughts away from past pain, in terms suggestive of phrenology: "I felt I was getting on; not lying the stagnant prey of mould and rust, but polishing my faculties and whetting them to a keen edge with constant use" (82). But phrenology does not exclusively represent forward motion, any more than neurology codes only historically mired impasse. Dames argues convincingly

---

15. For similar examples, see 161, 239, 244, 268, 273.

that in *Villette* the phrenological gaze serves not only to taxonomize people, but to challenge them to make a choice: "between past reticences and present opportunity" (121). The discourse of phrenology as clinical practice does typically code forward progress in *Villette*; however, when phrenological discourse is instead employed to describe the narrator-protagonist's interiority, it can signal psychic fragmentation and resultant narrative blockage. As Rachel Malane observes, we can see the influence of phrenology in Brontë's vision of a mind composed of discrete faculties capable of "autonomous activity" (73). Malane suggests that ongoing conflict among these personified faculties dissociates Lucy from her own mental processes (73).

The predominantly static nature of the phrenological model—while existing faculties might be developed or neglected, their relative power and nature are innate—means that it can describe mental paralysis just as readily as mental application. Indeed, Lucy employs the phrenological theory of discrete faculties to describe her unproductive mental struggle after parting from Graham following her recuperative stay at La Terrasse. She spends several hours absorbed in silent mental conflict on the question of whether or not Graham will write her and if so, whether and how she should reply. She first submits for an hour to the stern admonitions of "Reason," a faculty she terms a "Hag," "vindictive as a devil . . . envenomed as a step-mother," that counsels her to hope for nothing better than the opportunity to "work for a piece of bread" (229). Lucy personifies her own rationality as a figure of cruelty with no natural ties to herself. She then succumbs to the "divine, compassionate, succorable influence" (230) of "Imagination" (229), and her unspecified fantasies blend into sleep and dreams. The result of the conflict among Lucy's self-will and personified faculties is an extended period of wakeful cognition, without resolution on the question that gnaws her psyche. This paralysis differs from that which Lucy suffers during her bouts of nervous disorder: It follows from deliberate effort to work through a problem, and results from divisions categorically inherent in human consciousness. Unlike nervous collapse, this unproductive stasis does not issue unbidden from a bodily reaction. Brontë demonstrates no allegiance to either phrenological or neurological modes of describing the psyche, but interlaces both discourses to differentiate qualitatively distinct mental processes that can coexist within the same consciousness.

Juxtaposition of phrenological and neurological models of interiority has implications not only for the plausible depiction of characters' varied psychic states, but for the functions characters can serve within novelistic discourse. Deployment of different psychic models can expand or limit a character's capacity to generate narrative, as demonstrated by the variation in imagery

Lucy uses to compare Graham's feelings for her and hers for him near the close of the novel. The contrasting imagery within the passage illustrates not just differing degrees of affection between Graham and Lucy, but fundamentally dissimilar patterns of mental function:

> Graham's thoughts of me were not entirely those of a frozen indifference, after all. I believe in that goodly mansion, his heart, he kept one little place under the skylights where Lucy might have entertainment, if she chose to call. It was not so handsome as the chambers where he lodged his male friends; it was not like the hall where he accommodated his philanthropy, or the library where he treasured his science, still less did it resemble the pavilion where his marriage feast was splendidly spread; yet gradually, by long and equal kindness, he proved to me that he kept one little closet, over the door of which was written "Lucy's Room." I kept a place for him too—a place of which I never took the measure, either by rule or compass: I think it was like the tent of Peri-Banou. All my long life I carried it folded in the hollow of my hand—yet, released from hold and constriction, I know not but its innate capacity for expanse might have magnified it into a tabernacle for a host. (457)

The compartmentalization of affective and intellectual faculties is literalized in the architectural figure of a mansion with many rooms—each of fixed size and serving a discrete function and clientele—corresponding to the phrenological chart, which assigns a specific location to each mental capability and assumes established dimensions, hence delimited potential, for each faculty. The description of Graham's feeling for Lucy is couched in terms of an ongoing capacity for psychic experience of a set degree and kind: Lucy always "might have entertainment, if she chose to call," within a narrowly circumscribed realm of affection, yet "gradually, by long and equal kindness, he proved" that that his admittedly limited ability to feel for her will never diminish. As in phrenological science, Graham's psyche (alternately termed "thoughts" and "heart," denoting both intellectual and affective processes) is here a cohesively constructed but inherently divided set of predetermined, outward-turning (social, civic, professional) aims.

Lucy's psyche, in contrast, is figured as possessing the facility for growth and willed modification. Lucy's feeling for Graham, poignantly cast as the magical tent that a palm can contain but that expands exponentially if released, is capable of increase or restriction by its possessor's conscious choice. It is also mobile: Unlike the rooms of a mansion, it can be "carried." As in the neurological rather than phrenological understanding of embodied consciousness, Lucy portrays her own capacity for love—the only aspect of her psyche that she here shares—as a fluid interaction between inherent predisposition (her feeling for Graham, an "innate capacity"), conscious cultivation (her choice to restrain it), and social interaction (her regulation of her feeling for Graham implicitly follows from her perception that his feelings for her are less significant to him). It is not simply a question of control or indulgence of a given capability, but a process enmeshed in Lucy's personal history. Also, this is a model of the psyche that acknowledges the possibility of deliberate and successful concealment. Lucy describes compression and shielding of her feeling for Graham ("folded in the hollow of my hand," it is moderated in Lucy's experience and hidden from the view of others). Moreover, this feeling is the only aspect of her own psychic life she here chooses to divulge for the reader, in contrast with her wry delineation of the various components of Graham's mental structure. However much Brontë may wish to privilege the tidy and forward-looking phrenological model of the mind, she allows her narrator to embrace the less fully knowable, more dynamic model aligned with contemporary neurology. Lucy's feeling for Graham is something of which she "never took measure by rule or compass." In assessing her own character, Lucy rejects the phrenological method, which asserts that measurements of the living body code an individual's meaning and potential. She affirms that at least some aspects of psychic life are and should be unseen, and their scope unbounded. Brontë does not here enter into scientific debate. Rather, she deploys the contrasting ideologies—human character as fixed and knowable versus human character as fluid and multiplicitous—to explore different novelistic models of interiority. The neurological model offers the ambiguity and potential for transformation that catalyze a narrative, and it is ultimately the one most fitting for this narrator-protagonist. Competing Victorian models of mental function offer Brontë logic to structure a narrative defined by competing drives to elide the past, and to communicate one's history.

The moments of psychic blockage, emotional transitions, and unbidden returns of memory that Brontë constructs through phrenology and neurology produce narrative oscillations centered on Lucy's experience of loss. These patterns correlate with what we would now call trauma narrative. Nineteenth-century science offered culturally credible structures to explain the narrator-protagonist's vacillations between goal-directed action and self-defeating collapse, between intense attachment to past affections and stern excision of them from her narration. Phrenology disavows memory; neurology embeds it in the body and repeatedly brings it to the fore of the story's action. The juxtaposition and interrelation of phrenological and neurological rhetoric enables Brontë to represent a multilayered consciousness. Lucy's mind is shaped at the substrata by its past and embodied experience, yet capable of transformation, self-direction, and movement toward integration and healing.

SHIPWRECK AND THE SHATTERED PSYCHE

Nineteenth-century mental science gives Brontë language for interplay among consciousness, body, and experience, but this discourse falls short of communicating the full impact of devastating personal loss. Here she turns to a metaphor rich in cultural and religious significance: The key image for trauma in *Villette* is shipwreck. *Villette* invokes shipwreck imagery explicitly and at length in only three places, although sea and storm imagery recur throughout. Gilbert and Gubar note that in moments of emotional turmoil, Lucy substitutes descriptive water imagery for narration of actual events, which is "as much a camouflage as a disclosure" (418). Water imagery is a multivalent symbol for Lucy's emotional life, alternatively framing spiritual struggle and interpersonal relations. But the shipwreck imagery serves a specific function, emblematizing the central experience of loss that undergirds Lucy's subsequent emotional, spiritual, and socioeconomic struggles.

Brontë's deployment of sea and shipwreck imagery mobilizes broader nineteenth-century cultural language. Margaret Cohen argues that imaginative representations of seafaring transformed across the eighteenth and nineteenth centuries: an uneven progression away from showcasing the mariner's craft, an expression of human mastery and agency, and toward depersonalized depictions of the ocean's sublime power, as typified in Turner's shipwreck paintings.[16] *Villette*'s shipwrecks bear traces of both discourse traditions, at times emphasizing attempts to retain or reclaim agency but finally turning away from individualized experience altogether. Mandy Swann argues *Villette*'s shipwreck imagery codes specifically female forms of desire, destruction, and loss, particularly in reference to Homerian epic and the Christian Bible. In addition to these layers of symbolic meaning, however, shipwreck also had immediate emotional resonance for early-Victorian reading audiences, given its everyday impact on trade, investments, and the lives of British families, many of whom lost a loved one at sea.

Shipwreck was a daily occurrence in the early nineteenth century, when Brontë's final novel is set (Lincoln 155). Affordable pamphlets purportedly relating firsthand accounts were rapidly produced following important wrecks, later anthologized, and read by British citizens at all class levels (Lin-

---

16. See *The Novel and the Sea*, especially 106–31.

coln 159). By the 1830s, the advent of the rotary press and dropping price of periodicals carried sensational shipwreck narratives to a wider audience (Burg 2). Of course, newspapers also reported on shipwrecks. Historian Margarette Lincoln calls the sharing of shipwreck narratives through print media "part of the process of public mourning" (155) and argues that "iconography of the sea was powerful chiefly because the actual power of the sea was so frequently impressed upon those living at the time" (158). Shipwreck narratives publicly codified, in this period, the maxim that women and children should have first access to lifeboats (Burg 1)—a point of chivalrous national pride for the British, but also a practice that ripped families apart under horrific circumstances.

While composing *Villette* in 1852, Brontë would likely have read reports of the wreck of the *Birkenhead,* a transport carrying British troops and their families, which ran aground on an uncharted rock off the coast of Africa in January of that year (Burg 1). Lifeboats had insufficient space, and women and children were evacuated while husbands and fathers stayed behind to probable demise; in some cases, wives were reported to be forcibly pried from their doomed husbands (Burg 1). The agony of this separation from family amid crisis, and the guilt of surviving at the expense of a perishing loved one, resonates with the emotional life of Brontë's final heroine, Lucy Snowe. Widely published accounts of British and American civilian wrecks in the 1840s and early 1850s often tell a more unsavory tale of human interaction in crisis, that of "every man for himself," with physically weaker women and children likelier to die (Burg 3–7). This ethos also speaks to the moral universe Lucy inhabits, in which the socioeconomically strong repeatedly push aside the vulnerable. Shipwreck resonates with Lucy's ethical dilemma of survival in the face of overwhelming loss, both in the moment of struggle and in the aftermath.

The centrality of shipwreck in Lucy's psychic life is evidenced by its structural importance to her narrative. The figure of the shipwreck appears early, immediately following the Bretton episode, as the form taken by Lucy's recurrent nightmares, and also as the metaphor that communicates the impact of her youthful tragedy while shielding its details. It then reappears, in a domesticated form, as the healing "undersea" pause at La Terrasse after Lucy's collapse, a third of the way through the novel. Shipwreck finally takes literal form at the novel's close, in Lucy's reportage of storms that claim her fiancé's life, yet here, as at the beginning, she refuses to detail her loss. Instead, her narration pans back to take in the broad image of the many bereaved with whom she shares a lonely bond. The progression of shipwreck imagery reveals how Lucy's psychic trauma ultimately resists efforts to literalize or otherwise fix it in place. Analysis of the shipwreck passages on which Lucy's narration pivots

not only deepens our understanding of the character's wounded consciousness, but outlines a theoretical framework for traumatic experience as conceptualized before Freudian psychoanalysis or current neuroscience.

The figure of the shipwreck is introduced to explain what occurs when
Lucy's six-month stay at Bretton, in her fourteenth year, concludes. When
Mrs. Bretton receives a letter whose contents trouble her, Lucy first mistakenly
assumes it to be bad news of the Snowe household (6). It seems probable that
communicable illness forms at least some part of the Snowes' misfortunes,
and that Lucy was sent from home to escape contagion, as Madame Beck's
children later are when a sibling falls ill. Lucy's description of what follows
the Bretton stay conveys the shock of her disrupted youthful security, even
as it withholds actual events. Anticipating the reader's expectation of a young
girl's happiness "to return to the bosom of [her] kindred," Lucy states that "the
amiable conjecture does no harm, and may therefore safely be left uncontra-
dicted" (35). She then proceeds to contradict it, but only in a hypothetical
narrative:

> Picture me then idle, basking, plump, and happy, stretched on a cushioned
> deck, warmed with constant sunshine, rocked by breezes indolently soft.
> However, it cannot be concealed that, in that case, I must somehow have
> fallen over-board, or that in that there must have been a wreck at last. I too
> well remember a time—a long time, of cold, of danger, of contention. To this
> hour, when I have the nightmare, it repeats the rush and saltiness of briny
> waves in my throat, and their icy pressure on my lungs. I even know there
> was a storm, and that not of one hour nor one day. For many days and nights
> neither sun nor stars appeared; we cast with our own hands the tackling out
> of the ship; a heavy tempest lay on us; all hope that we should be saved was
> taken away. In fine, the ship was lost, the crew perished. (35)

This passage would recall, for Brontë's contemporary readership, real-life shipwreck narratives. Key details map onto survivor Captain Edward C. Wright's
account of the then-recent Birkenhead wreck, published in newspapers,
including the *Yorkshire Gazette*: Deceptive calm precedes disaster, as "the sea
was smooth at the time"; the sudden change upon impact, as "the rush of
water was so great" that those in lower decks "died in their hammocks"; the
extended battle for survival as survivors of the initial impact cling to wreckage, hoping currents will carry them to land ("Wreck of the Birkenhead Troop
Ship" 3). So detailed is Lucy's description, so similar to eyewitness reports like
Wright's, that one is tempted to read it as an account of an event that actually occurred to Lucy. Yet when crossing the channel to Villette, she answers

Ginevra Fanshawe's inquiry about whether she is "fond of a sea-voyage" by saying that her "*fondness* of a sea-voyage had yet to undergo the test of experience: [She] had never made one" (53). For all her concealment and misdirection, Lucy hates a deliberate spoken falsehood, and misses no opportunity to criticize Catholic foreigners for tolerance of lies. It is doubtful she would resort to a needless lie in answer to a fellow passenger's casual question. It follows, then, that Lucy's recurring dream of being the sole survivor of a shipwreck emblematizes rather than literally repeats the origin of her plight. However, as Elisha Cohn notes, "the simile doesn't have stable one-to-one correspondence" (61), and it is difficult to fully identify the narrator-protagonist with any one perspective within the story. This instability accords with the fracturing and self-alienating character of traumatic experience.

Lucy's mode of introducing the shipwreck invites the reader to participate vicariously in her own youthful shock at the reversal of expectations. She asks us to "picture [her], then, idle, plump, basking, and happy," giving readers an emblem of blissful, passive girlhood, dozing trustful of her security, confident the very forces of nature conspire only to promote her peace ("rocked by breezes indolently soft"). She then contrasts this conjured tranquility with the real terror of her own experience: If Lucy's journey through adolescence is a sea-voyage, it concludes in no safe arrival at the port of adulthood, but instead in a storm that shatters her household, plunges her into a battle for survival, and locks her psyche in perpetual struggle with this adolescent agony. As Cohen observes, survival of real-life shipwrecks required "the ability to wait, amid danger and physical distress" (24). Not only does a shipwreck bring about sudden loss of life and goods, it halts the progress of any survivors, leaving them clutching wreckage, awaiting rescuers who may never arrive. Lucy cannot shake free of her catastrophe; she avows herself an old woman within retrospective narration, but informs us the nightmare yet recurs. Shipwreck is an apt metaphor for trauma: It communicates not only the overwhelming effect of the traumatic event, but its ability to shatter the victim's sense of agency, leaving her unable to progress, clinging tenaciously to remnants of the past, in need of another's aid to move forward.

The violent cessation of progress and loss of agency, which cannot be recovered without assistance, connects the emblem of the shipwreck with psychic trauma. This first shipwreck passage also speaks to the nature of traumatic memory, and to the way trauma can seem to implicate victims in their own suffering. Lucy asserts she can "*too well* remember a time—a long time, of cold, of danger, of contention" (emphasis mine). What might it mean not just to remember, but to "too well remember" an experience? At stake here is the character of traumatic memory. Van der Kolk's influential research posits traumatic memory as relentlessly literal: flashbacks and nightmares that repeat rather than assimilate the event.[17] Brontë, more than a century earlier, was working within quite different models of materialized consciousness. Further, as previously discussed, she co-opts medical discourse not to endorse any particular scientific model of psychic function, but instead to delineate the lived experience of different psychic states, and achieve desired narrative effects. Unlike the veterans in van der Kolk's studies, whose nightmares bring back an instant of trauma in accurate detail, Brontë's protagonist endures dreams that emblematize, in the physical sensations and psychic states of one catastrophic emergency, an extended period of affective pain and socioeconomic loss. Lucy recalls, vividly and involuntarily, the physical and emotional sensations of her traumatic experience: "cold," "danger," and "contention." They are visceral and dehumanized; they might as easily describe perceptions of a trapped non-human animal as a young lady beset by worldly cares. These sensations assault Lucy in a dream that metaphorically, not literally, repeats her youthful experience of bereavement, fear, and economic dislocation, including the resultant fragmentation of stable identity captured by the dream's shifting perspective. By depicting a widely resonant emblematic trauma rather than the specific and likely more mundane one of Lucy's personal history, Brontë departicularizes her protagonist's loss. It moves beyond the realm of individual pathology to become a cultural figure for the experience of impoverished, isolated women who share Lucy's circumstances but not her precise experiences.

Another key point this passage conveys is how psychic trauma can implicate victims in their own injury: The victim feels, unfairly, as if she is in some way responsible for the traumatic event. Lucy asserts that as the storm dragged on, "we cast with our own hands the tackling out of the ship." While the language of the passage makes an obvious religious parallel in the shipwreck of St. Paul the Apostle, the image of crew and passengers tossing gear and possessions overboard to lighten the vessel also calls to mind the pained parting from beloved material things, like home and heirlooms, that would necessarily follow from financial ruin. It also suggests the discarding of hopes, ambitions, and affections by which Lucy attempts to protect herself from further pain. The circumstances of traumatic loss force victims to make agonizing choices and to engage, actively though unwillingly, in painful actions. In Lucy's case, it might involve making arrangements to sell a dead loved one's possessions in order to satisfy a debt, and it clearly entails attempts to close herself off from affection, passion, and self-assertion. Both her emotional guardedness

---

17. See especially "The Intrusive Past: The Flexibility of Memory and the Engraving of Trauma" by van der Kolk and Otto van der Hart in Cathy Caruth's collection *Trauma: Explorations in Memory* (1995) and van der Kolk's more recent book *The Body Keeps the Score* (2014).

and her resistance to active and ambitious roles (teaching, acting, dancing at a ball, pursuing scholarship) are evidence of this kind of emotional casting out. At Miss Marchmont's, Lucy puts the case thus: "I had wanted to compromise with Fate: to escape great agonies by submitting to a whole life of privation and small pains" (38).

This attempted cosmic bargain fails, bringing about the collapse that engenders the second shipwreck episode. First Miss Marchmont's death, which forces Lucy out of seclusion, then expanded duties at the school and developing interest in Graham and Paul interfere with Lucy's plan to wall herself off from social and emotional involvement. When isolation returns during the long vacation, Lucy's tenuously preserved psychic balance is thrown off keel. A week of stormy weather finishes the work unbroken solitude had begun. Subjected to an atmosphere that fuels her memories, grief, and desire while cut off from social outlets that might bring relief or distraction, Lucy's mind cracks under the strain of the tempest. The result is her most serious mental and physical breakdown of the novel. Its linkage to earlier shipwreck imagery is made explicit by Lucy's declaration that the cup of suffering from which she drinks is "filled up seething from a bottomless and boundless sea" (159). Following her confession and subsequent collapse in the streets during a raging storm, Lucy is conveyed, unconscious, to La Terrasse by the priest and a serendipitously nearby Graham. Lucy recovers at her newly rediscovered godmother's hands, surrounded, surreally, by familiar childhood objects in a foreign context: furniture from Bretton, a portrait of Graham as a boy, even needlework executed by a young Lucy and gifted to Louisa Bretton. Lucy has already recognized Dr. John as her old playfellow John Graham Bretton, and here reveals to him, as well as the reader, their connection, clearing one source of confusion. She conveys her disorientation and attenuated agency in terms that not merely repeat, but rewrite and reinterpret, the previously introduced nightmare of shipwreck.

At La Terrasse, Lucy perceives that the shipwreck of her dream has at last plunged her under the waves—but finds this experience not so intolerable as she feared:

> My calm little room seemed somehow like a cave in the sea. There was no colour in it, except that white and pale green, suggestive of foam and deep water; the blanched cornice was adorned with shell-shaped ornaments, and there were white mouldings like dolphins in the ceiling-angles. Even that one touch of colour visible in the red satin pincushion bore affinity to coral; even that dark, shining glass might have mirrored a mermaid. When I closed my eyes, I heard a gale, subsiding at last, bearing upon the house-front like a

settling swell upon a rock-base. I heard it drawn and withdrawn far, far off, like a tide retiring from a shore of the upper world—a world so high above that the rush of its largest waves, the dash of its fiercest breakers could sound down in this submarine home, only like murmurs and a lullaby. (181)

While the first metaphorical shipwreck rends Lucy from her childhood home, this one places her in a new domestic sphere and reunites her with her closest equivalent to living family. Her account of the first shipwreck focuses on efforts to stave off impending disaster and stay above water; this one accepts and embraces the plunge into the boiling depths, where she finds not the anticipated annihilation but comfort and protection. The first passage remains in the realm of metaphor, reporting the storm and shipwreck as if they were real to convey the impact of Lucy's actual suffering without revealing details. This passage, in contrast, merges imagined sea cave with actual Victorian home, connecting the symbolic dream realm of passion and loss to Lucy's mundane everyday reality of poverty and obscurity. Just as she acknowledges that the pincushion is a pincushion, yet notes its resemblance to coral, Lucy is beginning to see feasible connections between her outer and inner realities. This passage marks Lucy's progress toward reintegrating her scattered psyche and bringing the psychic and social/material registers into meaningful relation. It indicates a turning point, after which she takes an increasingly active role in her life and begins to articulate her needs and desires to those around her. Notably, Lucy wore mourning attire when she left from London about a year prior (53), but at La Terrasse she is persuaded by Louisa Bretton to don a pink dress (207–8). Lucy begins to define her identity beyond her experience of grief.

At the moment of the collapse that precipitated her arrival at La Terrasse, Lucy embraces powerful emotions she previously sought to foreclose. In her final moments before losing consciousness in a literal storm and psychic turmoil, Lucy declares, "My heart did not fail at all in this conflict; I only wished that I had wings and could ascend the gale, spread and repose my pinions on its strength, career in its course, sweep where it swept" (163–64). There is longing for oblivion in Lucy, who tells us that after her collapse her soul "reentered her prison with pain, with reluctance, with a moan and a long shiver" (165). Nonetheless, the transition from an impulse to fight or flee the sources of her recurrent psychic discord, to an attempt to face and accept them, indicates the beginning of Lucy's conscious effort to shift her relationship to her trauma and redirect the path of her life. In the second shipwreck passage, descent into the depths offers refuge, albeit of a qualified sort. The intense fear of drowning from the earlier nightmare passage is entirely absent from this daydream. The wind and waves that break the ship and cast its crew into the sea in the first passage reappear as the continuing storm outside the window of Lucy's room. Perceived from the inverted perspective of her half-imaginary, half-familiar undersea cave, they are but distant noise, not immediate threat; their sounds are reduced to "murmurs and a lullaby," such as a child might hear as she falls asleep. Lucy calls this room of respite her "submarine home": the first domestic space she lays any claim to since childhood, although one that exists below the surface of ordinary life. As Judith Butler has argued with regard to the force of repetition in language, traumatic repetition need not mean exact repetition; indeed, the compulsion to repeat can provide the opportunity to reinscribe, and paradoxically, a kind of agency "derived from the *impossibility* of choice" (124). While Lucy cannot prevent the return of her trauma, she can modify her response, thereby changing the experience. Embracing the metaphorical shipwreck, she gains a measure of control; the energy once spent attempting to maintain an impossible divide between psychic and social realities can be productively redirected. After her first, failed attempt to tell her story (to the priest) and the collapse and recovery that follow, Lucy pursues in earnest her search for a witness, beginning with her willingness to have her identity known to the Brettons.

When Lucy's search seems likely to end happily in her upcoming marriage, one final shipwreck intercedes. The brief final chapter of *Villette* brings news of a disaster at sea implied to claim Paul's life:

> The wind shifts to the west. Peace, peace, Banshee—"keening" at every window! It will rise—it will swell—it shrieks out long: wander as I may through the house at night, I cannot lull the blast. The advancing hours make it strong: by midnight, all sleepless watchers hear and fear a wild south-west storm.
>
> That storm roared frenzied for seven days. It did not cease till the Atlantic was strewn with wrecks: it did not lull till the deeps had gorged their full sustenance. Not till the destroying angel of the tempest had achieved his perfect work, would he fold the wings whose waft was thunder—the tremor of whose plumes was storm.
>
> Peace, be still! Oh! A thousand weepers, praying in agony on many shores, listened for that voice, but it was not uttered—not uttered till, when the hush came, some could not feel it: till, when the sun returned, his light was night to some! (495)

What is striking about this passage, in contrast with the previous shipwreck descriptions, is its depersonalization and lack of realistic detail. The first shipwreck passage recounts a metaphorical tale so richly imagined as to seem like a real event; the second fuses accurate descriptions of Lucy's surroundings with an equally precise account of their place in her imagination and memory. Lucy provides concrete detail and individualized perspective on the imaginary shipwrecks while insistently departicularizing the real one.

This passage moves farther away from Lucy's individual perceptions as she moves from anticipation to certainty of catastrophe. The first paragraph retains Lucy's unique vantage point, recounting her emotions and actions. The narration pauses with a dash each time she affirms that the storm is building, capturing her experience of breathless, silent waiting and disappointment. By the end of the first paragraph, when the storm has clearly become dangerous to ships at sea, the narrator makes a universalizing move, and we are concerned not with our narrator-protagonist Lucy, but with "all sleepless watchers." By the second paragraph, not only has Lucy effectively written herself out of narration, but the storm instead has achieved dominance as a personified character to which humanity is an object for consumption. We have moved from a specific woman's embodied perceptions to a detached though dramatic account wherein faceless men and women are devoured by supernatural forces.

Jarring as this shift to the mythic register may seem following the intense interpersonal drama and mundane domestic detail of the preceding chapter, it is not without precedent in the text. The motive and meaning of Paul's West Indian voyage have been consistently pushed to the edge of Lucy's narration, though she provides enough clues for alert readers to piece the story together. Amidst the strange, glittering, hallucinatory clarity of Lucy's observations of the fête in the park, she briefly outlines intertwined motives of the "secret junta" (460) of Père Silas, Madame Walravens, and Madame Beck. The priest seeks to wrest his favored pupil from the "heretic" Lucy, the elderly matron wants the wealth of a well-run plantation, and the directrice desires to kill off the man she could not win rather than see him wed a rival (461–62). If we trust Lucy's account, the combined machinations of envy, avarice, and wrath prevail upon her "Christian Hero" (398) to undertake shadily drawn and morally dubious pursuits administering a plantation likely reliant on enslaved labor.[18] We later learn Paul was meditating his proposal to Lucy while he consented to the voyage that, by making Madame Walravens independently

---

18. The plantation is located in Basse-Terre, the capital of French-controlled Guadeloupe. Although slavery had been abolished there by *Villette*'s publication, it would likely have been in practice during the earlier time frame of the novel's setting. On *Villette*'s engagement with histories of enslavement, see Mark Celeste, "Metonymic Chains: Shipwreck, Slavery, and Networks in *Villette*" (2016).

rich, would relieve the financial burden preventing him from marrying. Not only does Lucy have motive for rage that she never directly expresses at the role this unholy trinity plays in her lover's death, she also has reason for some measure of guilt. Considered in this context, the odd depersonalization of description and displacement of agency onto supernatural forces within the final shipwreck passage is a necessary gap for an unbearable truth. The morally dubious knot of socioeconomic motives that brought about Paul's voyage and therefore his death are replaced by the motiveless fury of a mythic being, be it folkloric "Banshee" or Christian "destroying angel."

The elusive and allusive final paragraph of this passage brings us squarely into the realm of Christian myth, referencing the words of Jesus that calmed the storm at sea, noting that in this case they came delayed and too late. The reader makes out the implication of death in the line "when the hush came, some could not feel it . . . when the sun returned, his light was night to some!" Yet Lucy avoids directly stating that Paul Emmanuel is among those lost. Similarly, she avoids openly indicting God's inattention to human prayers by not explicitly naming the story of Jesus on the sea of Galilee, from which the words, "Peace, be still" are taken, as that which she contrasts with her own experience. The final chapter of *Villette* provides ample clues to Paul's ultimate fate, but declines to say definitively that he never married Lucy, or to describe her reaction to news of his death. What might motivate these omissions?

Lucy and her author each have reasons to avoid closure. On the level of narrative realism, Lucy's narration of her own story cannot end conclusively, because without a suitable witness, a trauma survivor cannot assimilate the overwhelming threat or loss and reintegrate her fractured psyche. Just as the totality of her childhood loss was unacceptable, so is the subsequent loss of M. Paul, who as her fiancé was not only her confidante but also her newfound source of affection, social respect, and financial stability, as her family had been in childhood. Without a witness for this second, unbearable loss, Lucy cannot resolve, but can only repeat, her experience of threat, shock, and grief. Rather than providing closure, the final chapter drives the reader back into the text with a new understanding of the significance of its narrator's evasions, repetitions, and omissions. By narrating her experience of shock, pain, and exclusion, Lucy creates meaning out of her meaningless suffering.

Villette's use of trauma as narrative structure achieves more than just a believable depiction of psychic pain. It also obliges its audience to rethink what counts as a story. Given the developmental mandate of realist Victorian fiction, readers expect the narration of a series of logically connected events motivated by and revealing plausible interiority. In *Villette*, Brontë creates a different kind of realist novel. While Ginevra and Paulina's conventional marriage-plot stories represent the expected narrative of causally linked (indeed, predictable) events, Lucy's story of trauma is told differently—through the relation of a series of intense psychic and physical experiences, wherein the powerful emotion and sensation of memory grafts unexpectedly onto a seemingly trivial or unconnected interaction or object. As Ann Cvetkovich argues, due to the "overwhelming nature of physical and emotional stimuli" involved in traumatic experience, rather than proceeding as a conventional narrative, "the memory of trauma . . . may instead consist of a series of intense and detailed, yet fragmented, psychophysical experiences" (*Archive* 98). As narrator, Lucy recognizes the difficulty inherent in capturing the powerful sensations and emotions of significant memories in a conventionally progressive realist narrative. Attempting to describe the exhilarating shock of M. Paul's gift of the externat at Fauborg Clothide, she muses, "Certain junctures of our lives must always be difficult to recall to memory. Certain points, crises, certain feelings, joys, griefs, and amazements, when reviewed, must strike us as things wildered and whirling, dim as a wheel fast spun" (486). Emotional experiences of great intensity defy conscious categorization and resist sequential ordering; their impact is visceral and disorienting. To make sense of the disjunction between Lucy's passionate, painful, or morbid inner life and her generally mundane daily experience, and to mediate between memories of sudden, total loss and the present reality of dull routine, *Villette*'s narration knits the two together in ways the reader will often find jarring. In large part, Lucy's unreliability as a narrator owes to the fact that the story she seeks to communicate is not the one she appears to be telling.

Emphasizing developmental aspects of Lucy's narration, Brenda Silver outlines how *Villette* manipulates both conventional and socially rebellious potential readers, creating an audience that might comprehend how unreliability is forced upon female narrators by socioeconomic circumstances that limit possibilities. Silver argues that "rewriting the traditional novel to illustrate the limited plots available to women in literature, as in life, [Lucy] has survived the destruction of romantic fantasy and grown into another reality" (110–11). While I find compelling Silver's claims about the engagement of different reading audiences, I remain skeptical of arguments for Lucy's personal development. As Susan Anne Carlson observes, although Lucy's professional life continues and her economic status improves over the course of her long life (only a small portion of which composes the story's action), Lucy remains "trapped in her mental prison" and unable to "escape her own damaged self," incapable of growth beyond her pain (19). The continued repetition of her shipwreck nightmare (35) in the present day of the novel's narration underscores this failure of progression. The narrator-protagonist's refusal to effectively close her narrative implies not only that Lucy's romantic desires remain unfulfilled, but also that the narrative itself has not yet achieved its goal. By linking the denial of Lucy's needed witness to the denial of a more socially legible narrative goal, an anticipated marriage, Brontë's novel couches the desire for psychic reintegration in terms to which her contemporary readers can affectively respond.

Ending not with the anticipated "Reader, I married him," but instead with anxiety-producing uncertainty, Brontë subjects the reader to a mediated version of the uneasy dread that has characterized Lucy's tortured consciousness throughout the novel. Although we don't directly experience her loss, we do experience, through our own discomfort at the novel's evasive conclusion, an anxiety similar to though less intense than hers. The proclamation that opens the final chapter of *Villette*—"Man cannot prophecy" (493)—locates the threat of loss not in Lucy's specific story, but in universal human experience, insisting that the future is never securely knowable. This ambiguous ending forces the reader, like Lucy, to circle back to the beginning in search of answers: Lucy's final loss of Paul repeats Miss Marchmont's story of the death of her fiancé, which opened Lucy's journey. By involving the reader in the narrator-protagonist's experience of trauma, *Villette* works to produce a reading public who might serve as witness to the plight of the numerous women, many doubtless beset by personal tragedy, who were socially invisible as individuals, yet hypervisible as the depersonalized problem of "redundant women." *Villette* restructures novelistic form to construct a reading audience both Lucy and Brontë know does not yet exist.

By shifting the focus of narration from a search for a husband to a search for a witness, Brontë allows a woman distinguished neither by wealth, beauty, illustrious heritage, nor sparkling wit to make her perspective as central in art as it is peripheral in society. *Villette* is the story of Lucy's attempts to tell her story, and her discovery that it is far easier to give a clear narrative of a luckier young woman's story—Ginevra's or Paulina's—than her own, which both begins and ends in grief and social marginalization. There are two layers to Lucy's task of bearing witness: her actions and words as a character within her own narrative, seeking the right interlocutor, and her choices as a narrator, attempting to convey to an audience that craves closure the terrible weight of uncertainty.

CHAPTER 3

❧

"I *Have* a Choice"

Emily Jolly Reframes Women's Agency

R eaders are familiar with the division of Victorian female characters
between selfless domestic angel and desiring, disruptive antiheroine.
It manifests, for instance, in the contrast between Paulina and Ginevra
in *Villette*. Emily Jolly, a protégé of Charles Dickens once popular in her own
right, is particularly interested in female protagonists who mediate across
these categories. Her narrative innovations pick up where Charlotte Brontë's
leave off: Jolly's fictions often chronicle female self-development *after* the
desired marriage has been achieved (*Jane Eyre, Shirley*) or permanently foreclosed (*Villette*). Like Brontë, she constructs heroines whose thwarted desires
lead to intermingled psychic and bodily suffering.

Jolly, of course, failed to attain Brontë's canonical status; indeed, her work
is unavailable in modern critical editions, although much of it is now accessible online through digitized nineteenth-century texts. Subject matter and
generic experimentation may account for the limited interest Jolly's fiction
has garnered from twentieth- and twenty-first-century readers, critics, and
publishers. Jolly's protagonists struggle to balance domestic and creative
commitments. Her earliest freestanding novels, *Mr. Arle* (1856) and *Katherine
Evering* (1857), most closely follow a marriage plot; subsequent fiction increasingly experiments with structure and genre. Whereas the standard marriage
plot entails a choice between suitors, each of whom embodies a different set
of cultural values, Jolly's oeuvre introduces a crucial third element: creative

or intellectual work. Here, her fiction may more closely follow Germaine de Staël's *Corinne* than it does British models.[1] Jolly's female protagonists often rely upon art not only as an outlet for aspirations toward power but more simply for income. She frequently tells stories situated at the lower edges of the middle class, where families desire education and lay nominal claim to gentility but suffer economic strain. These heroines have more in common with Eliot's Mary Garth, whose monetized learning keeps her struggling family whole, than they do with Rosamond Vincy, whose musical skill ensnares eligible suitors, or Dorothea Brooke, whose intellectual ambitions are enabled by comfortable income. Jolly's characters are frequently defined not only in relation to family and suitors, but as working painters, composers, musicians, actors, writers, and instructors in these fields. Jolly takes female protagonists' work lives as seriously as she does their personal lives, and conflicts often turn on the intersections. For instance, the novelist protagonist of *Mr. Arle* grapples not only with social stigma that follows her dissenting father's renunciation of his Anglican living, but also with her lover's scruples over the creative vocation by which she supports her family.

Jolly's female characters do not fit comfortably within critical dialogues about patriarchal oppression and feminist rebellion common to the important feminist recovery work of the 1970s through 1990s, which brought a number of overlooked female authors to renewed prominence.[2] Her heroines are to varying degrees both assertive and accommodating. Characters initially portrayed as fiery and defiant (Bruna of *Bruna's Revenge*) may gradually reveal interest in traditional domestic affections, and those introduced as conventionally pious and self-sacrificing may develop agency and desire for independence (Ann of the same novella). Neither trajectory is expressly celebrated or condemned. Jolly's fiction depicts the life of an educated nineteenth-century woman as a series of trade-offs and negotiations, often driven as much by financial pressures as personal feelings, with satisfactions and disappointments alike attached to the choices of work-focused independence and family-centric domesticity. Jolly neither openly impugns patriarchal norms nor acts as their apologist; rather, she works within the system to analyze and communicate its harmful effects on both women and men, and sometimes to

---

1. For a discussion of de Staël's *Corinne* as a female novel of self-development centered on artistic vocation, see Ian Duncan, "The Bildungsroman, the Romantic Nation, and the Marriage Plot," especially 17–19.

2. On achievements and limitations of recovery feminism, including its privileging of perceived rebellion in authors and characters, see Talia Schaffer, "Victorian Feminist Criticism: Recovery Work and the Care Community," and Pamela K. Gilbert, "Feminism and the Canon: Recovery and Reconsideration of Popular Novelists."

imagine alternatives. She is neither a Sarah Grand nor an Eliza Lynn Linton. Her fiction is difficult to place, which may account for her near-absence, thus far, from critical dialogues.

Although her heroines do not *always* marry, Jolly is interested in marital relationships. Her novellas *A Wife's Story* (1855) and *Witch-Hampton Hall: Five Scenes in the Life of Its Last Lady* (1864) track self-development within marriage rather than leading up to it. These texts are markedly different in tone and genre, but I connect them for the informative contrast they show in the outcome of a parallel narrative situation. In each, a young woman who has suffered great loss enters marriage with a guilty secret and consequently endures worsening psychic turmoil. Precipitating events are excluded from the discourse: in *A Wife's Story*, death of family, and in *Witch-Hampton Hall*, rape and resultant pregnancy. In a pattern that echoes vacillations of the courtship plot, each protagonist hesitates between sharing her emotional life with her partner or concealing it from him. The divergent fates of Annie and Lady Ana are tied to the traditionally patriarchal values of the one husband and the more reciprocal vision of marital responsibility embraced by the other.

Close analysis of both texts demonstrates how Jolly employs interrelated strategies of generic manipulation and engagement with medical discourse to prompt readers to reexamine their assumptions about the gender binary in intellectual and emotional life. The association of reason with masculinity and emotion with femininity has a long-standing Western philosophical tradition.[3] These divisions intensified and became increasingly medicalized with the advent of the industrial revolution and related gendered divisions of labor (Moglen, *Trauma* 2–3). As Rachel Malane argues, "the gendering of emotion as female and intellect as male became the base of more detailed discussions about the sexes' cerebral functions" in Victorian science (23). Medical insistence on connections among the brain, nervous system, and reproductive organs intensified contrasting views of men's and women's mental and physical attributes (Malane 33). Rather than rejecting or ignoring this discourse, Jolly works within its terms to show how socioeconomic and cultural aspects of patriarchy produce the very mental instability that Victorian physicians chastised or bemoaned in female patients.

Annie Warden's hysteric episodes and Lady Ana's nervous exhaustion encourage readers to critically rethink women's embodied experience of psychic pain. In *A Wife's Story*, the protagonist's hysteric symptoms are initially triggered by her honeymoon and worsened by having children, but the text

---

3. See especially Susan Bordo's "Feminism, Western Culture, and the Body" in *Unbearable Weight: Feminism, Western Culture, and the Body* (2003).

implies Annie's hysteria originates not in sexuality or reproduction (dominant medical explanations) but rather through the stifling of her intellect within conventional patriarchal marriage. *Witch-Hampton Hall* similarly engages and critiques cultural and medical assumptions about the relation of female sexuality to mental dysfunction, selecting as its protagonist a woman whom Victorians would classify as "fallen." Lady Ana declines into symptomology of nervous exhaustion, but she is not doomed to the conventional "downward spiral" by her premarital sexual experience. Instead, her ambiguously somatic and psychic ailment is ascribed to socially mandated deceptions she must employ because she is culturally barred from communicating her experience of rape. Restoring open dialogue with an accepting intimate partner and loving family allows her to heal and provides an upward narrative arc.

Savvy generic choices make these potentially controversial topics accessible to a broad Victorian audience. In *A Wife's Story*, the mode of sentimental fiction, and strategic deployment of rhetoric of sensibility, presents the narrator-protagonist as a penitent matron, enabling her to chronicle the decay of her mental acuity and self-control without openly indicting the gender norms and economic systems that caused it. *Witch-Hampton Hall* engages still more sensitive material, with a plot predicated on the consequences of rape. The structure and generic conventions of gothic stage melodrama enable Jolly to avoid direct articulation of material too graphic for mainstream Victorian readership, while also focusing attention on the psychic experiences and social choices of the protagonist and avoiding potentially prurient attention to sexual violence. Taken together, these novellas offer a model of fictional engagement with female experiences deemed "unspeakable" within Victorian culture; they create a socially legible framework for analysis of what we might now term women's trauma responses to gendered socioeconomic barriers and interpersonal violence. Rejecting the strictures of the marriage plot and bildungsroman forms, these novellas deconstruct cultural myths and scientific hypotheses that imagined reproductive function as the primary arbiter of women's psychic lives.

SUBLIME HYSTERICS AND
THWARTED FEMALE INTELLECT

A Wife's Story, published serially in Dickens's *Household Words* in 1855 and later in book form with collected short stories, explores the ramifications of disordered mental states not only for power relations within marriage, but also for the development and expression of female intellectual creativity. Jolly's depiction of her narrator-protagonist's descent into and recovery from so-called madness both reflects and critiques contemporary scientific understandings of female mental disorder and woman's domestic role, shifting blame from biological to socioeconomic factors. Its narrative structure encourages the reader to participate in such a critique. The narrator's seemingly unaccountable perceptions and conduct require readers to implicate themselves in the character's social transgression. In trying to make sense of the story's plot, readers inevitably find clues that exculpate her and instead indict her society. Through engagement with both late eighteenth- and nineteenth-century scientific models of mental function and contemporaneous shifts in understanding of sensibility, sentimentality, and the sublime, *A Wife's Story* participates in ongoing debates about the interconnections between gender, affect, and creativity, appropriating key gendered divisions within medical science and aesthetics in order to demonstrate their socioeconomic and cultural basis. Its evasive narrative strategy allows Jolly to develop sympathy with reading audiences that might resist overt critique of patriarchal marriage conventions.

Jolly gives us what the historical record seldom provides: the first-person perspective of a woman whose extreme and disruptive psychic episodes are branded "madness" (153, ch. 5), though in Victorian medical terms, she would likely be termed hysteric. As she introduces herself, Jolly's narrator-protagonist, Annie Aston, is "rather small, generally very quiet in manner, not beautiful, and not plain" (97, ch. 1), yet she has a vigorous, moody inner life precariously contained within her decorous, unobtrusive exterior. Briefly, the events of the novella are as follows: A clever, orphaned young governess marries a good-hearted, handsome, and eligible gentleman, her dead brother's friend Harold Warden, who knows nothing of her "real nature, its force, its aspirations, its vehement unrest" (97, ch. 1). Annie, an aspiring composer, skilled pianist, and avid reader of poetry, eventually comes to regard the intellectually limited Harold with what she reluctantly terms "something like disdain" (124, ch. 2). Early in their marriage, she meets a friend of his whose tastes and intellect are better suited to her own, but her propriety averts her from pursuing even a platonic relationship with this ideal match, and her husband never guesses her true feelings. Nonetheless, the marriage deteriorates as the wife's mental health declines. Annie experiences increasingly extreme emotional outbursts and nervous episodes that bring her under a doctor's care and estrange her from husband and children. After another altercation, Harold gallops off recklessly and is seriously injured.[4] Believing him dead, Annie

---

4. This accident's obvious parallel to the death of Miss Marchmont's fiancé in *Villette*—likewise dragged by his own horse—is one of many connections between the texts.

swoons into a debilitating fit. Shortly thereafter, their small son and daughter are afflicted with a fever that claims the boy's life. The wife and daughter gradually recover, and the husband's survival is revealed. The contrite wife, believed by herself and others to be the source of the family's troubles, accepts her husband's moral superiority and humbly lives out her married life.[5]

Although canny readers might connect Annie's artistic persona to Romanticist aesthetic and ideological investments, the pre-Victorian setting is not made explicit until a concluding fictional editor's note explains that the repentant Annie has died after many years as an esteemed matron. Therefore Annie, who throughout her narrative seems to present herself as the Victorian woman's peer, comes to emblematize the gradual reining in of sensibility and retrenchment of the gender binary that typified English cultural life over the first half of the nineteenth century. On its surface, the novella endorses accepted Victorian attitudes about femininity, women's domestic role, and the causation of female mental disorders.

When *A Wife's Story* is contextualized within the range of Jolly's fiction, its discordant elements are thrown into relief. *Caste* (1857), her complex second novel, finds no solution in matrimony for its trade-class protagonist, who is like Annie a gifted pianist. After an ill-judged marriage to an aristocrat goes violently awry, she finds solace in the successful administration of a business dealing in sheet music. In spite of its generally light tone, Jolly's short story "My First and Last Novel" (1858), a social comedy about a naive wife's efforts to aid her financially strapped husband by secretly writing fiction, raises serious questions about how gender inequality negatively affects both the marriage bond and women's creativity. Her later story "All in the Wrong; or, the Tamer Tamed: A Story without a Moral" (1862) abandons the light tone in its examination of the devastating impact of both inherited property and traditional gender relations in a tense account of a love triangle at an idyllic country estate. While the story ends with an ostensibly happy marriage, a malicious struggle for dominance underpins interactions between friends and lovers, and the female protagonist's much-feared, now-dead father haunts the young people through the influence of his shockingly unjust will. Some later novels make explicit Jolly's skepticism about the coexistence of romantic partnership and female intellectual and creative fulfillment. After a disappointing love

---

5. Jolly's initial draft killed off the husband and both children, leaving the protagonist suffering alone. Charles Dickens, while enthusiastic about Jolly's manuscript, advised in a July 7, 1855, letter that she "spare the life of the husband, and one of the children" in order to "soften the reader whom you now as it were harden" (Dickens, *Letters* 677). Her compliance with this requested change, allowing the reader some hope and comfort, doubtless made the story more appealing to broad audiences.

affair, the protagonist of *Pearl* (1868) chooses her career as author over a wife's role even when a highly suitable match presents himself. The title character of *Bruna's Revenge* (1872) makes the alternative sacrifice, giving up her acting career for marriage and the companionship of her longtime female friend. Jolly's fiction evinces ambivalence about the feasibility of women's balancing artistic/intellectual pursuits with domestic satisfactions. While her work represents patriarchal conventions in increasingly violent terms, at the same time she seeks a vision of male–female relations in which greater equality would benefit both partners. Viewed as an early point in this progression, *A Wife's Story* seems less an endorsement of the status quo than a case study in its psychological impact.

Assuming *A Wife's Story* critiques rather than endorses traditional gender relations, to what aspects of a Victorian woman's lot does it ascribe blame for its protagonist's mental unraveling? A comparison to Brontë's *Villette,* with which *A Wife's Story* shares significant and perhaps deliberate parallels, is useful. *A Wife's Story* and *Villette* alike explore interconnections between disordered psychic states, feminine social roles, financial hardship, and loneliness. Both focus on a bereaved teacher-governess, the impoverished orphan daughter of a genteel family, whose reserve and propriety mask a vivid and passionate inner life and seething resentment for her spoiled charges. Jolly's Annie, who loves to read poetry and to play and compose music, retreats to the garden behind her unappreciative employers' home to vent "grief, scorn, or impotent rage" (100, ch. 7), just as Brontë's Lucy Snowe, whose appreciation of the arts is deep though largely passive, seeks a private outlet for tears and contemplation in the garden of Rue Fosette. Both, to the shock and dismay of their employers, receive an offer of marriage that promises to end their refined drudgery. Here the stories diverge. For Lucy Snowe, the improved social status and financial security offered by her suitor are conveniently merged with the emotional, spiritual, and intellectual fulfillment of joining her life with that of the person who understands her best. For Annie Aston, however, the engagement that seems to rescue her is something she rapidly comprehends to be a financial and social promotion but not the hoped-for "communion, the perfect sympathy, which [she] fancied was to take all the pain of over-fulness from [her] soul" (103, ch. 1).

Whereas *Villette's* bereaved protagonist is denied her expected emotional solace by her fiancé's sudden death, Annie is denied these things because she marries a man she cannot respect on an intellectual level, despite her sincere gratitude. Unlike the fiery, perceptive Paul Emanuel of *Villette,* himself marked by tragedy, the cheerful and good-natured Harold Warden is intellectually incurious, unable to share his new wife's passion for nature and the arts, much less to sympathize with her fiercely haunted inner life.

In spite of her good-faith effort to feel the love she believes she ought to feel, Annie cannot shape her relationship with Harold into her vision of what marriage should be. By dividing the social and financial security of marriage from the emotional satisfaction that is so often its corollary in Victorian fiction, and by focusing on the potentially devastating consequences of a decision to marry rather than the events leading up to it, *A Wife's Story* emphasizes the role economic factors play in psychic and domestic life. Annie's initial pain owes not only to grief at her parents' and brother's deaths, but also to the shock of socioeconomic demotion and the daily strain of dreary work where she is treated as a mere functionary, conditions that align with Laura Brown's delineation of insidious trauma in positions of economic precarity.[6] Subsequently, Annie is tormented not only by the denial of the sympathy and understanding she craves—as is Lucy Snowe—but also by the knowledge that she willingly chose a marriage that could not deliver these things in order to escape the humiliation she faced earning her living as a single woman. In spite of its seeming endorsement of the status quo, communicated through Annie's sentimental contrition, *A Wife's Story* more directly challenges conventional notions of femininity and domestic happiness than does *Villette*.

A Wife's Story also resonates with Victorian scientific and cultural anxieties about female education. Medical concerns that the rigors of study could cause women reproductive harm were common Victorian arguments against equal access to education and professional opportunity (Malane 49). For instance, in 1840 the influential neurologist Thomas Laycock faulted overapplication in musical study, especially the pianoforte popular with marriageable young ladies, as a significant precipitating factor in the development of hysteria (140–41). Annie, of course, is an ambitious pianist. As previously discussed, Victorian mental science tended to view reproductive function as overdetermining of female mental health. Laycock understood hysteria as an ailment of the nervous system specific to women (6–8), and most prevalent in those at the beginning or the end of their childbearing years (8). He correlated "hysterical symptoms" with menstruation in some women (45). Pioneering Victorian psychiatrist Henry Maudsley articulated a broadly accepted view in claiming that "woman has no honourable outlook but marriage in our present social system: if that aim is missed, all is missed" (*Physiology* 203). Even as Victorian mental

---

6. See "Not Outside the Range: One Feminist Perspective on Psychic Trauma," especially 110–11.

science regarded pregnancy and childbirth as instigators of mental instability, it espoused the belief that women's innate capacity for emotion and intuition best suited them for child-rearing (Malane 23). Thus, those very life events acknowledged as catalysts of mental disorder were implicitly recommended to promote mental health. Such internal contradictions did not diminish the cultural cachet or professional authority of scientific pronouncements regarding gendered intellectual capabilities. The seemingly objective investigations of neurology, physiology, and even phrenology lent credibility to theories of the gendered mind because they based their assertions about mental ability on measurable material phenomena.[7]

Jolly's novella is clearly inflected with Victorian medical understandings of women's nervous ailments, particularly hysteria. Physician Robert Brudenell Carter, her contemporary, identified typical hysterical symptoms as "a short attack of laughter or sobbing" or "very energetic involuntary movements," sometimes followed by "a period of catalepsy or coma" (1002). Annie passes rapidly from hyperactivity or peaceful elation to frigid anger or frantic distress, at times swooning into semi-consciousness or descending into nervous exhaustion after a wearing expenditure of emotion. Her symptoms accord with widely held Victorian medical beliefs that the female mind and nervous system were inherently excitable and prone to sudden outbursts and transitions (Malane 23).

Nonetheless, Jolly's depiction of the onset of Annie's illness calls into question conventional expectations about the genesis of women's psychic disorder. Annie's earliest outbursts occur in response to marital disagreements prompted by Harold's lack of respect for her intellectual passions, notably poetry, music, and nature. When Annie admires an imposing vista of the Scottish Highlands with spiritual fervor, declaring that "my soul strove and struggled, it essayed to dilate wide enough to take in all the glory, the grandeur," Harold shows no reaction, instead engaging in "light talk and laughter [that] pained me" (125, ch. 2) until she asks him to be quiet. She nearly faints from the intensity of her reaction to the landscape, and when Harold attempts to steady her, she informs the reader, "The calmness of his half-pitying look, irritated me yet more." Annie explodes into a "torrent of wildly passionate words" that she does not repeat to the reader, but which she "would have given more than my life to recal [sic]." She soon descends into "bitter tears" (126, ch. 2), begging her husband's forgiveness.

Apart from the altercation it provokes, the contrast between Annie's and Harold's reactions to the landscape implies critique of contemporary expecta-

---

7. See Malane ch. 1.

tions about male and female intellectual capacities. It is useful to contextualize Annie and Harold's first argument not only within nineteenth-century
scientific discourse of hysteria, but also within discussions of the related and
differently gendered discourses of the sublime and sensibility. These were
prominent concerns of moral philosophy, aesthetics, and literature in the late-
eighteenth- and early-nineteenth-century milieu in which the story's main
action likely occurs. Annie's pleasure in solitary contemplation of the natural world, her enthusiasm for its threatening or excessive aspects, her intense
but nondogmatic spirituality, and her artistic creation whose sophistication
outpaces fashion (musical composition) ally her with Romantic poets, particularly the young Wordsworth and Coleridge. The grand, imposing scale
of the landscape that occasions Annie's first argument with Harold and her
awed, passionate reaction indicate the presence of a sublime natural object
and a philosophically refined and emotionally intense response. Harold's reaction, by contrast, is pedestrian; the couple's conduct reverses gender roles in
Coleridge's much-repeated tale of travelers admiring the cataract in which a
lady's aesthetic ignorance in calling it "the prettiest thing I ever saw" becomes
the butt of the joke and the emblem of feminine intellectual limitations.[8]

When Annie's mental effort "to make God's things [her soul's] own, con-
taining them" fails, she gives herself over to "strife and pain, and impotent
self-abasement" (125, ch. 2), comprehending that she can neither abandon nor
achieve her desire to fully experience, appreciate, and understand the scene
before her. Annie's attempt to negotiate an intellectual and spiritual relationship to the sublime object certainly involves an ambitious assertion of her
mental powers. However, her attempt ends not in a sense of domination and
closure that validates her aspirations, but rather in a state of mental flux in
which she neither cedes her desire for synthesis with the grandeur of the
other nor claims intellectual mastery of the object she contemplates. Annie's
response to the landscape falls in line with Barbara Freeman's characterization
of "the politics of the feminine sublime" as "taking up a position of respect
in response to an incalculable otherness" (12). Annie demonstrates potential
for an aesthetic and spiritual discernment that recognizes both her individual
ambition for mastery and the limits of human control. This very capacity for
simultaneously desiring and ceding intellectual control, which can enable a
sophisticated aesthetic and spiritual response, will later be corrupted into the
agency-seeking, agency-destroying swoons of hysteria.

While in keeping with the feminine sublime as defined by Freeman,
Annie's response to the landscape also bears comparison to that more con-

---

8. Ian Balfour relates the history and discusses the implications of this anecdote (324–25).

ventionally feminine intellectual and emotional pose, sensibility. The culture
of sensibility shares scientific heritage with nineteenth-century theories of
hysteria: the hypothesis that consciousness has a material manifestation in
the nerves, which gained ground from the late seventeenth century and was
by the close of the eighteenth century a widespread conviction among the
English intellectual elite, and a primary basis of psychological description in
novels (Ahern 16–17). The man or woman of sensibility responds to environmental stimuli with intense emotion, most typically, in fiction, sorrow at
witnessing virtue in distress or intense love for one's object of affection. While
regarded as a moral virtue and mark of social distinction in mid- to late-
eighteenth-century Britain, sensibility was also cause for concern on account
of its capacity to pain its virtuous exemplar (M. Ellis 5–6). Further, by the
close of the eighteenth century, critiques of sensibility and its more narrowly
circumscribed literary subset, sentimentality, had gained purchase, notably on
the grounds that an instinctive emotive response might as easily be negative
as positive, and a professed sentiment may lack sincerity, seeking a reputation
for virtue unearned by charitable actions (Ahern 26). While philosophically
distinct from the sublime and possessing very different cultural connotations,
sensibility intersects with responses to the sublime, in ways particularly inter-
esting to discussion of Annie Warden's mental and physical states.

Markman Ellis argues sensibility displays "a complex logic akin to the
sublime, that discovers pleasure in distress and misery, albeit that sensibility is a sublime untouched by transcendence" (6). This apparent inability to
intellectually transcend environmental influences might be said to differentiate between, on the one hand, the (typically masculine) encounter with the
sublime and, on the other, the (typically feminine) transport of sentiment
or, given a more scientific and less sympathetic valence, swoon of hysteria.
Within the context of amatory and gothic narratives, the "young woman of
refined sensibility" is beset by "conflicting passions" or "engaged in a struggle
between her desire and her sense of duty," and "as a result of these moments
of passional excess, she falls into a state of cognitive and physical paralysis demonstrated by her maintaining a frozen physical attitude or, swooning,
suffering a complete loss of consciousness and ending up in a heap on the
floor" (Ahern 40). The heroine's swoon accords with the outwardly visible
physical manifestation of Annie's response to the sublime. Yet, as the reader
of her first-person narrative knows, a different mental phenomenon is at work
within Annie.

While the conflicts of sensibility typically focus on social relations—one's
emotive rapport with another person or with humanity more broadly—Annie's
inner conflict in this scene stems from her attempt to position herself, as an

individual creative intellect, in meaningful relation to the vast divine creation manifested in the natural world. But Harold, who has resisted Annie's attempts to include him in her intellectual pursuits, cannot discern such a difference, and exercises his characteristically weak powers of interpretation on outward physical signs alone. The conflict between husband and wife arises when Harold (not unreasonably) misreads the physical signs of Annie's intellectual and spiritual response to the sublime object as a purely emotional and physical transport of sensibility. The reader, privileged with knowledge of Annie's inner life, sees that like William Wordsworth, she is struggling to negotiate her intellectual and creative relationship with the natural world; Harold's dismissal of her enraptured response to the landscape effectively casts her as a self-tormenting Marianne Dashwood, swooning sorrowfully over dead leaves. To be treated with benign disdain by her intellectual inferior is more than Annie's patience can bear, and her explosive anger and immediate contrition follow. Later that evening, Harold is willing to dismiss the altercation, which seems, to Annie, evidence of his lack of mental subtlety, and she intimates to the reader, "I throned myself on an imagined elevation of intellectual superiority, and scorned his childlike singleness of heart" (126, ch. 2).

As Harold unwittingly stifles his wife's intellectual creativity over the course of their marriage, Annie begins to display similar bouts of mental overload and concomitant physical paralysis or collapse without the positive intellectual and spiritual component evident in her response to the Scottish landscape. Within their first year of marriage, her transports degenerate into emotional excess typical of both hysteria and overblown sensibility, composed, in Annie's case, of intense and conflicting waves of impotent rage and punishing guilt. As her marriage deteriorates, Annie's capacity for intense emotive response degrades from its starting point as a potentially powerful tool for moral refinement and intellectual creativity into a hazardously excessive and partially calculated hysterical display. As Fred Kaplan suggests, "the notion of sentimentality as insincerity, as false feeling, even as hypocrisy, became increasingly strong" (17) as the nineteenth century progressed; hence, the shift in motives and meanings of Annie's emotions correlates with declining trust in the cultivation and expression of moral sentiment between the beginning and the midpoint of the nineteenth century.[9]

---

9. In their introduction to the collection *Nervous Reactions: Victorian Recollections of Romanticism*, Joel Faflak and Julia M. Wright relate Victorian unease with inadequately restrained excesses of affective and bodily sensation in Romantic literature to the Victorians' growing valorization of morality as defined through duty, propriety, and self-control. They suggest this led to pathologization of "nervousness," which once denoted the bodily basis for energy and sympathy.

Annie's transition from woman of feeling and inspired artist to socially crippled hysteric and manipulative wife also inherently critiques a key gendered division within Enlightenment philosophy, that between the sublime and the beautiful. Ironically, when Annie's laudable but, by eighteenth-century philosophical legacy, gender-atypical response to the sublime is quashed by her simple husband's well-meaning insensitivity, she begins to learn the sly, deceptive domination that Burke associates instead with the sublime's implicitly lower counterpart, the conventionally feminine and winningly weak and submissive beautiful.[10] Annie's "fiendish" power over her husband is exercised through the seeming weakness of an "uncertain temper" and subtly manipulative expressions of disdain (127, ch. 2). Jolly traces its genesis to an argument touched off by the husband's failure to share his wife's appreciation of the sublime. The author thereby effectively ascribes female association with the alternative power of the beautiful not to inherent feminine nature but instead to socially constructed gender roles. Because Annie must at least superficially submit to her husband, even as she recognizes his intellectual inferiority, she is obliged to cultivate different, and morally dubious, intellectual capacities.

MARRIAGE, MATERNITY, AND MENTAL UNRAVELING

Early in her marriage, Annie has "seen, or fancied that [Harold] would expect from [her], only an implicit and child-like obedience" (123, ch. 2). The obligation to defer to her intellectual inferior, simply because she has married him, makes Annie feel "inclined to rebel" (123, ch. 2). The couple's early quarrels all follow the same pattern: Harold fails to appreciate an intellectual or spiritual passion of Annie's; she becomes angry and says something hurtful, then, regretting her unkindness, displays frustration and contrition through behaviors and bodily responses Victorians code as hysterical. In between these outbursts, which are portrayed as genuinely beyond Annie's control, she plays upon her developing reputation for instability to exact through fear, concern, and embarrassment the compliance she cannot win from her husband through reasoned and straightforward debate. While Annie's behavior follows stereotypical negative feminine patterns, its motives and causes are shown to be quite different from those on which Jolly's contemporaries blamed hysteria and women's limitations generally. Annie's developing mental weakness and volatility proceed not from lesser intellectual capacity, but rather from her

---

10. Frances Ferguson outlines Burke's explication of how the beautiful, and implicitly the woman, problematically dominates through appealing weakness (50–53).

intellectual superiority. Her emotional excitability, while figured as an innate aspect of her temperament, is linked to her intelligence, which is distinguished by both perceptiveness about the arts and receptiveness to the beauty of the natural world. Jolly suggests that the accepted dividing line between reason and emotion, as materially based mental functions, is far from clear-cut.

For Annie, intellectual acuity is intertwined with powerful emotion, and emotional well-being cannot be cultivated apart from intellectual development. Having knowingly entered into marriage with a slow-witted but generous man to escape poverty and drudgery, she is at once frustrated by his intellectual inadequacy and wracked with guilt at her inability to be satisfied with his simple kindness. For example, after an argument over Harold's failure to appreciate Annie's musical composition, the tearful Annie informs the reader, "That night I lay awake with the miserable consciousness that I had done no good, but great harm,—that now, indeed, poor Harold's heart must be wounded . . ." (130, ch. 3). Such inner conflict catalyzes her hysterical episodes, in this instance, one that renders her "restless," "feverish," and "very ill" for "many days after" (130, ch. 3).

Socioeconomic systems, not biological ones, trigger Annie's mental distress. While out of alignment with nineteenth-century medical accounts of hysteria causation, which leaned heavily on the notion of women's inherent biological susceptibility to environmental pressures, Annie's escalating patterns display noteworthy, though not exact, parallels with current theorization of psychic trauma. Contemporary medical formulations of PTSD hold that its psychological and related physiological symptoms are triggered by external events (even if some individuals are biologically predisposed to develop the disorder, rather than a short-term trauma response, from traumatogenic stimuli). Clinical accounts of PTSD also now emphasize the role of social support, or lack thereof, in recovery, a topic to which I shall return later in this chapter. Similar to the twenty-first-century PTSD case, Annie develops debilitating psychological and physiological patterns as a result of an experience of abrupt loss in combination with social and economic contexts that intensify, rather than resolve, her suffering. The financial hardship and social stigma inherent in her governess position all but oblige her to accept any reasonable marriage offer, without consideration of the suitor's temperament and capacities. Once married, she sincerely seeks an appropriate outlet for her intellect and emotions within the marriage bond but finds herself thwarted by Harold's intellectual inadequacy. Annie's spiral into hysteria begins when the development of her powerful intellect and nuanced spirituality is arrested by the intolerable necessity of deference to her intellectual inferior. As she later embraces her new maternal role and attempts to trade her gender-atypical aesthetic creativ-

ity for the culturally sanctioned biological and social creativity of motherhood, her psychic disorder further escalates.

In addition to complicating the scientifically assumed divide between reason and emotion, Jolly also modifies contemporary medical opinion regarding the role of childbirth and maternity in mental disorder. As previously
discussed, the prevailing medical opinion was that the physical upheaval of
pregnancy and childbirth could destabilize delicate female brains, but that
child-rearing was the task women's sympathetic and emotive minds were best
suited for: Caring for children should naturally promote a mother's mental health. Annie's experiences reverse that conventional wisdom. She finds
immediately after the birth of her first child, "there was a long interval during
which I thought I was at peace," because "physical weakness made quiet and
stillness grateful, and the new great joy seemed to fill and satisfy my soul"
(151, ch. 5). The physical exhaustion following childbirth reduces Annie to
a mental state in which the passive and childlike behavior idealized in the
domestic woman is, for the first time in her life, genuinely welcome. After
the birth of her daughter, Annie explains that she "gave up everything to my
child, and Harold thought me a paragon, a perfect example of self-denying
love" (152, ch. 5).

Ironically, it is her very attempt to make motherhood the whole goal of
her existence—the most culturally appropriate goal—that ultimately drives
Annie further into psychic disorder. As her daughter grows and is joined by a
son, Annie's need to be the only source of love and meaning in their lives, as
they have become the only source of love and meaning in hers, alienates her
both from them and from their father. Her intense jealousy of the children's
affections, irrational at first glance, becomes more understandable when one
considers that, with her intellectual and artistic aspirations foiled, her parents
and siblings long dead, and her marriage unsatisfying, they are literally all
Annie has to live for. Annie's dilemma vividly illustrates what Kelly Oliver
has termed "maternal melancholy" (*Colonization* 110), wherein the mother,
denied access to positions of power within a patriarchal culture, is only able
to relate to the social order through her child, and invests her whole identity
in the child (111). Not surprisingly, Oliver notes, this responsibility is overwhelming to most children (111).

Annie's consuming love is off-putting for her children, who feel emotionally smothered. Of her relationship with her growing son, Annie laments, "He
would turn from my wild love to meet his father's calm tenderness. The older
he grew, the more plainly he showed this preference" (152, ch. 5). The children's
clear partiality toward their father then becomes the primary source of fric-
tion in the marriage and the main trigger for Annie's increasingly frequent

and intense emotional outbursts. Maternity, not as biological fact but as cultural construction, is shown to produce the very feminine mental instability, ill health, and unhappiness it was widely believed to alleviate.

The ambiguous status of hysteria, as a scientific, moral, and cultural category, made it a useful catchall for behaviors and subjective experiences that would otherwise call into question a woman's moral fitness as a member of the community. In a demonstration of agency, it is Annie herself, not her husband, who calls in a doctor for consultation, having learned Harold is pitied in their social set as "the poor gentleman who had a mad wife" (153, ch. 5). But Annie's agency proves illusory. Dr. Ryton explicitly offers her the choice of virtue or sanity: "Mrs. Warden reflect! Do you remember when I was last sent for to attend you? Do you mean to confess that that humiliating wildness of passion was voluntarily indulged?" (153, ch. 5). Annie is asked to acknowledge a temporary loss of reason in order to protect her virtue. She can and indeed must take an active role in defining her experience, but she is forced to reduce the nuances of her unhappiness—bereavement, guilt, longing, and resentment—into two simple categories. Either she admits she is "mad," to use the term her social set employs, thus conceding that she is incapable of sustained rational thought and self-control, or she claims that she is sane, and is branded "selfish" and "wicked" (153, ch. 5) by her doctor for engaging in behavior that distresses her family. The assumption underlying Dr. Ryton's analysis is that any rational and moral woman would appreciate the comfortable home that Harold Warden provides. Annie is insufficiently disruptive for the asylum, but not calm and content enough for proper society, so she allows herself to be sequestered as a hysteric rather than have her domestic dissatisfaction recognized by her community.

Dr. Ryton's investigation of Annie's instability is based entirely on observation of immediate symptoms and makes no inquiry into either the family tragedy that preceded her marriage or the history of her interactions with her husband. Therefore, the attentive reader is privileged with an understanding of Annie's motives that the doctor lacks. Often *A Wife's Story* obliges the reader to determine Annie's motives by interpreting her actions and interactions because the motives other characters ascribe to her, and even those she herself espouses in moments of contrition, fail to account for her behavior. Annie declares that her dilemma results from her unique circumstances, choices, and temperament, but the interactions she describes instead show that her distress is the inevitable result of women's socioeconomic and cultural position. In puzzling out the discrepancy between the claims Annie makes and the events she describes, the reader is drawn into critique of accepted nineteenth-century scientific, aesthetic, and cultural assumptions regarding gender.

An active reader notices striking incongruities between the narrator-protagonist's self-presentation and the evidence she marshals to contextualize and perhaps excuse her behavior, seemingly against her declared intentions. Annie frames her story with an explanation of the personal history that shaped her temperament and a declaration of her particular moral failings. As the novella opens, she asserts that her experience of being orphaned has aged her emotionally beyond her years (97, ch. 1). While she does not share her story of bereavement, she makes clear that this loss has changed her, and she renders in painful detail the degrading manner in which she is treated as a governess and the resentment it provokes. Thus circumstanced, Annie explains, she mistakes the fond memory of old times that her brother's friend Harold evokes for affection for Harold himself (98, ch. 1), and confuses her gratitude for Harold's kindness with romantic love (97, ch. 1). At the story's close, her explanation is a moralizing mea culpa rather than a justification, but it is no less particular: She concludes their suffering as a couple resulted from her being a "sinful wife" (186, ch. 7). Yet as previously discussed, the interactions she outlines demonstrate that the problems in the Wardens' marriage driving Annie to mental disorder and Harold to despair are in fact rooted in socially constructed patriarchal gender roles dictating a wife's submission to her husband, and associating femininity with affect and self-abnegating nurture rather than intellect and self-assertion. Without any open challenge to the status quo of gender relations, indeed, despite a superficial endorsement of them, Jolly demonstrates that her contemporary marriage system limits women's potential and distorts family affections. Nowhere in *A Wife's Story* do we find the open critique of women's position considered so offensive by contemporary readers in, for instance, *Jane Eyre*. Yet active readers analyze the substance of Annie's interactions with Harold and notice that her declarations are at odds with the events and attitudes she describes.

Ironically, as she narrates a story that enables and encourages readership to critique Victorian domestic life, Annie is recording the history of how she herself gradually lost all capacity for such critique. Annie's hysteria allows her to vent unhappiness without openly challenging her husband's authority, yet it is a false or transitory agency. It implicitly grants the power of interpreting her behavior to a rigidly patriarchal medical authority, which forces her to choose between two equally unpalatable labels, "madness" and "wickedness," both of which are socially alienating, and moves her farther away from the relationship of genuine reciprocity that she desires. *A Wife's Story* demonstrates that disordered mental states might effectively critique women's social position within Victorian fiction, but in lived experience could only further diminish a woman's social agency. Its title is significant: It is not "Annie's Story" or even "Mrs. Warden's Story," but "*A Wife's* Story," a tale of the erasure of individual female identity within patriarchal marriage. Yet by opening a space for readerly critique, Jolly enables wives entertaining themselves with *Household Words* to engage in the rational questioning her heroine no longer can. By investing this recognizably conventional Victorian wife and mother with the sensibility of a thwarted Romantic poet, Jolly, like her protagonist, achieves through manipulation what she cannot accomplish by reasoned and straightforward debate.

REWRITING THE DOWNWARD SPIRAL: SEXUAL FALL AS LIVE BURIAL

Jolly can, however, imagine a marital relation of genuine reciprocity and sympathetic connection. She selects, for what may be the sole idealized and fully imagined romantic partnership of her oeuvre, a female character that, in the majority of contemporaneous fiction, would be doomed to solitude and shame. Despite more complex social realities, Victorian fiction—and likewise cultural discourse—is notably reticent with regard to active, affirmative life trajectories available to women who lose their virginity prior to marriage. Whether portrayed with opprobrium (Esther in Gaskell's *Mary Barton*), sympathy (Hetty in Eliot's *Adam Bede*, Emily in Dickens's *David Copperfield*), or even admiration (Gaskell's *Ruth*, Hardy's *Tess of the D'Urbervilles*), their narratives typically conclude in social isolation and/or penitent demise. In mainstream Victorian fiction, the socially validated position of wife and (legitimate) mother appears unavailable to the "fallen woman," regardless of whether the character's premarital sexual experience is presented as resulting from deliberate choice, or violence, or ambiguous circumstances. As Lynda Nead suggests, perpetuation of the downward spiral narrative within fiction and visual culture assuaged bourgeois anxieties about the social chaos female unchastity was believed to incite. She explains, "Temptation—fall—decline and death. This narrative provided a linear coherence; it posed the 'problem' of deviant femininity which was then resolved through the process of narration. Its sequence was seen as the unveiling of reality, the revelation of truth" (*Myths* 140–41). The fallen woman's social and then actual death contained the threat she posed to established sexual and economic order.

Jolly's *Witch-Hampton Hall* offers a significant departure from the standard narrative pattern. This unique novella depicts an aristocratic rape survivor who becomes first a clergyman's wife with a guilty secret (swapping her illegitimate son for her sister's dying baby) and then an esteemed matron whose husband loves her no less for having had a child out of wedlock. In contrast with canonical Victorian texts and mainstream culture, which by and large equate female sexual fall with irretrievable loss of both virtue and agency, Jolly's novella insists upon a gender-neutral ethical framework that values empathy (feeling with the partner), sympathy (feeling for the partner) and integrity, and eschews the dominant association of inviolable female body with pure female psyche. Turning to mental science to explain the fallen woman's loss of agency, and telling her story in a gothic rather than a realist register, *Witch-Hampton Hall* implicitly undermines the truth claims of narrative traditions that cast the sexually compromised woman as impure and/or incapable of social reintegration. In order to recognize the significance of *Witch-Hampton Hall*'s departure from mainstream narratives of female sexual compromise, it is crucial to understand that the historical record suggests Victorian culture failed to meaningfully distinguish between female sexual experiences resulting from choice and those resulting from violence or coercion. A rape survivor such as Lady Ana would face the same social barriers as a woman who consented to a sexual relationship (a point to which I shall return). *Witch-Hampton Hall* excavates and challenges assumptions about embodied female virtue that underpinned the all-too-familiar narrative of the fallen woman's social and spiritual descent. In striking contrast with narratives that kill off this character or sentence her to exile, Jolly's novella allows Lady Ana to retain her place in her family's ancestral home, respectably integrated in the surrounding community. *Witch-Hampton Hall* grants its heroine the markers of narrative approval typically afforded to the virtuous Victorian heroine: a loving marriage with a preferred suitor and stable social participation. The close of her story far more resembles the fate of Dinah Morris, Hetty Sorrel's pious foil, than that of Hetty herself.

Crucial to *Witch-Hampton Hall*'s revision of the fallen woman story is rejection of shame, the affect Victorian culture overwhelmingly associated with female sexual impurity, and its substitution with guilt, a mental state more productive of choice and action. The distinctions drawn between guilt and shame by philosophers Bernard Williams and Kelly Oliver usefully elucidate why a protagonist who feels guilty rather than ashamed is more capable of progression, in terms of both psychological growth and narrative momentum. As Oliver explains, "shame is about identity while guilt is about action" (*Colonization* 12). Jolly's protagonist regards not her sexually compromised state, but rather her deceptions, as the basis of her blameworthiness. As a rape victim, Lady Ana locates her sense of culpability not in her identity as "fallen woman" (no longer virginal and indeed pregnant out of wedlock) but rather in her related subterfuge. As her deceptions are socially mandated, they may lead the reader not only to exculpate Lady Ana, but also to critique the social structures that silence victims of sexual violence and oblige its concealment. As Lady Ana's sense of guilt is grounded in action (the baby swap), she is able to develop a recuperative course of action to repair the harm her deception causes and thereby reestablish her integrity. By shifting the psychic consequences of sexual fall from the realm of shame to that of guilt, Jolly's novella restores the fallen woman's agency, allowing her protagonist a narrative more complex than the predictable downward spiral.

Rewriting the downward spiral into an upward narrative arc requires Jolly to both acknowledge the Victorian fallen woman's loss of agency and reimagine it in terms different from those that dominated her contemporary sociological discourse. By manipulating generic conventions and drawing upon contemporary science, she reframes the cultural meaning of Lady Ana's mental paralysis. As Amanda Anderson has shown, the fallen woman's fundamental loss was understood to entail far more than virtue: "A pervasive rhetoric of fallenness in mid-Victorian culture . . . constitutes sexually compromised women as lacking the autonomy and coherence of the normative masculine subject" (1). *Witch-Hampton Hall* replaces this rhetoric with two alternative means of accounting for its protagonist's attenuated agency: on the metaphorical level, the gothic convention of live burial, and on the literal level, the scientific concept of depleted nerve force. The trope of live burial communicates the weight of the fallen woman's social exclusion and psychic torment without the moral disapprobation characteristic of conventional Victorian commentary on sexual impurity. The terminology of nervous depletion allows readers to understand the fallen woman's loss of agency not as self-fulfilling moral prophecy, but instead as a socially conditioned physiological weakness that restorative conditions might remedy. These very different strains of discourse work in tandem to represent the protagonist's sexual fall in terms that preserve its emotional impact, yet remove the sense of permanent stigma and irredeemable exclusion that fallenness usually entails in Victorian fiction.

Before proceeding to detailed analysis, it is helpful to review the complex plot and unusual structure of *Witch-Hampton Hall*. As the subtitle, "Five Scenes in the Life of Its Last Lady," indicates, *Witch-Hampton Hall* eschews cohesive narration in favor of an episodic style that mimics stage melodrama, particularly the gothic subgenre.[11] *Witch-Hampton Hall* capitalizes on the episodic structure of stage melodrama not only to keep violent and offensive

---

11. Its other commonalities with melodrama include a handsome, virtuous hero; an irredeemably evil villain, whose designs on the heroine drive the plot; an active, daring, suffering heroine; and a plot heavily dependent upon concealment and subterfuge (see Booth 16–26). It shares further characteristics with the gothic subgenre that flourished on late-eighteenth- and early-nineteenth-century stages: problems of inheritance, a gloomy manor, and a heroine threatened in the isolated countryside (Booth 68–69).

actions in the margins, but to focus the reader's attention instead on the affective and ethical consequences of sexual violence and sexual experience within patriarchal culture. The novella is divided into a present-day introduction and five "scenes" set in an unspecified past. In the prologue, a nameless narrator describes the remote location and gloomy aspect of the titular hall, claiming knowledge of its former inhabitants through an ambiguously supernatural vision. "Scene I" opens as adolescent Lady Ana confronts a villainous suitor on the steps of her family hall. We learn from their dialogue that he has raped her and will destroy her reputation if she does not marry him and thereby give him her fortune. She angrily rejects him. Later that evening, Ana's recently married younger sister, Emma, arrives with her husband Sir Lionel. Their dialogue reveals that Ana, who like her sister loved Sir Lionel, pursued a flirtation with her attacker in order to redirect Sir Lionel's interest toward Emma (who loved him more) and to distract herself from the impending loss of both sister and potential suitor.

From here on, the novella explores the consequences of deceptions that follow from Lady Ana's sexually compromised state. Scene II opens later the same year at Sir Lionel's manor, where Emma is near death after a difficult childbirth. The doctor warns that if Emma's sickly baby does not rally, the grief will kill her. Aided by her old nurse, Ana switches her thriving newborn by her rapist for her sister's now dead child. The third scene takes place six years later at Witch-Hampton Hall. Lady Ana, who has lived in self-imposed isolation, receives a proposal of marriage from Witch-Hampton's rector, whom she loves. Fearing the injury to her would-be husband's reputation should her "shame" (III 199) be revealed, she initially rejects him. The old nurse, however, pitying her darling's loneliness, persuades Ana to allow her to explain the situation to the suitor and let him decide. She marries believing her fiancé knows the truth; in fact the nurse only shared that Ana loved her sister's husband and recoiled in maidenly modesty from her unrequited love. After the marriage, the nurse confesses the deception to Lady Ana and admonishes her to keep the secret for the sake of her husband's happiness. Scene IV takes place shortly after the marriage, at Witch-Hampton Hall. As Emma and her children keep company with Ana, we witness young Lionel's aggressive misbehavior, his unwillingness to heed Emma's direction, and his instinctive deference to the commands of his "aunt" Ana, who openly dislikes him. Later, Ana worries aloud to her old nurse that her attacker will return to destroy her marital happiness. The nurse reassures her, revealing that in a chance meeting with the man, she without directly lying led him to believe that Lady Ana was dead, a suicide, and her child dead as well. The final scene takes place ten years later, at Witch-Hampton Hall, following a family row with young Lionel, who has been expelled from school. Ana, after the recent deaths of both her attacker and her old nurse, is now the only person living who knows the secret of young Lionel's parentage. Her health has mysteriously declined. Recognizing that the boy's rebellion owes something to his consciousness both that he is different from his siblings and that his revered "aunt" resents him, Ana is at last moved to pity and affection for her child. Unable to bear secrecy any longer, she reveals to him their true relation. She then collapses in a faint, to be revived by her husband, to whom she privately confesses the full truth. Her husband is shocked and grieved. But rather than send her and the illegitimate boy away, as she suggests, he affirms his unchanged love. Lady Ana recovers her health and lives out her life with her husband and newly claimed son.

In accounting for how Jolly builds her protagonist toward this atypically affirmative conclusion, I seek not only to unpack the rhetorical framework that stigmatized sexually comprised women, but to delineate means by which those rhetorics might be challenged from within traditional patriarchal culture. Literary genre (gothic) and scientific discourse (nervous economy) provide authorial tools to reframe the affective experience of the sexually compromised woman. First, I examine how Jolly employs the gothic convention of live burial to change the ethical terms of Lady Ana's social isolation while maintaining its emotional weight and significance to the character's mental life. I explore parallels between the Victorian social category of fallenness, wherein shame acts as a psychic barrier, and the gothic literary convention of live burial, wherein the material barrier is arbitrary and thereby lacks ethical authority. Mapping sexual fall onto live burial undermines the ethical grounding of the social convention that isolates sexually compromised women. Jolly's novella combines the gothic trope of live burial and the scientific concept of depleted nerve force to separate sexual fall from moral decline and thus reimagine it as a biological phenomenon and social calamity that sympathetic support can remedy. *Witch-Hampton Hall* does not challenge assumptions that sexual experience outside of marriage is a disruptive, undesirable, and potentially isolating event in a woman's life, but it removes that event from its proscribed, morally condemnatory conventional narrative.

In spite of its persistent stigma as less serious and complex than the realist novel, gothic fiction has, conversely, been aligned by some critics with upheavals in the accepted social order and female challenges to patriarchal authority.[12] Gothic's potential to convert contemporary socioeconomic problems (for instance, women's entrapment in patriarchal legal systems) into symbolic

---

12. See especially Diane Long Hoeveler's *Gothic Feminism: The Professionalization of Gender from Charlotte Smith to the Brontës* (1995) and Anne Williams's *Art of Darkness: A Poetics of Gothic* (1995).

narratives (innocent maidens seeking to escape locked castles) makes it an effective means of approaching controversial subject matter in a manner accessible to mainstream audiences. Furthermore, live burial, a specifically gothic mode of entrapment, provides a resonant metaphor for the position of the sexually compromised Victorian woman. Both live burial and the Victorian concept of sexual fall are characterized by complete social and psychic isolation without the cessation of consciousness. The shunned sexual profligate and the gothic victim walled up alive in an underground cell are alike cursed with intense awareness that their existence drags on although they cannot engage with the social world. Jolly's novella capitalizes on parallels between the gothic convention of live burial and the Victorian rhetoric of fallenness not only to explore the interiority of the sexually compromised woman, but also to write the fallen woman's narrative into a genre where it can have an affirmative ending. Indeed, "Female Gothic," as Anne Williams defines it, always entails the heroine's "rebirth," within "a world where love is not only possible, but available," after being "rescued at the climax from the life-threatening danger of being locked up, walled in, or otherwise made to disappear from the world" (103–4). By telling Lady Ana's story in this gothic register, Jolly selects for her protagonist an upward narrative arc.

   Witch-Hampton Hall is situated, through setting, themes, and characters, within the gothic tradition. Traditional British gothic novels appearing between the 1760s and 1820s were characterized, according to David Punter, by "an emphasis on portraying the terrifying, a common insistence on archaic settings, a prominent use of the supernatural, the presence of highly stereotyped characters and the attempt to deploy and perfect techniques of literary suspense" (1). Despite these fantastical characteristics, they are also noteworthy for insistence on historical authenticity, often communicated by devices such as supposed interpolated manuscripts (Kiely 10). Maggie Kilgour associates the genre with "a revolt against a mechanistic . . . view of the world," noting that gothic villains are "frequently an example of the modern materialistic individual taken to an extreme, at which he becomes an egotistical and willful threat to social unity and order" (11, 12). Published forty years after the waning of the gothic era proper, *Witch-Hampton Hall* demonstrates all of these characteristics, with some modifications. Moreover, its protagonist bears comparison to the most memorable heroine of Victorian gothic, Catherine Earnshaw: passionate, commanding, unafraid to roam the moors or even strike a blow.

   In spite of discordant elements, the gothic can, as Eve Sedgwick has shown, be understood through formal organizing principles, which *Witch-Hampton Hall* manipulates to communicate the fallen woman's social isolation. Sedgwick argues for the coherence of gothic conventions under the designations of "the unspeakable" and "live burial" (4–5). For instance, a manuscript might be damaged beyond legibility or a character die before communication of vital information, rendering the lost words unspeakable. A protagonist might be confined in an isolated location or literally buried alive, or family or lovers unjustly sundered, isolating a living individual from that to which he or she should be joined, constituting live burial. These conventions, Sedgwick asserts, figure "the self to be massively blocked off from something to which it ought normally to have access," when typically "there is both something going on inside the isolation . . . and something intensely relevant going on impossibly out of reach" (12). The arbitrariness of the barrier is characteristic of this division (13). Lady Ana's profound social isolation echoes that of the walled-in prisoner of the traditional gothic (consider, for instance, the imprisoned mother of Radcliffe's *A Sicilian Romance*). Her vitality is physically encased in the cold, barren confines of her sepulchral family hall just as it is socially constrained by her secret. Mainstream Victorian discourse surrounding female sexual fall, which posits an impassible social barrier the sexually compromised woman is powerless to breach, offers a striking parallel to Sedgwick's representation of the plight of live burial in gothic fiction. Shame is the barrier that dooms the fallen woman to exist separate from human community: As Dickens's Mr. Peggotty explains, his beloved niece Emily stays away because "shame steps in, and keeps betwixt us" (*David Copperfield* 631). Lady Ana likewise perceives her sexual experience as a barrier between herself and the affection she desires. She isolates herself from family and tells her suitor, "I must not marry anyone. There is something stands between. I am not what you think me" (III 198). The fallen woman's shame is conceptualized as a physical obstruction walling her off from community participation.

Strictures on the social outlets available to fallen women existed within a cultural context that placed a high value on integrity and that was therefore especially attentive to deceptions. With chastity as the cornerstone of female morality, however, women were largely omitted from moral and social negotiations contingent upon reversible ethical distinctions.[13] Scholars document that in lived experience (as opposed to dominant cultural discourse and artistic representation), the fallen woman was not necessarily either repentant or excluded from respectable social participation.[14] But the Victorian novel is

---

13. On the importance of deception within a culture that venerates truth-telling, and women's exclusion from this discourse, see *The Power of Lies: Transgression in Victorian Fiction* (1994) by John Kucich.

14. For discussion of nineteenth-century sociological accounts that outline British and French female sex workers leaving the trade for marriage or for other employment, see Steven

clear about acceptable alternatives for a woman who loses her virginity prior to marriage: death, as in the case of Gaskell's Ruth, or penitent, celibate exile, as with Dickens's Little Emily in *David Copperfield*.[15] In the conventional Victorian fallen woman narrative, penitence may save the soul, but both social and practical fate follow from the transgressor's irredeemably tainted physicality: The socially respected, economically secure position of wife and (legitimate) mother is closed off to her. Within Victorian fiction, if not nineteenth-century British history, the fallen woman, like the victim of live burial, is doomed to exist in contemplation of an impassible barrier between herself and the life she ought to lead. Even Jolly's Lady Ana, who from the start differentiates between the social implications and ethical ramifications of her sexual experience, nonetheless finds a declaration of love from a suitor ignorant of her history "strange as music from heaven heard by one in hell" (III 198).

While acknowledging the social stigma of sexual fall, *Witch-Hampton Hall* differs from mainstream Victorian explanations of that isolation. Sociological discussions of fallenness assumed that the physical experience of losing virginity prior to marriage determined a woman's mental, social, and bodily downward spiral. Anderson identifies "the Victorian category of fallenness" as "a historically determined, and typically gendered, conception of attenuated agency or fractured identity" (23). In both fiction and cultural discourse, the female fallen state was defined against implicitly masculine qualities: rationality, control, and action (Anderson 36). It differentiated not only a sexually impure woman from her upstanding sisters but, more essentially, feminine ethical capacities from masculine ones. Thus, the conventional, passive Victorian feminine virtues of placid endurance and a trusting, affectionate nature

---

Marcus, *The Other Victorians: A Study of Sexuality and Pornography in Mid-Nineteenth-Century England* (1966) and Amanda Anderson, *Tainted Souls, Painted Faces: The Rhetoric of Fallenness in Victorian Culture* (1993).

15. Emily declines subsequent marriage opportunities, living quietly with her uncle. A second-tier character can be granted some measure of respectability after a "fall" if penitent, but only offstage: Martha of the same novel, who marries after emigrating to Australia. Anthony Trollope's Carrie Brattle, of *The Vicar of Bullhampton*, lives celibate, unable to achieve the social respectability of marriage. Eliot's Hetty Sorrel, who adds infanticide (albeit unintentional) to impurity, must pay doubly for her corporeal sins, dying in exile. Elizabeth Gaskell's heroine Ruth loses her governess post when her history is revealed and dies of the illness she contracts from her seducer while serving as his nurse. Even Mrs. Vanstone in Wilkie Collins's *No Name*, who lives unmarried in an otherwise conventional Victorian household for many years, meets delayed punishment when she loses her husband in an accident; her life in the birth of her one legitimate child, which dies; and her daughters' fortune to the legal consequences of illegitimacy. Collins presents a more positive picture of a fallen woman's lot in *The New Magdalen*, when Mercy Merrick, a rape victim like Ana, marries respectably; however, Mercy and her husband emigrate to America to avoid scandal. These disparate cases are linked by the social exclusion the fallen woman's lot entails.

could be, in a corrupting environment, converted into blank fatalism and sexual availability. Whether radical and sympathetic or conservative and condemnatory, mid-Victorian sociological accounts of prostitution frequently blamed social forces and environment, with contributing factors ranging from the limited availability of well-paid work to the immoral influence of theater and novels (Anderson 54, 58–59). Yet as Anderson observes, what seals the prostitute's fate, according to Victorian commentators such as William Tait and W. R. Greg, is her internalization of society's moral condemnation: Her unquestioning acceptance of the social edict that she is permanently contaminated causes her to recoil from "respectable" would-be rescuers (58–59, 62–63). Diana Peschier's recent research into Victorian asylum records affirms that the deep stigma attached to illegitimacy sometimes produced shame and guilt leading to suicidal behavior and child abandonment in real-world unwed mothers like Jolly's Ana (25).

Jolly's rendition of her protagonist's response to sexual fall differs significantly from dominant discourse by portraying a woman who did not choose to lose her virginity but who, unlike the stock fallen woman, insists on her ability to make choices afterward. Historical evidence suggests that within mainstream Victorian culture, a woman who lost her virginity through rape would garner sympathy but nonetheless be regarded as "fallen": fundamentally altered in spiritual character as well as bodily state.[16] Indeed, throughout the nineteenth century, the same language of "seduction" could be employed in formal contexts to describe rape and consenting sexual relationships.[17] While such a cultural attitude troubles and offends twenty-first-century readers, the circumstance of rape allows Jolly to sidestep the problematic question of women's sexual agency in seduction. By making her fallen woman a rape survivor, not an abandoned lover, Jolly evades and arguably interrogates her culture's conflation of women's bodily and moral purity, instead locating Ana's moral dilemma in her management of the consequences of her "fall." Ana's initial rejection of culpability enables her to retain psychic and social autonomy.

Lady Ana's self-assertion combines ethical judgment, physical activity, and verbal self-expression. Readers are introduced to Ana after she has led her attacker on a horseback chase to the steps of her family manor, where she

---

16. In her study of convent-based rehabilitation centers for fallen women, historian Susan Mumm notes that "while penitentiary casebooks often demonstrate great compassion for these young victims [of rape and incest], there is never any suggestion that a prolonged and formal course of repentance was inappropriate for women who had lost their virginity by force" (530–31).

17. See, for example, Lynda Nead's discussion of London Foundling Hospital intake forms and interviews, "Fallen Women and Foundlings: Rethinking Victorian Sexuality" (181–83).

resists his matrimonial advances. "I *have* a choice" (I 187), Ana declares as she scorns her rapist's claim that she must now marry him to save her reputation, which he calls her "honour" (I 188). She then cuts him across the face with her riding crop. Lady Ana insists that she retains the capacity to choose her own fate and distinguish right from wrong. Such insistence, while signaling an understanding of virtue consistent with the Victorian valorization of integrity, is also vexingly at odds with gender norms. Ana's subsequent sense of wrong-doing stems not from her sexually compromised body but instead from her active participation in deception. After substituting her baby for her sister's, she prays "for God's forgiveness, and that He would bring good to those she loved out of the evil of her lying work" (II 194). Her self-castigation originates not in the bodily reality of her situation but in her social misrepresentation of it. Within a novelistic tradition that overwhelmingly figured female sexual contamination as an impassible moral and social gulf, Jolly's novella instead identifies Lady Ana's *deception* as her misdeed: a transgression that can be reversed. In so doing, Jolly presents the sexually compromised woman as an active individual capable of growth, change, and social reintegration, unlike the stock fallen woman, who remains locked in a static state of self-accusation.

NERVE FORCE AS PSYCHIC AGENCY, WITNESSING AS SOCIAL REINTEGRATION

Witch-Hampton Hall rejects the downward spiral narrative that assumes the moment of sexual fall deprives a woman of her power to act and choose, yet it remains crucially interested in the problem of attenuated agency. Jolly's novella correlates attenuated agency not with sexual impurity, but rather with deprivation from affirmative social contact. The decisive, assertive action that Lady Ana displays in rejecting her rapist's marriage proposal, concealing her pregnancy, and substituting her child for her sister's requires social support: the emotional and practical aid of her old nurse, a mother figure. Rather than immediately losing her power of self-assertion after the sexual assault, Ana collapses into pathological inaction more than a dozen years later, following the death of her old nurse, the only remaining person with knowledge of her sexual violation and the birth of her child. Ana develops an ambiguous ailment that combines psychic and somatic symptoms. Jolly capitalizes on the Victorian diagnostic category of nervous exhaustion to present her protagonist's mental collapse as both morally neutral and recoverable. Yet in contrast with Victorian medical discourse, which recommended rest and isolation to cure nervous breakdown, *Witch-Hampton Hall* figures social participation as central to the recovery of psychic agency. The timing of Lady Ana's mental collapse, and the social rather than somatic means by which she recovers, make *Witch-Hampton Hall* prescient of modern understandings of the interpersonal conditions needed to heal mental trauma. In order to restore psychic agency and achieve social reintegration, Ana must fully reject shame, assuage her guilt through corrective actions, and share her experience of threat and loss with accepting interlocutors.

My analysis of Lady Ana's experience of guilt (in relation to acts of concealment and misrepresentation) and shame (in relation to her identity as "fallen woman") draws upon the elaboration of these concepts by philosophers Bernard Williams and Kelly Oliver. Williams and Oliver associate shame with the subject's internalization of the imagined perceptions of others. Williams usefully distinguishes guilt from shame, identifying guilt as arising from "an act or an omission . . . that typically elicits from other people anger, resentment, or indignation," and for which "an agent may offer . . . reparation" (89). Shame, on the other hand, originates in "something that typically elicits from others contempt or derision or avoidance," which may be "an act or an omission, but it need not be: it may be some failing or defect" (B. Williams 90). In her discussion of shame related to such forces as sexism, racism, colonialism, and homophobia, Kelly Oliver contends, "those excluded or abjected by the dominant values are made to feel ashamed, not about something they have done but about who they are. Shame is directed at the very being of the marginalized subject" (*Colonization* 114). Recent psychological research with PTSD sufferers finds a statistically relevant relationship between an individual's feelings of shame and her resistance to social support networks, with greater shame correlated with more severe PTSD symptoms (Dodson and Beck 109–10). Whereas shame, grounded in identity, shuts down the subject's ability to act, guilt, arising from action, can catalyze further action. As discussed, mainstream Victorian discourse associates female sexual fall with shame and concomitant loss of agency. *Witch-Hampton Hall,* by ultimately rejecting shame as the affect appropriate to the fallen woman, and by substituting guilt linked to specific actions, recovers the fallen woman's agency and shifts female virtue from a passive to an active realm.

Witch-Hampton Hall represents shame as an externally imposed devaluation of Lady Ana's core sense of self. The text makes clear that in the immediate aftermath of her rape, Lady Ana rejects the equation of female sexual impurity with moral wrongdoing, and instead holds her attacker, not herself, wholly to blame. When she refuses to marry him and he threatens her reputation, Ana's attacker warns, "You are not one to bear *shame* meekly. You have no choice left; you must marry me" (I 187). She replies, "That 'shame' which you have given me, which you think me too simple to understand, has freed me from you forever" (I 87). The placement of "shame" in quotation marks is critical: It demonstrates that not just the author, but the protagonist herself, questions the validity of the shame her culture assigns to sexually compromised women. Ana's construction—"That shame *you* have *given me*"—positions her shame as something imposed upon her by her attacker, indeed, as an extension of the physical rape. Moreover, she attempts to turn her injury into a paradoxical source of liberation: It has "freed [her] from [her attacker] forever." By implication, Ana might have married this man had he not raped her, if only to avoid the loneliness of watching her sister go off to live with the man she herself once loved. Having experienced her attacker's full brutality and divined the greed that motivates him, she now rejects him entirely.

Witch-Hampton Hall is vitally concerned with the distinction between social opprobrium, which it aligns with a devalued identity, and ethical culpability, which it aligns with a selfish or dishonest action. Lady Ana assigns full culpability for the rape to her attacker, refusing to cede her agency to judge and act. She accuses her attacker of having "done me, a weak girl, the worst wrong a man can do a woman—one human creature another" (I 187). She emphasizes her physical defenselessness at the hands of a more powerful man ("me, a weak girl"), underscoring the injustice and violence of the attack, while simultaneously placing her attacker's wrongdoing in a gender-neutral ethical category (not just "the worst wrong a man can do a woman," but the worst wrong "one human creature [can do] another"). Despite this unequivocal condemnation of her rapist, Ana perceives the cultural necessity of removing herself from social interaction, as a sexually compromised and pregnant unmarried woman. She later avows to her old nurse that as "a woman whose shame might at any moment be in all mouths" (III 199), she must not marry. Acknowledging the social opprobrium sexual fall entails, Ana nonetheless distinguishes between the shame of her status as fallen woman and the guilt she associates with the deception of the baby swap, referring to "my shame, and since, my sin" (III 200). Her "shame" is the socially imposed identity of "fallen woman"; her "sin"—the wrongdoing that triggers guilt—is concealment and misrepresentation.

Interaction with the old nurse, an accepting and rational interlocutor who knows the truth of the events that have shaped Lady Ana's emotional life, enables her to separate shame from guilt. Ana can rely on her old nurse for reassurance of her value, competence, and lovability; for practical support; and perhaps most importantly, for validation of her own perspective on the rape, which mainstream gender ideologies undermine. The old nurse's support is consistent and modulated to Lady Ana's immediate needs. For instance, in the aftermath of the attack, the nurse, suspicious but not yet certain of Lady Ana's situation, mirrors the girl's lack of eye contact yet surreptitiously studies her changed manner, then provides her with the affectionate assurance she needs to face the company waiting below. When Lady Ana asks, "Do I look as usual, nurse? Is all right with me?" the nurse replies, "Yes, my pet. They will say you are fairer than ever, my queen" (I 189). Later, the nurse provides invaluable practical aid, first caring for the unwanted baby and then misleading Ana's rapist, who returns to harass her. Most crucially, the nurse helps Ana maintain a stable perspective on the formative calamity of her life despite community and cultural pressure to see it differently. She reminds the married Ana of her growing son's real birthday, which his "parents" do not know or keep (IV 204), and she places the returned rapist in perspective as a "villain" to be outmaneuvered when Ana is inclined both to fear him and to reproach herself for her anger (IV 208). Such support cannot make Ana happy in spite of her tragic circumstances, but it enables her to maintain a coherent sense of self in the face of a potentially shattering crisis. Not only can she reject self-blame for the rape, she can even question God's justice: "What had I done that He let my orphan weakness cry out in vain?" (III 195). Supportive, validating interaction, the text demonstrates, allows an individual to differentiate social opprobrium from ethical culpability.

Loss of her only confidante shuts down Lady Ana's ability to contextualize her experience and affirm its particularity. After both her rapist and her old nurse, the only others with knowledge of her attack, have died, Lady Ana's concern shifts from actions and measurable consequences to abstract ideals and affective urges. We learn "this isolation of hers had in it something which she felt to be frightful. The condemnation to perpetual silence roused in her a wild, a mad desire to proclaim her sin, ay upon the housetops" (V 210). Denied an affirmative interlocutor, she internalizes the shame her culture assigns to sexually impure women. In this passage, what is meant by "her sin" remains ambiguous: previously, "sin" had referred to Lady Ana's dishonest actions, but in this context it appears to comprehend having an illegitimate child as well as representing that child as her sister's son. As Oliver has demonstrated, an external witness—an individual capable of empathetic response to one's articulated experience—is crucial to the maintenance of subjectivity (*Witnessing* 15). Modern psychoanalytic and psychiatric discourse emphasizes the importance of the empathetic interlocutor for the psychic health of survivors of trauma, such as rape. In his discussion of Holocaust survivors, psychoanalyst Dori Laub argues that "only when the survivor knows he is being heard, will he stop to hear—and listen to—himself" (71). Twenty-first-century medical research has demonstrated that social factors (external to therapy) influence both PTSD risk and recovery, and that strong social support targeted to specific needs is crucial to healing.[18] In Ana's case, the loss of such an interlocutor leaves her to contrast her feelings of self-reproach (triggered by young Lionel's behavior toward her sister) and anger (at Lionel's father and by extension at the boy himself) with an ingrained cultural expectation of what she ought to feel toward her child and his father. The socially mandated pride and affection do not fit her case; the experience of rape that originated her feelings is culturally unspeakable. Lady Ana cannot maintain her long-standing perception of the events surrounding her rape, uncharacteristically downplaying her sense of violation and attempting to rewrite her youthful experiences into a more conventional romantic narrative. Following the rapist's death, "he was not so much the man who had foully wronged her as the man who had once loved her, though in a wild and savage fashion, towards whom she had not been blameless" (V 210). Never before did Ana suggest her financially motivated attacker might have loved her.[19] Without a witness to confirm her interpretation of events, Lady Ana loses her grasp of the social and economic forces (i.e., patriarchy, property) that play into her experience of suffering.

Social isolation causes Lady Ana to replace her concerns about the practical consequences of her deception, such as Lionel's negative influence on her sister's family and the risk to her husband's public reputation, with an internalized sense of wrongdoing: self-reproach for not being able to feel the "right" emotion. She trades guilt, which registers her perception of the consequences of her actions and develops her conscience, for shame, a far less productive emotion that leads only to fruitless self-rebuke. She wishes she could "expiate her crime of hate toward the father" through "love paid to the son," yet she cannot regard her son as other than "a thorn [planted] to fester in the flesh of those she loved" (V 211). Her self-recrimination has shifted from her

---

18. The importance of social support in PTSD outcomes is well documented in twenty-first-century research. Anthony Charuvastra and Marylene Cloitre review research in psychiatry and neuroscience to argue that "social support . . . is among the most powerful influences in both risk for and recovery from PTSD" (302), but the "psychological value of positive social support often depends on who gives the support and whether the support offered matches a specific need" (307). They also find that interpersonal traumas (particularly rape) are likelier to produce PTSD symptoms than traumas of a nonpersonal nature (such as natural disaster) (303–4). More recently, psychologist Paul Frewen and psychiatrist Ruth Lanius document how accepting relationships with friends, families, and intimate partners, as well as community integration and perceived societal support, positively influence the trauma survivor's recovery (284–87).

19. At no other point has Lady Ana indicated any possibility of love between herself and her attacker. For his part, he makes clear that his desire to marry her is directly linked to property (I 187), and she not only tells him, "I loathe you" (I 187) but later declares to her sister, "I never loved him" (IV 202).

failure to do the right thing (tell the truth) to her failure to be the right thing (a loving mother), and the latter failing, she perceives, cannot be remedied. The weight of this anguish is indicated by her failing health.

The novella represents Lady Ana's reaction to her psychic isolation not as simple anguish but as illness. After a family altercation with the rebellious teenage Lionel, Ana's brother-in-law warns that "Ana, ever since old nurse's death, has seemed so weak and ill that she is not fit to bear the shock of such scenes" (V 209). The narrator intimates that Ana suffers "a nameless illness, a trouble more of mind than of body, but telling surely upon her physical condition" (V 210). Her observable symptoms are severe depletion of bodily and mental strength and concomitant despair: She tells her husband, "I shall never be better till I am dead" (V 210). She has also "learnt to dread sleep and her own fevered dreams" (V 211).

Lady Ana's shame-ridden torpor accords with the scientific concept of depleted nerve force current in Jolly's day. In symptomology, Ana's mysterious illness, "more of mind than of body," bears comparison to neurasthenia. Her inexplicable exhaustion, sensation of fever, sleep disturbance, and overwhelming hopelessness coincide with common medically identified neurasthenic symptoms (Abbey and Garfinkel 1639–40). Neurasthenia, a gender-neutral or masculine-coded ailment whose complaints might range from "headaches and insomnia to complete mental collapse," was considered "a fairly genteel form of nervous exhaustion," producing "quietly anxious" sufferers, whereas hysterics were deemed "troublesome and uncooperative" and believed to have "crossed the boundary of acceptable behavior" (Archimedes 36), like Jolly's earlier protagonist, Annie Aston Warden. Physicians explored genogenic (hereditary), chemogenic (neurophysiological), and psychogenic explanations for neurasthenia, typically treating these possible causes as not mutually exclusive but, potentially, mutually reinforcing (Chatel and Peel 1406–07). Although it was not until the 1880s that popularization of the discrete category of neurasthenia gave physicians a coherent diagnostic vocabulary, the Victorian medical discourse on nervous exhaustion was voluminous, if unfocused, by the mid-Victorian period (Oppenheim 92).

When Jolly published *Witch-Hampton Hall* in 1864, some scientific consensus had been reached regarding the causation of nervous exhaustion such as that which Ana's symptoms suggest. The metaphor of the brain as voltaic battery, and the nerves as electric wires, was by then commonly employed to figure an individual's nerve force: It might be depleted by overexertion, but rest could recharge it (Oppenheim 81). A sufferer of nervous exhaustion had, in effect, run herself down with excessive emotional, intellectual, and/ or physical exertion (Oppenheim 81). According to medical historian Janet

Oppenheim, it was feared that this total depletion of energy could lead to "not merely a lower level of vitality, but to the very loss of selfhood" (87). In the throes of shattered nerves, individual will and self-identity disappear (87). Mid-Victorian theories of nervous exhaustion afford a concept of attenuated agency and fractured identity parallel to that ascribed to the fallen woman. Crucially, however, nervous breakdown, considered a somatic ailment with psychic effects, carried minimal social stigma (Oppenheim 12).

The Victorian medical community overwhelmingly prescribed rest and quiet for sufferers of nervous exhaustion, but in Jolly's novella, recovery of psychic agency instead depends on a supportive social network. By reestablishing connections with empathetic interlocutors, Lady Ana recovers her cohesive selfhood and sense of agency, which allows physical healing. The shift occurs when a crisis changes how she perceives her son's motives, enabling her to empathize with him. After young Lionel is dismissed from school in disgrace, she regards him no longer as the culmination of the worst traits of both her rapist and herself, but instead as a lonely, unhappy person, with whom she shares a common experience of psychic isolation. She feels "stirred with pity as she saw how the proud boy held himself aloof, felt himself unloved and alone" (V 211). Ana realizes that young Lionel's unhappiness and related misbehavior stem from his intuitive awareness that he is different from his so-called siblings and that she, the person whom he perceives himself to be most like, feels contempt for him. Empathy with her son allows her to move beyond the shame of her identity as fallen woman (and doubly, as unloving mother), and to instead feel only guilt at the harm her deception has caused her family (especially young Lionel). Accordingly, she resolves to take action to repair that harm by confessing the truth to her husband. Ana is once again able to locate her blameworthiness in actions rather than identity, and therefore to act: She reflects, "It was not now *what* she had hidden, so much as the fact that she had hidden it through these long years of his love, that seemed to her the most dreadful part of that which he should have to learn and she should have to tell" (V 211). When she begins to feel an empathetic connection with her son, the act of deception, which can be reversed and remedied, is once again the focus of her self-criticism.

In the affectionate reaction of her son, and more critically the affirmative response of her husband, we see the groundwork for Ana's recovery. Although her husband is "stunned" (V 214) by her confession, it is not sexual impurity, but "the sin of her long deceit" (V 214) that troubles him. Even so, "he never doubted but that he loved her still" (V 214), and he asks his wife, "How must my love have failed and fallen short, not teaching you to trust me?" (V 214). He locates the change in their marriage in his own perceptions, not in her character: "I have loved you, not knowing—now I know. That is a change in me, and how have you changed from the being I have loved?" (V 215) Without denying the bitterness of their now shared experience, he encourages her to face the coming trials with him. If, as Oliver suggests, "love and agency are both activities of subjectivity . . . necessary for a sense of self, let alone a sense of self-worth" (*Colonization* 124), we might directly link Ana's affirmation by her husband to her subsequent recovery. Empathy with her child enables Lady Ana to move past shame, and a sense of responsibility toward her family obliges her to act to reverse her guilty deception. With her husband's acceptance, Lady Ana finally assuages that guilt by taking on the task of raising her difficult son. The stereotypical fallen woman is benumbed and paralyzed by shame. Jolly's protagonist both feels and acts.

Lady Ana's subsequent life entails sacrifice of self to family in her taxing "incessant watch" (V 215) to keep the passionate young Lionel on the path of right. While such a fate may discomfit modern feminist readers, it significantly revises the fallen woman narrative, placing the sexually compromised Ana in the company of morally upstanding (and sexually pure) Victorian heroines. Within Victorian culture, Nead has shown, "the purity of domestic life was maintained by the influence and attendance of the respectable woman" (*Myths* 33) who cultivates a moral atmosphere within her social networks and is in turn herself shielded from the physical and moral harm of public spaces (33–34). Ana is integrated into her community as a clergyman's wife and a devoted mother who serves as a moral guide to her child. She does not flee or die upon confession of her extramarital sexual experience. Her conclusion resembles that of Esther Summerson, a beloved, a self-effacing doctor's wife and matron at the close of *Bleak House* (1853), much more than that of Esther's "fallen" mother Lady Dedlock, who rejects contact with her adult daughter; leaves her affectionate, forgiving husband; and dies of exposure in a winter storm at her lover's grave. Unlike Jolly's Lady Ana, Dickens's Lady Dedlock tells her daughter, "I must travel my dark road alone, and it will lead me where it will" (579), regrettably unable to breach her isolation, even as the distraught Esther longs for a connection. The narrator later explains Lady Dedlock has "[shut] up the natural feelings of the heart, like flies in amber, [spreading] one uniform and dreary gloss over the good and bad, the feeling and the unfeeling, the sensible and the senseless" (851). In her novella published just a year later, Jolly significantly revises her mentor's rendition of the fallen woman's psychic life. Through her capacity to feel empathy for, and accept empathy from, other people, Lady Ana achieves the social integration that, in Victorian novels, signifies success and virtue. Whereas Lady Dedlock seems numb to the pain her self-immolation causes both Esther Summerson

and Sir Leicester Dedlock, Lady Ana perceives and responds to both her husband's anxiety at her illness and her son's pain at her rejection. This capacity
for emotional connection and ethical response is Jolly's crucial innovation in
her depiction of the fallen woman.

   Witch-Hampton Hall revises not only its contemporary discourse on fallenness and femininity, but crucially, our understanding of masculine virtue
in the Victorian age. Mainstream Victorian culture framed the wife's role as
providing emotional support, without any expectation of equal psychological
nurturance from her husband (Tosh 54). Ana's husband, however, understands
equitable sympathy as the hallmark of successful marriage. His empathy is
signaled early, when he is drawn to the song through which she expresses her
pain and resistance. Seeking refuge from her anger in music, the lonely Ana
joins her voice with those of the birds in "a wild, rich flood of passion-fed,
untutored song" (III 196). Arriving on an unannounced visit, her future husband informs Ana that "I stood below at the avenue gate in the black shadow,
and listened till a vague, superstitious fear trembled through me, and I almost
doubted if it were the earthly singing of a mortal maiden," calling her singing
"the crowning enchantment of your enchanted valley" (III 196). The music
he appreciates is not a young lady's entertainment for company, but artistry
that proceeds from her most authentic emotions. This forms a marked contrast with Annie Warden's husband, who encourages her music as a ladylike
accomplishment but finds her compositions boring and even alienating, and
never inquires about the emotions that shape them.

   In contrast with cultural discourse that coded passivity and chastity as
female virtue, *Witch-Hampton Hall* locates gender-neutral moral virtue in an
individual's commitment to act with responsibility and integrity toward those
they love. In the gothic convention of live burial, Jolly finds a means to communicate the extremity of the fallen woman's psychic and social isolation and
her sense of attenuated agency, while refusing the morally freighted downward spiral narrative. The mid-Victorian scientific concept of depleted nerve
force provides a credible alternative explanation for the protagonist's attenuated agency, and figures that lost agency as both recoverable and morally neutral. *Witch-Hampton Hall* does not challenge the construction of extramarital
female sexual experience as undesirable and disruptive, nor does it question
the assumption that devoted domesticity is a woman's highest calling. But
Jolly's novella removes the moral stigma conventionally attached to the sexually compromised woman, and in so doing, it imagines both her subjectivity
and her narrative progress in more complex, active terms. Even as it endorses
female domesticity, Jolly's depiction of Lady Ana redefines a woman's "purity"
as her determination to act ethically and with empathy. When Ana meets her

would-be husband to say farewell after asking her old nurse to communicate the truth of her history, she stands "white and calm: the holy might of her love gave her power so tacitly to honour the untarnished purity of her soul and will" (III 199). Jolly co-opts language suggestive of the domestic angel's chastity even as she insists a woman's ethical worth be defined by her ability to act with fairness and compassion rather than by her sexual history. By insisting on Lady Ana's "will" to act rightly, *Witch-Hampton Hall* rejects the downward spiral theory that robs the fallen woman of agency.

Taken together, *A Wife's Story* and *Witch-Hampton Hall* offer a socially focused account of the causation of women's psychic disorder, challenging medical theories grounded in reproductive physiology. But just as important, they also provide an alternative vision of domestic partnership as a dynamic, visceral, ongoing negotiation, distinct from the static promise of happiness the traditional marriage plot presents. Even Victorian novels that track their characters through satisfactory marriages (Celia Chettam in *Middlemarch*) or desperately unhappy ones (her sister Dorothea Casaubon) typically present the initial engagement as overdetermining: A compatible husband offers stability; an incompatible or irresponsible husband produces strife. Keeping a tight focus on the interactions of a single couple from engagement through years of married cohabitation, these two examples of Jolly's fiction take into account not only the choice of suitor but also quotidian choices—what to share, what to hold back—that build respect or resentment between a couple. In so doing, these texts imply close connection between well-regulated marital communication and women's mental health.

CHAPTER 4

∼

Wilkie Collins and George Eliot Confront Accidents of Modernity

Wilkie Collins's *No Name* (1862) and George Eliot's *Daniel Deronda* (1876) share concerns of the sensation era their publication dates approximately bookend. Both thematize ethical and emotional consequences of accident and chance within a period of rapid industrial and economic modernization. Their plots are shaped by deadly physical accidents, social interactions enabled or curtailed by rail travel, and unexpected financial reversals. They interrogate the moral underpinnings of evolving marriage and inheritance law, particularly psychic risks to women and to illegitimate children. Both novels feature female protagonists whose unusual and unsettling beauty, penchant for acting and self-display, and mental and verbal quickness are inextricably linked to nervous sensitivity that, under stress, transforms into nervous pathology. These female protagonists are morally ambiguous, neither heroines nor villains. Gwendolen's and Magdalen's shifting characters are formed through geographical mobility and financial uncertainty, and positioned in opposition to traditional patriarchal family mores. The insecurity and volatility of the protagonist's perspective produces a fragmentary and halting narrative that unsettles readerly expectations. *No Name* and *Daniel Deronda* feature key departures from the respective structural norms of the sensation novel and the multi-plot realist novel. These novels derive formal uniqueness from the intense, unstable modern economic and material forces that act upon and constrain the embodied consciousness of the female protagonist.

No Name and *Daniel Deronda* document and critique the era of sensation, a period when technological and economic transformation hit home for middle-class British citizens. Reflecting on their contemporary culture, these novels pose two broad questions: What does it mean to be an ethical woman in a modern world? How is it possible to be a healthy person in a modern world? The 1860s saw cultural shifts across British life: gender dynamics, national identity, economic behavior, and the everyday experience of technology. It is useful to concisely review salient transitions. 1857 was a pivotal year, setting into motion changes that would reshape the fortunes and opportunities of many British citizens. International financial crisis was precipitated by failures of American railway and insurance companies, affecting the investments of numerous individuals, including Britons (Henry 29). Simultaneously, the 1857–1858 Sepoy Rebellion introduced a shocking sense of the vulnerability of British dominance and civilian British bodies abroad. The rebellion triggered brutal retaliation and brought sweeping changes to the administration of the Empire's largest and most symbolically important colony. Meanwhile, the 1857 Matrimonial Causes Act and opening of the Divorce Court in 1858 not only substantively changed the legal options available to aggrieved spouses; they also inaugurated a thriving business of divorce court journalism, which aired domestic dysfunction for a wide audience (Surridge 133). British financial regulation was also evolving at mid-century. The Limited Liabilities Act (1855) and Companies Acts (1856 and 1862) changed patterns of investing, normalizing shareholding by the century's close (Itzkowitz 121): a shift from tangible (land) to intangible (shares) property as the cornerstone of wealth. Everyday experience was further transformed by visible incursions of industrial modernity into the daily lives of nonfactory workers: what Nicholas Daly terms "the industrialization of transport, communications, and entertainment . . . of consumption and leisure" (*Literature* 4–5). Adult Britons of the 1860s would have experienced a marked sense of the difference between their lives and those of their grandparents, including embodied experience as well as the legal and economic landscape.

The genre reviewers dubbed sensation fiction was part of this transformation. Marlene Tromp argues that sensation fiction, which "both derived from and revised realist fiction" (3), developed a "seemingly counter but functionally medial discourse to high-culture fiction and realism" (13). Both *No Name* and *Daniel Deronda* employ sensation elements, particularly attention to physical embodiment, to communicate culturally unspeakable aspects of their protagonist's dilemmas. Anxieties about sexual behavior shape key aspects of these conflicts and figure prominently in critical discussion of Magdalen and Gwendolen. But in these novels financial precarity triggers at least as much physiological shock and intense emotion. Tamara S. Wagner argues that as modern forms of speculation developed in the Victorian era, financial instability became literary shorthand for broader uncertainties about the consistency of selfhood (5). In connecting *No Name* and *Daniel Deronda,* I read both novels as meditations on the increasing fluidity of identity, and heightened awareness of risk, characteristic of 1860s British culture. Nervously sensitive Magdalen and Gwendolen embody misfires in the readjustment of British self-identity to a modernizing world: In social experience and lifestyle, they are products of rapid economic and technological change, and yet they are temperamentally, one might say physiologically, unfitted for the very cultural shifts that define their experience.

SENSATION AND EVERYDAY SHOCKS

Sensation fiction of the 1860s features scandalous (sensational) content and also plays upon the reader's bodily responses (sensations) to suspense and surprise. Circumventing the porous distinction between sensation and realist fiction, my analysis considers how both *No Name* and *Daniel Deronda* respond to a culture of sensation, powered by new technologies, within their rapidly modernizing world. Sensation fiction thematizes the interplay between distracted reverie and focused attention characteristic of life within industrialized urban society (Daly, *Sensation* 9–10). The genre's rise is intimately connected to the history of the railway, which produced an expanded reading public of harried commuters. Trains also furnished the means for abrupt plot reversals and exciting chases within the novels these readers consumed. Sensation novels—which Nicholas Daly aptly terms "a bracing cocktail of nouveau Gothic, Newgate novel, and crime journalism" (*Sensation* 16)—exist in dynamic relation with their cultural moment, reflecting and reproducing its sensibilities and habits of thought.

It has become a critical commonplace that sensation authors domesticated and modernized gothic vices. Fueled by the concurrent vogue for journalistic coverage of corruption and violence in high life, sensation novels feature well-bred gentlefolk, inhabiting recognizably contemporary settings, engaged in bigamy, murder, and fraud and falling prey to madness. Cultural gatekeepers saw danger in sensation fiction's fusion of the deviant and everyday; as Winifred Hughes writes, "when crime is represented as routine, not to mention universal, the critics start to bridle in self-defense" (40). Sensation plots were all the more shocking because readers were denominated as feminine and refined: Emily Allen observes that when a reader is invoked by the sensation narrator, that reader is most commonly addressed as a lady (409). Not just women, but *ladies,* were invited into close conversation with transgressive subjectivities.

Reflecting uncertainties of an emerging credit economy, sensation plots often turn upon the unreliability of once-trusted social indicators of class, character, and more fundamentally, individual identity. Relatedly, the genre's broad readership—from working through upper classes—meant that in consumer habits they engendered, these novels muddled the role of literary taste as a marker of class affiliation (Daly, *Sensation* 7). Sensation was also threatening as a visceral influence on potentially naive or volatile readers. Ann Cvetkovich remarks, "Critics repeatedly emphasized the emotional state produced by the sensation novel, the form that 'preaches to the nerves,' rather than the content of the novels themselves. Sensational content was simply the vehicle for sensational affect" (*Mixed Feelings* 20). Blurring hierarchies upon which a class-stratified patriarchy relies, sensation fiction similarly mobilized the affective and physiological responses of lady and scullery maid. In a decade of rapid political transformation—reaching its crescendo with the second Reform Bill of 1867, which enfranchised many working men—such popular fiction drew intense disapprobation from genteel critics and social commentators.[1]

In both politics and fiction, defying gender norms proved more contentious than redefining class-based social participation. The 1857 Divorce Law made full divorce (with option to remarry) less expensive and complicated, placing it within the reach of some middle-class husbands (Stone 372). But there remained strong parliamentary opposition to expanding women's ability to sue for divorce, reflecting intractable sexual double standards (Stone 375). Similarly, John Stuart Mill's amendment including unmarried women's suffrage in the 1867 bill expanding men's political representation, which initially gained steam from a female-coordinated effort of press promotion, was defeated in the House of Commons (Bostick 125–27). Within debates leading to the groundbreaking Married Women's Property Act of 1870, discussions of class privilege subsumed arguments based on gender equity, as lawmakers focused on the unequal protections of wealthy brides, who could have a settlement, and poor ones, who were entirely at their husband's financial mercy

---

1. Daly links anxiety about sensational culture, including fiction, to middle- and upper-class concerns about the crowd and political enfranchisement in the 1860s. See *Sensation and Modernity in the 1860s,* especially the introduction, "White Years," 1–25.

(Shanley 67). This political dynamic finds parallel in the plotlines of sensation novels, wherein heroes drawn from humble genteel backgrounds may triumph (Walter Hartright is the most dramatic example), but socially transgressive and desiring heroines of any class origin must be punished or at the very least, chastened (for instance Helen Talboys, Isabel Vane, Aurora Floyd, and, I argue, both Magdalen Vanstone and her realist counterpart, Gwendolen Harleth). Gender, to a greater degree than class, predicts success or failure of a sensation character's bid for greater agency and control.

No Name and *Daniel Deronda* introduce female protagonists who appear uniquely poised to challenge any constraints. Magdalen and Gwendolen are portrayed as different from the average woman of their social circle not only in character, but in physiology. Both are remarkable for their unusual beauty—unusual meaning rare in type, not necessarily superlative—and abundant vitality. Both display pallor that correlates not with illness, but with energy, and includes not only very fair skin, but uncommonly light eyes and atypical light-brown hair (Magdalen's is a tone "oftener seen on the plumage of a bird than the head of a human being" [13]). Magdalen's complexion of "creamy fairness all over" aligns with "overflowing physical health which strengthened every muscle, braced every nerve, and set the warm young blood tingling through her veins, like the blood of a growing child" (14). Gwendolen is critiqued by some observers as "want[ing] a tinge of colour in her cheeks," but praised by others for "warm paleness" that looks "thoroughly healthy" (12); she is readily capable of "a quick blush" (70), although only "when . . . taken by surprise" (107). As Pamela Gilbert argues, the blush, by mid-century, had transitioned away from its early-nineteenth-century signification as an "infallible index of character," demonstrating sudden self-consciousness of the innocent, to providing "a more complex sense of how appearance communicated emotional and psychological states" within a "body that produces, rather than merely housing, the subject" (104). The vigorous and adaptable pallor of Magdalen and Gwendolen communicates, in this context, their excess of nervous energy and corresponding susceptibility and volatility, which Eliot terms "iridescence of . . . character" (42). These character descriptions emerge within a racist cultural and scientific logic associating fair skin with civilization, but Magdalen's and Gwendolen's pallor signifies something more ambiguous. In both women, paucity of color reveals abundance of energy, as particularly concentrated in their eyes. Magdalen's "discordantly light" eyes enable "subtle transparency of expression" (13), Gwendolen's "dynamic . . . glance" (7) produces "the effect of unrest" on the stranger who meets her gaze: Their eyes, so central to human expression and sympathy, are at once unexpected and unstable. Both are described as taller than average, having the masculine advantage of being physically imposing, yet markedly feminine in form, retaining sexual appeal to suitors. Magdalen's movements recall "a young cat" (13), Gwendolen's a "young racehorse" (25): unpredictable animals. Magdalen and Gwendolen possess uniquely changeable temperament and appearance that they parlay, to their advantage, into acting a part, socially or onstage.

Perhaps more so than any other sensation novel, No Name thematizes the radical instability of social, legal, and embodied identity within a modern world. Collins's earlier protagonist Laura Fairlie is violently but temporarily stripped of her legal identity, name, and autonomy in The Woman in White (1860). But Magdalen Vanstone loses these things permanently, not through the scheming of a foreign interloper like Fosco, but rather through a combination of her father's careless error in his will and a railway employee's careless error on the line. Only by chance does the execrable Noel Vanstone profit. The randomness of Magdalen's suffering compounds its terror and anguish, and its linkage to the iconic catastrophe of the age—rail disaster—positions Magdalen as an emblem of fragile self-identity within industrial capitalism. Even her illegitimacy is presented as an unfortunate accident of circumstances disconnected from her social experience of stable, conservative bourgeois domesticity. Magdalen's monitory double, Mrs. Lecount, is a genteel-poor widow likewise tormented by Noel; the similar suffering of Magdalen's ostensibly respectable nemesis underscores women's vulnerability to sudden, unpredictable socioeconomic demotion. No Name diverges from readerly expectations in revealing its key secret—Magdalen and Norah Vanstone's illegitimacy—at the outset, relying on Magdalen's quest for recognition (or vengeance) rather than detection to fuel its narrative progress.

Daniel Deronda, which has been read both as heavily indebted to the sensation genre and as pushing limits of Victorian realism, offers a striking parallel in that its female protagonist's shattered self-identity, shocked by economic and physical accidents of modernity, likewise structures its departures from narrative norms.[2] Daniel Deronda shares sensational elements with No Name: a plot shaped by railway travel, telegram, and bodily accident; a genteel illegitimate family living in opposition to the father's lawful marriage; and the female protagonist's nervous susceptibility, which places her sanity in question. Set a decade before its publication, this realist novel shares the

---

2. Athena Vrettos argues that sensation tropes inflect Eliot's portrayal of Gwendolen's nervous disease (551–52). In Mixed Feelings, Ann Cvetkovich reads Daniel Deronda through the sensation genre and its structures of affect. There is a long critical history of reading Eliot's final novel as a kind of limit point to Victorian realism; Alex Woloch calls it "an exemplary instance of novelistic 'late style,' at once extending, merely recapitulating, and straining against the novelist's own previous works" (167).

less respectable genre's interest in the malleability of female social identity within modern economic and technological contexts. Like Magdalen Vanstone, Gwendolen Harleth has her social place defined through loss of her father "by an accident" (75). Gwendolen's sense of self is then redefined, in young adulthood, through her abrupt loss of fortune in another working of chance, the failed speculation that ruins family investments (233). Unlike *No Name*, which keeps us tightly focused on Magdalen's psyche and narrative outcome, *Daniel Deronda* takes substantial interest in a broader world, but, I argue, Gwendolen's destabilized viewpoint structures how readers experience it. Shifting focus from Gwendolen's domestic plot to Daniel's political one, the novel enacts the gradual dissolution of a young lady's self-identity within a world that cultivates her ego but offers no meaningful outlet for ambition. Yet, in its attentiveness to effects of both minor stressors and sudden shocks upon Gwendolen's sensitive nervous system, *Daniel Deronda* sounds a broader warning about the psychic and physiological impact of daily life under industrial capitalism.

Geographical and social mobility, coupled with awareness of risk and susceptibility to chance, are defining experiences for the protagonists of these novels. These are also defining experiences for any Victorian rail traveler. The railway, which facilitates key plot points in both novels, introduced average citizens to firsthand contact with industrial technology, while transforming commerce and social relations. Taking rail travel and the socioeconomic change it engenders as central to the era of sensation, I next outline how physiological and mental effects of train travel were understood in Magdalen's and Gwendolen's time, and how railway fears connected to broader anxieties about the volatility of a modernizing world.

OFF THE RAILS: MOBILITY AND RISK

In the mid-nineteenth century, the railway was the chief tangible means by which industrial capitalism reached the middle classes, for whom factory work was an abstraction or something encountered at a distance (Daly, *Literature* 20). As rail commuting increased, this physical contact with industrial technology became a common experience for people of both genders across the class spectrum. The jolting and vibrations characteristic of rail travel were feared both by laypeople and medical professionals as harmful to bones and tissue, to say nothing of commuters' anxiety at prospects of an accident or the more mundane mishap of a delayed train (Daly, 43). The railway also facilitated intermingling of the sexes, which threatened to transform gender relations, as Wilkie Collins himself once acknowledged in a letter (Daly, *Literature* 44). Wendy Parkins argues that female geographical mobility, facilitated by new technologies including railways within the mid-Victorian through intra-war period, was both practically and symbolically linked to women's increasing political and social agency in modernity (2–3). Gwendolen and Magdalen exemplify the assertive, geographically mobile young women associated with this social change. Their mental decline—portrayed as physiological in effects if not in origins—resonates with debates about public health consequences of railways and new technology more broadly. It is useful to consider the construction, and threatened dissolution, of Magdalen and Gwendolen's psyches within the context of the 1860s railway boom, and its real and perceived dangers to both social place and physical well-being.

The turn of the sensation decade inaugurated a period of intense medical study into the effects of rail travel. In February and March 1861, the *Lancet* ran an eight-part series on public health impact of railways (Harrington 39–40), which was popular enough to be reprinted the following year in bound editions. As the earliest comprehensive medical inquiry into rail travel within Great Britain, the *Lancet* series deserves considerable attention. It consolidates wide-ranging scientific examination of the physical and psychological risks Victorians associated with regular use of this new technology. While the effects of occasional but catastrophic accident are discussed, the *Lancet*'s primary focus is on everyday risks of repeated exposure. With the exception of a necessarily gender-specific section on miscarriage (termed "abortion"), the *Lancet* contributors pay little attention to sex difference as they outline varied health implications of phenomena, including "mild but constant vibratory motion" (15), rapid air circulation in carriages (33–37), muscle fatigue from "frequency, rapidity, and peculiar abruptness of the motion of the railway-carriage" (41), and the effect produced on vision and the brain by the quick succession of images passing outside (43–44). But the *Lancet* series returns repeatedly to mental stressors rail commuting occasions, cautioning through case studies, personal experience, and general observations that such anxiety has negative physiological effects, even in individuals who previously displayed no ill health. Reflecting on his seasonal seaside residence, Dr. Forbes Winslow describes the negative influence of commuting to city employment. Winslow recalls the fear of missing trains—and therefore professional commitments—that disrupted his sleep and enjoyment of breakfast, the "scramble for the morning paper and to get a seat" at the station, and the physical wear of the journey itself (39). He concludes that "fatiguing effects, mental and physical" (39), of railway commuting outweigh benefits.

Some contributors focus on how stressful rail travel may exacerbate or reveal existing flaws of physiology or character. One physician claims the "frequent excitement, and constant hurry and anxiety" seen in rail passengers might "prove fatal" in "certain unhealthy conditions of the heart" (39–40). Similarly, Dr. Waller Lewis, chief medical officer of Her Majesty's post, concludes from his study of employees that harm from regular rail travel reveals innate but previously undetected constitutional weakness, or results from not keeping regular habits of rest; he insists it does not make the vital and well-regulated man unwell (61–67). On the whole, however, the *Lancet* series emphasizes hazards to all frequent travelers from combined effects of ceaseless, low-grade anxiety and unnatural physical fatigue.

Anxiety did not result solely from stress about missed connections and appointments. Accidents, while comparatively rare, were well publicized, often in sensational terms, receiving lavish attention in illustrated weeklies as well as more sober coverage in respectable daily papers. Discussing mental effects of train travel on the passenger, the *Lancet* contributors describe the creeping anxiety in terms that may remind modern readers of our understanding of insidious trauma: Repeated false alarms and minor discomforts bring to mind that catastrophic harm, however statistically unlikely, is always near at hand; prolonged alertness brings fatigue felt physically as well as psychologically. It is worthwhile to quote a relevant passage at length:

> The mental condition of passengers by train is commonly, perhaps, sufficiently placid and unconcerned; but several eminently careful observers have, in their communications with us, alluded to an often experienced condition of uneasiness, scarcely amounting to actual fear, which pervades the generality of travelers by rail. The possibility of collision is constantly present to such persons. And every one knows how, if by chance a train stop at some unusual place, or if the pace be slackened, or the whistle sound its shrill alarm, a head is projected from nearly every window, and anxious eyes are on the look-out for signs of danger. So, too, the frequent lateness of trains, and the bad time which they keep, are causes of anxiety. The pace, also, prevents the traveler from that observation of natural objects and sights of interest on the road, which made coach traveling a source of mental relaxation and a pastime. The passenger is forced into subjective sources of mental activity; and where the tendency to excitement exists, this also, *quantum valeat,* must be esteemed an undesirable feature belonging to this manner of locomotion. (43)

The author focuses on how the presence of unfamiliar and intrusive sensory stimulus such as the whistle, and the absence of accustomed and grounding sensory stimulus in the form of "sights of interest," produces a state of "uneasiness" that hovers at the threshold of fear. The rail passenger encounters constant physiological reminders of impending harm, yet is prevented from meaningfully situating himself within his environment by visual means, let alone asserting bodily control. The result of this combined overstimulation and loss of agency is an inward turn: "Subjective sources of mental activity" are all that are left to the traveler. Interiority is, quite literally, produced through unhealthy industrial means. The "lateness of trains," previously discussed as a stressful inconvenience to commuting professionals, may be understood more ominously within this passage; late trains were sometimes to blame for collisions, including the high-profile and deadly 1856 Picnic Train Tragedy, also known as the Camp Hill Disaster, on the Northern Pennsylvania railroad.

The *Lancet* authors make clear that railway fatalities are comparatively rare: They cite multiyear statistics showing that a far greater number of Britons are killed in carriage accidents than train accidents (8–9). In London alone, seventy people perished and 910 were injured in coach and carriage accidents in 1860, whereas in the whole of Great Britain, thirty-seven were killed and 515 injured in railway accidents the same year (8). Nonetheless, the *Lancet* authors are attentive to the ways physical and mental stressors endemic to train travel focus the passenger on that unlikely, but overwhelmingly horrifying, possibility, and remind him of his entire helplessness should an accident occur. Anxiety related to railway accidents becomes a meaningful public health concern to legions of regular travelers who never experience one directly.

Such anxieties were far worse for those who witnessed death on the rails, even if they suffered no bodily injury. As early as 1861, physicians recognized that passengers who walked away seemingly unhurt from a railway disaster could manifest distressing physiological and psychological symptoms in the weeks that followed. The *Lancet* cautiously concedes, "It would appear, from the evidence on various trials which have been instituted to recover compensation from railway companies, that neither the direct shocks produced by the accident, nor the physical injury inflicted at the time, afford any trustworthy indication of those insidious results which may subsequently ensue at a more or less distant period" (112). Modern readers will recognize the delayed onset of symptoms that our current psychiatry associates with PTSD. Symptoms thus appearing may be physical, as with paralysis, tingling, or numbness, or mental, as with "slowly ensuing . . . intellectual derangement" (112). In reviewing the *Lancet* material, it is admittedly difficult to disentangle ill effects we might associate with head injury from those we might now ascribe to post-traumatic stress. In keeping with the tendency of pre-Freudian nineteenth-century psychiatry to ascribe psychological ills to material causes, the *Lancet* physicians identify "concussion of the nervous centres experienced during the shock" (112) as the origin of disruptions of physical, intellectual, or emotional function that present no evident injury as a cause.

Victorian medical concerns regarding the impact of rail travel on public health focus not only on the proliferation and regularization of new technology, but also on its misuses and outright abuses under insufficiently regulated capitalism. Rampant overwork of railway employees is cited by the *Lancet* as a risk factor for accidents, with the combination of good railway pay and "over-stocked labor-markets" ensuring those who complain of unsafe conditions would be readily dismissed and replaced, sustaining the status quo (12). A signalman interviewed admits being on duty for twenty-four consecutive hours, and one engine driver reports a thirty-six-hour shift without breaks for sleep, while a guard describes being in charge for three days and two nights; an anonymous official concedes these experiences are commonplace (11–12). Physicians express concern about errors such fatigue causes in even the most competent employees, recognizing a significant public health risk in unregulated work hours. At the turn of the sensation decade, the Victorian medical establishment acknowledged the inevitable ubiquity of rail transportation, treating its potentially harmful effects as hazards to be analyzed by experts and managed by travelers. They demonstrated keen awareness of how human greed, insufficiently checked by government regulation, multiplied the risks of regular close contact with this powerful industrial technology.

The advent of widespread rail travel created a paradox. On the one hand, it provided Victorians of both genders and of all but the poorest classes the opportunity to rapidly traverse the nation, and thereby the chance to seek economic opportunity and reinvent social identity temporarily or, potentially, with permanence, should they successfully establish themselves in a distant city. In this sense, the railway might be viewed as a path to greater social agency. On the other hand, the experience of train travel entailed dramatically diminished agency, in that for the duration of the trip the passenger's body was at the mercy of powerful industrial technology administered more for profit than for safety. As the *Lancet* contributors meticulously document in the first comprehensive study of rail travel impacts on public health, average passengers were uncomfortably aware of their vulnerability to catastrophic accident and to the more mundane consequences of a delayed train and resultant missed engagement.

Cultural productions worked to manage these unavoidable anxieties. Nicholas Daly and Paul Fyfe have explored how Victorian popular culture sought to master the incomprehensible suddenness of rail accident through representations in sensation drama and illustrated periodicals, which slowed the mechanical impact to a narrative speed allowing human intervention (drama) or rendering sudden catastrophe knowable through visual adaptation of its components to an established aesthetic framework (periodical illustrations).[3] Novels such as *No Name* and *Daniel Deronda*, I argue, execute a different kind of work in their engagement with industrial modernity and its inevitable accidents. Magdalen Vanstone and Gwendolen Harleth are recognizably modern subjects, exercising apparent agency through geographical and social mobility, deliberately breaking with traditions and mores of the prior generation, yet painfully conscious of their vulnerability within legal and economic systems that offer no meaningful protection. While sudden and sometimes fatal accidents lurk throughout their plots, including, in Magdalen's case, rail disaster, these novels focus more on anticipation of harm and accumulation of stressors, with their moments of greatest violence almost always occurring offstage.

TRAVEL AND TRANSITION IN *NO NAME*

Sensation fiction is deeply interested in its characters' bodily affective responses, and in provoking similar physically felt reactions from readers: gasps of shock, tears of sympathy, and quickened pulses of suspense. Even within this context, *No Name* is peculiarly attuned to interrelation between physical body, affective responses, and moral fiber. While the female protagonist's physical transformations are our primary focus, as Kylee-Anne Hingston has argued, Magdalen's volatile corporeality exists within a broader context that questions the consistency of physical selfhood. Hingston asserts, "Because all bodies in *No Name* show themselves to be elusive and different—even the presumably healthy ones—the text repeatedly undermines the concept of a stable, healthy body" (121). With its pervasive exploration of the mutability of identity through shock, stress, disguise, social position, and illness, *No Name* evinces unique concern for the fluctuations of moral and intellectual character in relation to modern embodied experience.

This interest finds keenest expression in descriptions of Magdalen's response to the revelation of her illegitimacy. No legal status more effectively foregrounds the unstable relation between material embodiment, social mores, and subjectivity. Illegitimacy is a passively acquired legal status in which the social transgression of an individual's parents has socioeconomic consequences for her. The illegitimate child's body is a record of a relationship unsanctioned by law or conventional morality. Jenny Bourne Taylor sug-

---

3. See Daly, "Sensation Drama, the Railway, and Modernity" in *Literature, Technology, and Modernity, 1860–2000,* and Fyfe, "Illustrating the Accident: Railways and the Catastrophic Picturesque in the *London Illustrated News*" (2013).

gests that the ascendancy of separate spheres ideology in the Victorian era furthered the stigma of illegitimacy, because "the illegitimate child becomes increasingly linked to the mother as women become increasingly economically and socially marginalized and positioned within marriage, as the centre of the home" (127). Norah and Magdalen, raised as if they were legitimate within a sheltered, conventional household and suddenly revealed as illegitimate, offer a unique window into the process by which the social meanings of illegitimacy impact an individual's experience of her own materiality. Norah, who dutifully accepts the new meaning ascribed to her, largely disappears from the narrative because she presents no challenge to existing social structures and thus can generate no plot. Magdalen, by contrast, fails to accept the legal and social meanings written onto her body, and her opposition gives the novel momentum.

Unlike her docile older sister, the newly orphaned Magdalen secretly listens under a window as their governess consults the family lawyer. She thereby learns without the mediations generally afforded a delicate young lady that she and Norah are "Nobody's Children" (143), at the mercy of their heartless uncle. When she later reveals her presence to the governess Miss Garth and lawyer Pendril, Magdalen exhibits "a changeless stillness on her white face . . . an icy resignation in her steady grey eyes" as she "repeat[s] the lawyer's own words back to him, exactly as he had spoken them" without "a tear on her cheeks" or "a faltering tone in her voice" (143). The exact terms of her loss are engraved in her memory, but she shows no bodily signs of affective response to them. Magdalen justifies her expedient in sparing Miss Garth the pain of confronting the disinherited daughters with their scandalous history, saying, "You have suffered enough for us already; it is time we learnt to suffer for ourselves" (144). Magdalen's journey to master her pain and affix to it her own meaning—not the one given her by conventional advisors like Miss Garth, yet still a socially legible meaning—is the genesis of the story.

Magdalen's eerie composure in the face of combined personal grief, economic hardship, and social stigma is perceived as unnatural and morally suspect, causing Miss Garth to exclaim, "You frighten me!" (144). In the immediate aftermath of the revelation, Magdalen is described as having flesh physically cold to the touch (143, 151), and she declares she cannot cry because "My heart is numbed" (144), demonstrating psychological and physiological symptoms of shock. She can neither express her pain in culturally appropriate words and tears, nor avoid its transformative impact and retain her old manner and appearance. Cut loose from her youthful understanding of the world by the double blows of her parents' deaths and discovery of their social transgression, Magdalen is unable either to deny the reality of calamitous change

or to accept the cultural meanings attached to it and the economic consequences that follow. In contrast to spirited Magdalen, who is rendered chill
and steady by the shock, reserved Norah responds with conventionally pious
expressions of sorrow and submission to fate and social law. Norah resolves
to earn her living as a governess; Magdalen fixes on the project of gaining
back her inheritance, directly referencing her father's wishes and her parents'
love. By refusing to accept the culturally mandated narrative for her life as
"Nobody's Child" and thereby to sanction society's condemnation of her parents, Magdalen unwittingly shuts herself off from the support and empathy
she would otherwise have received from Norah and Miss Garth. Magdalen's
response disturbs those who uphold conventional morality. By seeking to
reinstate the inheritance her illegitimacy invalidates, she, an innocent maiden,
implicitly condones the sexually transgressive choice her parents made.

Magdalen's reaction in early stages of shock suggests characteristics typical of trauma response: emotional numbness, repetition, and inability to comprehend and integrate the reality of the traumatic event. Her fixation on the
incomprehensible double catastrophe of orphanhood and illegitimacy drives
her quest to regain the inheritance. The novel's plot proceeds from Magdalen's
desire to integrate the opposed forces that have been set at odds within her
psyche by the knowledge of her illegitimacy and disinheritance. On the one
hand, there is her love and respect for her socially discredited parents, and on
the other, there are the cultural norms and legal processes that she accepted
unquestioningly in her youth, by which her parents, and by extension she and
her sister, are now condemned. Her quest to reclaim the inheritance is also a
struggle to reconcile these contradictory, but equally undeniable, aspects of
her experience. The protagonist's experience of trauma and social transgression directly fuels the novel's progress. It is not the secret, but Magdalen's
reaction to its revelation, that determines the plot of *No Name*.

Magdalen's failure to physically demonstrate affect through culturally
mandated outlets marks her inability to accept the totality of her loss, but it
disconcerts more conventional characters who prefer Norah's tearful submission to grief over Magdalen's chill composure. Even as Mrs. Vanstone hovers
between life and death, the difference between the sisters is evident. Miss
Garth peers quietly into Norah's room, where "the kneeling figure by the
bedside, told her that God's help had found the fatherless daughter in her
affliction" (108). Norah literally embodies a posture of individual submission
to fate and recognition of divine hand in tragedy. Magdalen's conduct demonstrates no such conventional pieties. Miss Garth finds Magdalen neither
sleeping nor praying but "pacing to and fro," her "sad young face" "locked
in its cold despair; the large light eyes look[ing] mechanically into hers, as

vacant and tearless as ever" (109). Magdalen's external absence of affect troubles Miss Garth, who expresses a wish that Magdalen could follow Norah's example. Magdalen replies that "Norah . . . feels no remorse. [Our father] was not serving Norah's interests when he went to his death: he was serving mine" (109). As the errand that took Mr. Vanstone on the fatal rail journey was moved up one day to accommodate legal business occasioned by Magdalen's engagement, she holds herself responsible for the calamity.

Magdalen's "remorse" at her unwitting participation in the chain of events leading to her parents' deaths is both a source of suffering and an obstacle to sympathy. But it is also an assertion of individual will against overwhelming external forces. Magdalen's resistance to chance resonates with broader currents in the novel's setting, and its time of publication. As Daniel Martin notes, No Name is set more than a decade earlier than it was written, during a period of overblown speculation in railways leading to economic crash, when countless citizens lost their fortunes to chance train-related mishaps more mundane, but no less financially devastating, than the one that leaves the Vanstone daughters penniless (191). If Magdalen can claim responsibility for the tragedies that befall her family, then whatever the cost in psychic pain, she has spared herself from conceding the randomness of mortality and misfortune. If her deliberate actions brought about the tragedy, then loss is neither random nor inevitable. Magdalen's remorse, which stokes her coldly burning rage, is no less than Norah's piety a ringing denial of the meaninglessness of modernity, the helplessness of femininity, and the insurmountable power of unjust laws.

Magdalen's flirtation with the abnegation of personal agency, and with denial of a meaningful moral framework for human interactions, comes in the desperate days leading up to her most daring action, marriage to Noel Vanstone. Dreading the means of her vengeance, Magdalen contemplates suicide, and goes so far as to purchase a bottle of laudanum to end her life. Numbly paging through a newspaper to pass time, she reads about a farm laborer who, deserted by his sweetheart, settled his irresolution as to whether he should kill her by tossing his spade in the air, as one might flip a coin. The laborer in the news story shoots the woman on the chance fall of a spade, ensuring his own execution. Magdalen, gazing out her bedroom window, determines that odd versus even numbers of ships sailing by within a given half hour will determine whether or not she drinks the poison. The passing ships decree that she shall live and hence marry. While she cannot decide whether to ascribe her grim salvation to "Providence" or "chance" (500), Magdalen ultimately defies both: She retains the bottle of poison rather than discarding it, so that she could at some later point make a deliberate choice to end her life if she deems her marriage unendurable. Magdalen's stubborn insistence on regarding life circumstances as the result of her own choices is ultimately self-destructive, and prevents her from processing loss in socially acceptable ways. Yet it also constitutes a form of resistance, an assertion of female agency in the face of patriarchal law, and human agency in the midst of an increasingly mechanized world where chance accidents literally derail the best-laid plans.

Ironically, it is the inflexibility of Magdalen's purpose in avenging her parents and accepting her own perceived blame in their deaths that fuels the changeability of her temperament and social self-presentation. Several early critics of *No Name* fixated on the fluctuations of Magdalen's character in relation to plot, expressing dissatisfaction with her unstable selfhood. In a generally favorable unsigned *Atheneaum* review, H. F. Chorley expresses unease at the dissonance between the appealing, richly drawn heroine's "good qualities," including "her beauty, her theatrical adroitness, [and] her courage," and the low scheming she employs them to forward (10). "There must be surely coarseness," he insists, "as well as meanness, in one capable of such expedients as these" (11). Chorley ascribes Magdalen's contradictions of character (described in implicitly classed terms) to the requirements of the author's (not the protagonist's) intricate plotting, suggesting "that Mr. Collins has become so possessed with his story as to be unaware that its necessities give his heroine a color and a character which he neither intended, nor may be able to perceive" (11). Relatedly, an unsigned review in the short-lived *Reader* expresses dissatisfaction with the mixture of mainstream domestic virtue and sexually forward scheming. It faults the English sensation novel, termed "a plant of foreign growth," for lacking the conviction of French depravity, and Collins for preserving Magdalen's respectability through marriage, thereby robbing the novel of "sensational grandeur" (15). The character is faulted, essentially, for being neither stainless angel nor lustful demon, and the plot denigrated for stopping short to preserve its heroine's conventional virtue from "the one unpardonable sin in our English code" (15). Mrs. Oliphant, in an unsigned *Blackwood's* review, drily notes the paradox that following Magdalen's "career of vulgar and aimless trickery and wickedness," "she emerges, at the cheap cost of a fever, as pure, as high-minded, and as spotless, as the most dazzling white of heroines" (170). The novel is here critiqued not for its female protagonist's duplicitous nature, but rather, for her sincere, thus unsettling or disappointing, contradictions. Magdalen's variability creates dissonance and unease.

Like its popular sensation peers Wood's *East Lynne* (1861), Braddon's *Lady Audley's Secret* (1862), and Collins's own *The Woman in White* (1859), *No*

Name features a plot heavily dependent upon characters' plausible assumption of disguise. *No Name*, however, is the only of these novels to consider at length, indeed to thematize, the psychological impact of material assumption of another person's identity. In *East Lynne*, Richard Hare the younger, a born gentleman, assumes the character of a working-class stable hand with sufficient credibility to live undetected for years while in danger from the law. Upon resumption of his actual identity, his speech and manner shift back to those of his accustomed station without any notable effort. His mental suffering during the period of concealment is linked not to the strangeness of assuming an entirely new identity, but instead to his native timidity, the threat to his life that necessitates hiding, and his pain at separation from loved ones. Similarly, when Isabel Vane lives with her ex-husband and children under the assumed character of a governess, her mental pain stems from grief at her changed position in the household, jealousy of her ex-husband's new wife, and self-reproach for her earlier impulsive desertion. Her changed role and assumed name do not threaten her stable core identity as Isabel Vane. Never is her inner sense of self compromised by the assumption of Madame Vine's character; her transformation relies entirely on bodily changes (gray hair and a scar) and details of dress, not any alteration of manner. Indeed, her refined deportment, cultivated through years of aristocratic society, makes Isabel desirable in her new position as governess.

In Wood's *East Lynne* and Braddon's *Lady Audley's Secret*, it is fear of detection, and strife at the circumstances that necessitate disguise, that threaten the mental well-being of characters who live under an assumed identity. In *The Woman in White*, however, Collins begins to consider the potentially devastating psychic impact of this common sensation plot device. Placed in an insane asylum under an assumed name by her nefarious and money-hungry husband, the previously stable though sensitive Laura Fairlie Glyde actually takes leave of her reason. Even after a rescue by her sister, both her memory of past experiences and her ability to cope with present necessities are badly impaired for months. Ascribed the name and life circumstances of a monomaniac, she loses her rationality and falls prey to debilitating extremes of emotion, finally regressing into a childlike state from which it takes her years to emerge. Two years later in *No Name*, whose title calls to mind the erasure and disruption of identity, Collins explores in more extensive and nuanced ways the psychic impact of taking on another person's appearance, name, and social position. Magdalen's assumption of new identities includes private theatricals, paid public performances, and impersonation. Her self-transformation is necessitated by disinheritance and facilitated by mobility: across country via rail, and throughout urban and suburban environments on foot.

Magdalen's highly mobile identity intensifies more typical fluctuations of embodied interiority within sensation characters—and readers who connect with them. In its emphasis on physiological response and identification with the suffering of fictional characters, sensation novels can condition socially normative emotional reactions. Cvetkovich claims that sensation fiction literally embodies social structures through production of affect that the reader experiences as a bodily and seemingly natural response to concrete representations of social interaction (*Mixed Feelings* 23–24). The affective experience produced through identification with a character such as Magdalen would be fragmentary and shifting: She not only experiences significant transitions, but adopts varied identities. Her complex interiority changes throughout the novel, but it is debatable whether the character can be said to develop through accumulated life experience as, for example, we might say that Jane Eyre's, or for that matter Aurora Floyd's, does.

As she moves through different geographical and cultural environments, crafting personas to suit her circumstances, Magdalen's patterns of speech, bodily mannerisms, and even thoughts sync with the imagined character with whom she identifies, gradually erasing her stable self-identity as her body wastes from the strain. It is crucial that Magdalen's corporeality is not merely presented as a sign to be read or misread in social interactions. The vividly imagined materiality of the protagonist's body forms the interface between Magdalen's psyche and her social context. Further, the reader who empathizes with the eerie numbness of her disbelief, the righteous indignation of her rage, the shudders of her dread, and the tremors of her anxiety is likewise drawn into the loop. Affect, the most palpably physical mental process, renders visible a crucial link between the material and the social that might otherwise be difficult to conceptualize. A rethinking of affective processes as at once materially based, manifest in nerves and other organs of perception and cognition, and at the same time socially constructed, rendered apparently natural through historically specific means, forwards this analysis. The affective responses Magdalen's transitions prompt from the reader are less predictable, and less standardized, than those provoked by, for example, the sorrows and regrets of the erring wife Isabel Vane or the terror of the bland innocent Laura Fairlie. In her extreme transformations of not only socioeconomic position, but character, and her related moral ambiguity, Magdalen Vanstone is a particularly modern sensation protagonist. The personas and disguises she undertakes attempting to reclaim her fortune amplify those shifts of self-identity increasingly common in an era when both economic and geographical mobility were becoming commonplace, risk was normalized, and accidents could produce sudden changes. Put simply, the mid-Victorian reader, like Magdalen, could board a train and act a new social part in another community; she could, like Magdalen, suffer a chance reversal, and find her financial position and social role abruptly transformed.

Collins's retention of the formal tools of narrative withholding—an interlacing of third-person and multiple first-person narration that obliges the reader to fill in gaps between available perspectives—here functions not to conceal information from the reader, but to communicate the fragmentation of Magdalen's identity in the midst of competing forces. The earlier *Woman in White* and later *Moonstone* both employ first-person narrators involved in the story's action, most of whom are deliberately collaborating to generate a document that produces coherent meaning from shocking, confusing, and threatening events. While they include interpolated letters, those documents are understood by the reader as deliberately positioned within more structured narration by a sympathetic first-person narrator involved in the story's action and serving as editor (Richard Hartwright and Franklin Blake, respectively), guiding the reader through the interpretation of evidence. In *No Name*, Collins instead employs third-person limited omniscient for the story's five "scenes" and integrates five "between the scenes" sections in which the narrative progresses through letters exchanged by characters and by memoranda of the dubious Captain Wragge. The third-person narration presents Magdalen as the novel's most attractive character but issues cautionary statements about her conduct and moral fiber. The interpolated letters, in contrast, provide unmediated access to Magdalen's self-representation to both friends and foes (which are, in this story, often interchangeable) and the other characters' often disapproving responses to and interpretations of her. The third-person narration presents Magdalen as viewed by an observer beyond the story's action, within a conventional and unified moral framework. Her speech and bodily reactions are offered for the reader's assessment, and she is made the subject of moralizing or excusatory narratorial comment. The interpolated letters, however, offer individualized assessments of her character and actions, filtered through diverse interests of other individual actors within her social milieu. The overall effect dramatizes the destabilization of Magdalen's once steady identity through conflicting perspectives on her character. It also showcases the limitations of both third-person omniscient narration and first-person narration, neither of which adequately account for the character and choices of contradictory Magdalen. Most sensation plots implicitly depend upon the divergence of external self-representation and core subjectivity: The outwardly respectable lady or gentleman proves to be a cruel malefactor. *No Name*, in contrast, is driven by its protagonist's attempts to negotiate a new confluence between interiority and external social and material experience following the violent split occasioned by her parents' deaths and the accompanying revelation of her illegitimacy. *Daniel Deronda* similarly derives narrative structure from its female protagonist's psychic conflict.

DIVERGENCE AND DISENFRANCHISEMENT
IN *DANIEL DERONDA*

A young man of mysterious origins heroically saves a virtuous young woman from mortal danger. In so doing, he uncovers clues that teach him his true identity and reunite him with his rightful inheritance, placing him in a respected leadership role. In the course of his adventures, he chooses between an alluring femme fatale and the domestically minded maiden whose life he preserved, and his selection of the "right" woman, who echoes his developing social values, crowns his mature happiness. A young lady raised at the mercy of a cruel patriarch is briefly freed to explore her own power. But incomprehensible calamity strikes, and she makes a wicked bargain to recover stability. Tormented by a new oppressor and consumed by regret, she reaches out for aid, only to multiply her suffering as her desired rescuer turns away.

These are the same story, seen from different subject positions. The dual plots of Eliot's final novel, which proceed in productive tension with one another, elaborate very different arguments about the meaning that can or should be made of their contemporary society. Figuring both British high society and the multi-plot novel as in need of reinvigoration, *Daniel Deronda* allows a disordered and disoriented position to guide its formal structure. Daniel and Gwendolen's related yet dissonant self-development unsettle the reader's confidence in the meaningful correspondence between private and public sphere concerns.

What constitutes the dynamic relation between Gwendolen's disappointment and Daniel's satisfaction? Following Annabel Herzog, I read the two halves as deeply interconnected. Whereas Herzog emphasizes parallels between Gwendolen's and Daniel's secret, socially unspeakable experiences within patriarchy, mine expands the focus outward, situating the two protagonists within a web of similarly constrained characters.[4] After outlining the narrative bifurcation of Daniel's and Gwendolen's stories, which shifts attention from Gwendolen's domestic society to Daniel's public network, I

---

4. Herzog identifies two interrelated secrets: "Gwendolen's traumatic relationship with her stepfather and Daniel's ambiguously remembered circumcision. Eliot's dislocation of the chronology of events and her recurrent use of figures of substitution that displace or *defer* meaning encrypt these secrets" (37).

explore parallels between Gwendolen's experience and other female characters, explaining how theories of nervous susceptibility and shock inform
the novel's structural alignment with Gwendolen's retrospective view of loss.
I then delineate corresponding adolescent instances of shameful shock that
connect Daniel, Gwendolen, and Mirah. *Daniel Deronda* employs language of
psychic shock to describe characters' pained recognition of how sexual and
monetary transactions intersect in a rapidly modernizing environment.

The dual plot structure encourages comparison of outlets for ambition
available to women and men of talent and genteel upbringing. Gwendolen's
plot is one of dissolution, the painful and terrifying breaking down of a social
order predicated upon subjugation. Daniel's plot is one of construction, the
building up of an evidently healthier social order governed by shared interests
and unifying traditions. The trick is that they are the same story, seen from
different subject positions. *Daniel Deronda*'s dual plot structure traces the
evolving self-knowledge of two protagonists joined by a bond of sympathy,
whose perceptions of their relationship diverge. The expanding rift in perspectives results not only from Daniel's shifting cultural allegiance but from
the normalizing pressure of gender roles as both characters move from adolescence into mature social participation through matrimony and, for Daniel,
the choice of vocation. The dual plot structure demonstrates vividly the extent
to which one's interpretation of the ethical import and affective significance of
events is shaped by a subject position contingent upon gender, class, ethnicity, and national affiliation. *Daniel Deronda* goes beyond providing its readers
access to viewpoints typically marginalized, stigmatized, or excluded from
public discourse. By showing us how two protagonists experience the same
chain of events in radically different ways, the novel encourages readers to
recognize the extent to which subject position shapes our interpretation of
the world.

I do not contend that *Daniel Deronda* presents its readers with any affirmative blueprint for the meaningful participation of individuals socially or
politically excluded from British imperial power. Indeed, it fails to imagine
a socially integrated and affectively satisfying alternative for a woman dis-
inclined to conventional domesticity. Further, it reproduces within Daniel's
supposedly hopeful proto-Zionist project the same patriarchal, imperialist structures it depicts as problematic within the British plot. Nonetheless,
through the connection between Gwendolen and Daniel, the novel renders
both structurally and thematically the unsteady alliance of feminine/private
and masculine/public concerns.

Without commenting upon gender dynamics, Alex Woloch has argued
for the structural interdependence of Gwendolen and Daniel as "dueling or

potential protagonists" who are "mutually co-implicated, and thus incomplete, centers within the narrative as a whole" (172). Gwendolen and Daniel are drawn together by their inarticulable bond of social disenfranchisement; both experience guilt and shame within a socioeconomic system that seems predicated on a psychic as well as monetary economy of scarcity, in which one must push aside the needs of others in order to meet one's own. But they are also repeatedly, and with growing intensity, driven apart by their mutual inability to see past the feminine and masculine positions to which they have been acculturated. To say that Daniel cannot marry Gwendolen on account of the revelation of his Jewish heritage would oversimplify the complex gender and class affiliations that divide them.

Questions of faith and culture aside, the two protagonists are in no position to marry one another at the novel's close. As they reach maturity, Daniel, aligned with economic and political life, and Gwendolen, aligned with domestic and affective life, lack common ground. Daniel's public-sphere ambitions are future-oriented; Gwendolen's domestic investments are increasingly retrograde, seeking return to the youthful courtship period that came before her grave error in accepting Grandcourt. The novel's vision of social organization cannot depict meaningful confluence between the public and private realms with which each has become increasingly associated. Daniel, whose "tastes were altogether in keeping with his nurture" (169), gravitates to the role of gentleman-politician Sir Hugo envisions for him (173, 176). He finds his sense of purpose only when the revelation of legitimacy allows him to take a socially validated place within patriarchal descent. He rejoices upon the revelation of Jewish patrimony as "something like a discovered charter warranting the inherited right that his ambition had begun to yearn for . . . what was better than freedom . . . a duteous bond which his experience had been preparing him to accept gladly" (744). Daniel can then take part in the material nation-building that his childhood with Sir Hugo Mallinger implicitly taught him to valorize. As a newly legitimatized son, he too can become a political leader. Joseph Kalonymos, his grandfather's friend, declares of Daniel, "You argue and you look forward" (725): Over the course of the novel, Daniel acquires the narrative momentum to carry a story into the future.

In contrast, Gwendolen, who "meant to lead" (39) but "cannot conceive of herself as anything else than a lady" (63), is a retrospective narrative force, increasingly bound in her shrinking domestic world and fixated on her single irredeemable error of displacing Lydia Glasher. Long after the wedding night revelation, she finds "the words of [Lydia's] letter kept repeating themselves" (424) inwardly, anchoring her consciousness in her past fault. Early in Gwendolen's marriage, "her confidence in herself had turned into remorse and dread; she trusted neither herself nor her future" (430). "Dread" is a key term for Eliot, broadly denoting poisonous brooding over errors that cannot be mended or spoken of. Marriage forestalls Gwendolen's forward momentum and fixes her gaze backward; this focus on irrecoverable past opportunity intensifies. Parting from Daniel in Genoa, "she was a banished soul—beholding a possible life that she had sinned herself away from" (701). Convalescing after the shock of witnessing Grandcourt's passing, the "only project she like[s] to speak of" is "to place her mother and sisters with herself in Offendene again, and, as she said, piece back her life on to that time when they first went there, and when everything was happiness about her, only she did not know it" (772). Gwendolen rediscovers her fragile will to live only when deprived of her social leadership, enveloped entirely within the life of affect she shares with her mother, focused on a return to what she perceives as her only brief moment of choice and possibility: domestic in nature. The novel's largely retrospective structure follows her backward-looking impulse.

The division inherent in the novel's plot and ambivalence of its ending offer an aesthetic structure for critique of the social systems that falsely divide psychic and affective life from political and economic. The filaments connecting these halves are the tense fibers of nerves, whose sensitivity and dysfunction Eliot delineates with scientific precision. It is crucial to attend not only the division within the novel's plot, but also how the text works to ally readers with Gwendolen's increasingly disordered perspective through repetitions as well as temporal shifts and discontinuities. Nicholas Dames notes how "in perhaps no other Victorian novel is the question of time so prominent, and so vexed" (*Physiology* 129). His nuanced reading locates *Daniel Deronda* within the 1850s to 1870s cultural moment defined by "ever more harried consumers, and ever more elongated artistic forms," particularly as typified by the musical compositions of Wagner, whose work Eliot knew intimately (*Physiology* 129). I share Dames's concern for the novel's situatedness within a fraught cultural moment. My different emphasis leads me to attend to how its repetitions, temporal disruptions, and elisions connect readers with Gwendolen's damaged and shocked consciousness, anticipating modern formulations of psychic trauma.

As Gwendolen's psyche structures our reading experience, her perspective is implicitly normalized even when her perceptions and responses may be termed pathological. Her developing psychic disorder and diminishing sense of self are enacted in the novel's formal structure: It first disorients the reader's sense of temporal order and then decreases Gwendolen's presence. Famously opening in medias res, *Daniel Deronda* introduces both Gwendolen and Daniel at a gambling resort on the evening she receives news of her family's financial reversal. The narrative then moves chronologically backward to provide first her, then Daniel's, then Mirah's histories. When the narrative returns to Gwendolen, she arrives home at Offendene to cope with her changed circumstances, and we follow her abortive contemplation of acting and governessing, Grandcourt's renewed courtship, and the wedding night revelation of his mistress's diamonds, which forces acknowledgment of the economic system that profits Gwendolen at another woman's expense. At this second substantial shock to Gwendolen, her plotline is abandoned entirely for thirty pages, and the final third of the novel subordinates its account of Gwendolen's matrimonial suffering to Daniel's developing knowledge of his Jewish heritage, related interest in Mirah, and attempts to renew family connections.

Gwendolen's third substantial shock, the detested Grandcourt's accidental drowning, nearly excises her consciousness from the narrative. Her confession to Daniel is narrated from his perspective, masking her interiority while communicating her intense guilt and suffering through dialogue, gestures, and bodily symptoms of nervous shock (688–97). The short scene of Gwendolen's leave-taking from Daniel in Genoa closes with her collapsed insensible on the floor (698–702); she then falls from our view for fifty pages while we focus first on the Gascoignes and then more substantially on Daniel (750–55). After Genoa, Gwendolen, once central, appears speaking in only four scenes in less than twenty of the novel's remaining hundred pages: an interlude with her mother (755–56); followed by family interactions regarding living arrangements, Grandcourt's will, and her desire to consult Daniel (760–64); then twice, most substantially, in submissive conversation with Daniel (766–72, 800–807). Daniel's gradual understanding with Mirah, and her father's shameful reappearance, take much of our attention. Gwendolen's final representation in the text is a brief letter she sends on the occasion of Daniel Deronda's wedding, assuring him that "it shall be better with me because I have known you" (810). This action creates symmetry between the first and second halves of the novel, being the inverse of Lydia's note to Gwendolen: offering a blessing, rather than a curse, on her ostensible rival's wedding day. Over the course of the text, Gwendolen's much-remarked egotism is shaken by accidental or unexpected events that cause emotional shock; the novel wears away the female protagonist's sense of self, and its very structure enacts her developing awareness of how small is her place in the world. Readers are not only told that "the world seemed getting larger round poor Gwendolen, and she more solitary and helpless in the midst" (803); we are made to feel it, as she would.

Gwendolen's descent into pathological nervous dysfunction is only the most intense manifestation of a broader dis-ease within the text. Her disordered perspective amplifies what the novel shows to be *typical* patterns of female consciousness within the constraints and stressors of her era.

"WOMAN'S LIFE": CONSTRAINED AGENCY AND FRACTURED NARRATIVE

Long prior to *Daniel Deronda,* mental strain recurs in Eliot's characters, with certain gendered differences. In earlier novels, Eliot's consideration of women's mental instability often focuses on anxieties about motherhood: in *Adam Bede,* Hetty Sorrel's "hidden dread" and subsequent impulsive infanticide; in *Felix Holt,* Mrs. Transome's lifelong "dread" at the guilty secret of her favored son's parentage. Moral guilt combined with belief that no action can assuage one's mental pain are the defining characteristics of these scenarios. Eliot's male characters sometimes display similar guilt and desperation about unspeakable knowledge. For instance, the corrosive mental effects of a secret can be seen, in varying degrees, in Hetty's lover Arthur Donnithorne, *Middlemarch*'s killer-by-omission Nicholas Bulstrode, and even *Felix Holt*'s Reverend Lyon, with respect to his concealment of Esther's true heritage. In *Daniel Deronda,* the title character, suspecting his illegitimacy, "connect[s] dread with unknown parentage" (207), both his own and Mirah's, and hesitates to pursue definite information in either case. Eliot recognizes that the more active and public nature of men's lives mediates, if not dispels, the combination of guilt and anxiety, which she repeatedly terms "dread," that through brooding turns to anguish in a sedentary and private domestic realm. In *The Mill on the Floss* (1860), comparing Maggie Tulliver's struggles to her brother Tom's, Eliot writes:

> So it had been since the days of Hecuba, and of Hector, tamer of horses: inside the gates, the women with streaming hair and uplifted hands offering prayers, watching the world's combat from afar, filling their long, empty days with memories and fears: outside, the men in fierce struggle with things divine and human, quenching memory in the stronger light of purpose, losing the sense of dread and even of wounds in the hurrying ardour of action. (405)

We see here the germs of the female-domestic-retrograde, male-public-forward division that characterizes the plot structure of *Daniel Deronda.* This passage also demonstrates Eliot's awareness of the discourse of nerve force: a vital energy that fuels unhealthy emotional excess if not dissipated through socially sanctioned outlets.

Within *Daniel Deronda,* all women experience socioeconomic stressors, but it is those who discern their status as commodities, and feel guilt and anger about their involvement in the system of sexual and commercial exchange, who cross the line into mental instability. Gwendolen is chief among them, and her hysteria has become a critical commonplace, grounding discussion of how the novel engages gender ideologies.[5] Victorian theories of hysteria connected its disruptions of mental function (brain and nervous system) to female reproductive organs and cycles (Malane 36–37). Commonly described hysteric symptoms included excessive emotionality and vacillation between hyperactivity and torpor. The pioneering psychiatrist Henry Maudsley, whose work Eliot knew, claims that in addition to "the usual hysterical convulsions," an episode may also or instead comprise "acute maniacal excitement, with great restlessness, sometimes tending to the erotic and obscene, evidently without abolition of consciousness; laughing, singing, or rhyming, and perverseness of conduct, which is still more or less coherent and seemingly willful" (*Body and Mind* 79).[6] While hysteria is a plausible medical frame for Gwendolen's psychological and bodily symptoms, some scholars have instead or additionally read her through related Victorian discourse of nervous sensitivity and shock, which downplays the importance of female reproductive physiology.[7]

Innate nervous "sensitiveness" such as Gwendolen's could presage hysteria, but was not itself considered a disorder. Nervous response, also called nervous irritability or excitability, was at mid-century understood as a necessary biological process (Malane 30). Nonetheless, physicians cited women's greater nervous excitability in establishing the biological basis of gender difference

---

5. Doreen Thierauf's "Tending to Old Stories: *Daniel Deronda* and Hysteria, Revisited" (2018) offers a thorough analysis based upon contextualization with scientific texts Eliot would have known. Marlene Tromp reads both Lydia Glasher and Gwendolen Harleth as employing hysterical language that challenges the dominant legal, religious, and ostensibly rational discourse Henleigh Grandcourt embodies (212–23). Athena Vrettos has argued "the form of Gwendolen's hysteria ultimately challenges and mimics the dominant narrative structure" (574) in making interior visions come true.

6. Both Maudsley texts cited in this chapter were in George Eliot and George Henry Lewes's library: See Baker 132.

7. Jane Wood reads Gwendolen in terms of nervous "tendency" (140) and how nerves facilitate "exchange between various aspects of individual experience: psychological, physiological, and social" (139). In *Shock, Memory, and the Unconscious in Victorian Fiction,* Jill Matus reads Gwendolen as "a susceptible and volatile subject" (147) primed to respond to "overwhelming experience" (147), but does not frame her as necessarily pathological or specifically hysteric.

(Malane 30–31). Jill Matus argues that Gwendolen's nervous susceptibility, dramatic though it may appear, would not be read as necessarily pathological by her contemporaries (*Shock* 151–52). As Matus observes, "rather than setting Gwendolen up as a diseased subject, the narrator calls her an 'intense personality,' which suggests that certain ordinary tendencies are exaggerated or writ large in her make-up" (*Shock* 152). Eliot accepted the central premise of nerve function articulated by her contemporary medicine—as Jane Wood explains, she "understood the nerves to be the operating mechanism converting sense experience into healthy or diseased consciousness" (136). Within *Daniel Deronda*, nervous disorder surfaces as dysregulation of emotional or physical response to sensory input or its social meaning: either numbness and frigidity, or inappropriate emotional intensity. Sustained apprehension of threat or insecurity, predominantly economic in nature, is shown to condition women characters for disordered reactions when faced with unexpected shocks. Gwendolen's instances of nervous dysregulation often originate in challenges to her sense of individual mastery, as when receiving her mother's news of vanished investments, she cannot emotionally or intellectually process the information and sits motionless "as if she had been jarred by a hateful sound and was waiting for any sign of its cause" (16). (This language recalls the *Lancet* rail travelers anxiously anticipating catastrophic crash after an unexpected noise.) Following this scene, Gwendolen stays up all night packing to return to Offendene, showing no apparent sorrow and minimal fatigue. Gwendolen's dramatic nervous outbursts occur within the broader fabric of smaller misfires like this one, in which her absence or excess of emotional and somatic response are perceived by other characters not as pathology but variously as self-control, self-absorption, high spirits, or temper. When we compare Gwendolen's ambiguously psychic and somatic symptoms to those that manifest in other female characters, parallels emerge, implying that whatever pathology inheres in her "sensitiveness" is broadly latent in modern female experience. My reading situates Gwendolen within a network of characters in its examination of the Victorian woman's regular stressors and everyday risks.

Daniel Deronda's portrayal of nervous disorder challenges dominant theories within Victorian mental science, which presented women's greater susceptibility to emotional extremes as inherent to female biology. Of course, Eliot earlier explored the extremes of *male* nervous susceptibility in *The Lifted Veil* (1859), whose narrator Latimer, always "a shy, sensitive boy" (6), emerges from a fever "fragile, nervous, ineffective" but apparently possessing a receptivity to other minds and future events amounting to clairvoyance (14). I shall return to the implications of Latimer's case for masculine nerves in chapter 5; its relevance to Gwendolen lies in the similar coupling of nervous sensitivity and unique power, and its implication that Eliot did not align nervous susceptibility exclusively or primarily with female physiology. Eliot's final novel instead presents women's nervous disorder as consequent of cultural and legal systems that constrain female economic agency, social freedoms, and to some extent, physical mobility. Maudsley held that gendered biological changes at particular life stages triggered pathological manifestations of nervous disorder (*Body and Mind* 78); Eliot reframes these triggers as predominantly economic in nature. *Daniel Deronda*'s female characters manifest hysteric symptoms when forced to confront their actual or expected exchange of sexual availability (including production of heirs) for financial stability: not only Gwendolen Harleth, but Mirah Lapidoth (in relation to the Count) and Lydia Glasher (in her interview with Grandcourt prior to his marriage). They undergo intense and dramatically embodied negative emotions, triggered by a shameful intersection of sexuality and property, producing a mental state in which capacity for intentionality is uncertain. Their mental distress follows from inability to accept a male-enforced financial arrangement related to a sexual relationship.

Within the genteel worlds these characters inhabit, even women who show no signs of actual instability live in perpetual self-reproach and anxiety. Lady Mallinger winces at the sight of Grandcourt, whose status as heir reminds her of "what she felt to be her failure as a wife—the not having presented Sir Hugo with a son" (279). Weary and fretful Mrs. Davilow indulges Gwendolen to mitigate her guilt at the unhappiness her second marriage brought her eldest child. Meanwhile, "the sad faces of the four superfluous girls" who are Gwendolen's unwanted and unlovely half-sisters hover undifferentiated in the background, emblematic of "those other many thousand sisters of us all—[each] having her peculiar world which was of no importance to anyone else" (229). The mental struggles of most female characters in *Daniel Deronda* coalesce around their perception that the only acceptable duty of a woman is timely marriage and the production of satisfactory heirs. Both their social status and their material comfort are contingent upon societal and even biological reproductive factors beyond their control.

Daniel's mother—who never meets any of the characters just discussed—is the novel's one portrayal of a woman who overtly challenges the proscribed feminine role and controls her economic destiny outside the boundaries of marriage and reproduction. As an actress, she is not only an artist, but an economic actor, taking responsibility for her finances through public work rather than, as a genteel lady should, relying upon her husband's support within the private sphere. In youth, she perceives that Daniel Charisi "never thought of his daughter except as an instrument" (662), "a makeshift link" (631) to community endurance through marriage and childbearing. Having "wants outside his purpose" (662), she surreptitiously secures musical training, marries a man she can rule, goes on the stage, and gives her son, Daniel, to an admirer to raise, because "I was living myriad lives in one. I did not want a child" (626). Content she has secured for her firstborn the youth and education she herself would have preferred, the Princess Halm-Eberstein shows no evidence of guilt at her choices.

The "choice" Gwendolen gets in the novel's third book is dubious: interwoven in evolving economic patterns beyond her control or full comprehension, and limited by her inability to imagine herself beyond the role of lady. Daniel's judgmental attention to Gwendolen's recreational gambling focuses the reader on her moral fallibility, particularly in relation to money. Gwendolen's engagement to Grandcourt follows shortly after her roulette play in the novel's chronology (although several hundred pages later in narrative discourse), inviting us to connect these actions. The narrator makes the parallel explicit when we are told that on her wedding morning, Gwendolen "wrought herself up to much the same condition as that in which she had stood at the gaming table" (354). Despite her guilty feeling, this final ill-fated gamble is precipitated less through Gwendolen's active decision than by the financial miscalculations of others. Her family's sudden ruin in financial speculation prompts her reconsideration of Grandcourt's romantic interest and the economic stability it could bring. Her agency is markedly constrained.

While Gwendolen regards the marriage market, recreational gambling, and financial speculation as different activities, the novel connects them as structurally similar economic patterns where women compete in games of chance whose rules they do not fully fathom. Gwendolen flees to the gambling resort of Leubronn to sidestep Grandcourt's proposal following Lydia Glasher's revelation. Claiming agency and defying her uncle's anticipated patriarchal pressure, she declares, "I don't care if I never marry any one. There is nothing worth caring for. I believe all men are bad, and I hate them" (154). It is the financial market—specifically, instabilities of 1860s speculation—that drives her back to England and ultimately to marriage with Grandcourt. By the mid-nineteenth century, gaming houses were illegal within Great Britain, and foreign resorts like the fictionalized Leubronn objects of polite disapprobation (Itzkowitz 123–24). Gamblers, nonetheless, justified their avocation by noting that the morally and socially ambiguous practice of speculation—defined as "buying and selling of commodities to benefit from changes of price"— was not substantively different, although legally permissible (Itzkowitz 124). The failed "great speculations" in mines through which Mr. Lassman "meant to gain" but "risked too much" (233) are condoned by long-suffering Mrs.

Davilow as "the will of Providence" (232) but impugned by Gwendolen, who cannot fathom that such a practice could be legal, as "people's wickedness" (233). Gwendolen's mother voices characteristically early-Victorian bourgeois views of laissez-faire economics as a divinely ordained self-regulating system; the daughter articulates doubts characteristic of the second half of the nineteenth century.[8] Henry suggests that the family's devastating losses should not be viewed as inevitable; rather, ignorance or poor guidance about investing are to blame: Mines were an especially risky speculation, and based upon Mrs. Davilow's description, the fictional Grapnell & Co. was not a limited liability corporation (160–61). Mother and daughter are both shown at the mercy of a broader realm of financial choices and chances that affect them profoundly but lie beyond their direct participation or even full understanding.

In the novel's symbolic system, Gwendolen's engagement structurally parallels the risk-based activities of gambling and speculation (where she has recently suffered losses). These connections follow broader cultural patterns wherein, according to Wagner, "speculation stood in as a synecdoche for an unstable financial system propelled by chance and, by extension, for speculative society at large," including the marriage market (8). Despite symbolic connections visible to the reader, what Gwendolen seeks in her marital choice is an escape from financial uncertainty, through alliance with the obsolescent system of land-based wealth inheritance that her suitor embodies. Marrying a respectable older landowner appears, falsely, to promise local centrality and influence as well as solid economic status (Schaffer, *Romance's Rival* 117–18). This promise of class stability, envisioned as "what Grandcourt might do for her mother" (294), finally inclines Gwendolen to accept him. She explains to Daniel retrospectively, "We became poor all at once, and I was very miserable, and I was tempted" (699). In desperation, having lost both her stake at the gaming table and her family property in the mines, and finding the labor market distasteful, unpromising, and alien, Gwendolen turns to the same mode of economic participation that failed her mother, marriage with the scion of an old family (not unlike the Harleths, who never condescended to recognize Fanny). Readers see parallels among recreational gambling, financial speculation, and the marriage market, which all entail chance, sudden change, and profiting from another's loss, but in her moment of (profoundly overdetermined) decision, Gwendolen perceives marriage into land-based wealth as a safer alternative to other forms of economic participation.

---

8. On this shift in public attitude, see Elaine Freedgood, "Banishing Panic: J. R. McCulloch, Harriet Martineu, and the Popularization of Political Economy," in *Victorian Writing about Risk* (2000).

Women's economic insecurity conditions Gwendolen's mental instability by precipitating emotional shock (notably from lost investments) and, within the Grandcourt marriage, sustained anticipation of imminent harm. The wedding night revelation that propels Gwendolen from nervous susceptibility into full hysterics is not only Lydia Glasher's justified rage at displacement, but equally recognition of her own similar economic and social vulnerability in relation to her newly married husband. Gwendolen's earlier interaction with Lydia prepares her for the psychic break of her wedding night. At the Cardell Chase archery outing, anticipating a proposal, Gwendolen receives an anonymous note requesting "if she is in doubt whether she should accept Mr. Grandcourt," she may "hear something to decide her" in secret (149). Immediately we are told "Gwendolen felt an inward *shock*" (149; emphasis mine): a term implying physiological response, similar to that of impact. No mention is made of Gwendolen's emotions, only her practical reflection, given in quotation marks to signal exactitude: "It is come in time" (149). "Dread," Eliot's key term for inward trepidation, surfaces as Gwendolen considers that she might miss the mysterious appointment and remain ignorant (151). Gwendolen registers a somatic response and apprehends a generalized threat.

When Lydia Glasher and Gwendolen Harleth meet, both represent their relation to Grandcourt and one another in predominantly economic and reproductive terms, not emotional ones. Lydia gestures to her nearby children, specifies that she left a husband and child for Henleigh Grandcourt, and pointing to her son, declares that Grandcourt "ought to make that boy his heir" (152). Gwendolen's only comment—"I will not interfere with your wishes" (152)—might as readily be made regarding a rental agreement as a romantic relationship. The plot elements are melodramatic; the dialogue, in contrast, is straightforward, restrained, and focused on economic consequences. Even Lydia's one statement of emotion—"it is not fair that he should be happy and I miserable" (152)—is couched concisely in terms of equity. The narrator specifies these "words were uttered in a biting accent, but with a determined abstinence from anything violent in tone or manner" (152). Throughout, narration emphasizes the formality of the women's interaction and bearing. Listening to Lydia, Gwendolen "felt a sort of terror: it was as if some ghastly vision had come to her in a dream and said, 'I am a woman's life'" (152). Gwendolen's feeling is not jealousy, hurt, or outraged pride—no social or complex emotions, but rather the basic physiological response to danger, "terror," within the impersonal context of "woman's life," not her specific relation to her rival or suitor. Reeling inwardly, Gwendolen maintains impeccable outward composure as she carries out her resolve to leave the outing and, if possible, the country without further conversation with Grandcourt. During an evening of gambling with the Langens shortly thereafter, typically vivacious Gwendolen displays emotional detachment she calls being "bored to death" and declares, "If I am to leave off play I must break my arm or my collar-bone. I must make something happen, unless you will go to Switzerland and take me up the Matterhorn" (14). The Cardell Chase encounter and its aftermath position Gwendolen's response to her triangulated relation to Lydia Glasher and Henleigh Grandcourt more in line with the symptomology of nervous shock than that of hysteria: sudden overwhelming fear followed by a period of numbness and personality change. This episode also foregrounds the economic consequences of Grandcourt's behavior to both women, and of Gwendolen's decision to marry or refuse him.

On the day she reneges upon her promise and pledges herself to Grandcourt, Gwendolen vacillates between conflicting impulses: the initially dominant "exulting defiance" (355) and the substrata of "dimly understood facts" and "deeply felt impressions" (354) related to both her displacement of Lydia and her own impending legal subjection to a man of dubious character. At Gwendolen's wedding there persists "an under-consciousness in her that she was a little intoxicated" (355): language suggesting a transient state of heightened energy and impaired judgment, preceding an inevitable crash. On the "railway journey of some fifty miles" (356) to Grandcourt's Ryelands estate her excitement builds, "with an increased vivacity as of a kitten that will not sit quiet to be petted" (357). By the time a carriage conveys the couple down the lane of Gwendolen's magnificent new home, "her usual susceptibility to changes in light and scenery helped to make her heart palpitate newly" (357), a phrase that invokes the interplay of emotional and somatic responses characteristic of nervous excitability.

Visual stimulus acts upon Gwendolen's constitutional predisposition, heightened emotional state, and latent memory. The narrator first asks if this sensation results from Gwendolen's satisfaction at gratified ambition, then offers an alternative explanation: "Was it alone the closeness of this fulfillment that made her heart flutter? or was it some dim forecast, the insistent penetration of suppressed experience, mixing the expectation of triumph with the dread of a crisis? Hers was one of those natures in which exultation inevitably carries an infusion of dread ready to curdle and declare itself" (357). In keeping with Victorian emphasis on the materiality of the psyche through the brain and nervous system, this passage insists on the raw physicality of perception and emotion. We attend the unsteady rhythm of Gwendolen's heart, the "*penetration* of suppressed experience" as memories invade her present moment, the "mixing" of different psychic states, like separate material components, that may cause her mood to "curdle," implying mental life has a texture. The surfacing of "suppressed experience" through physiological stimulus recalls Maudsley's assertion that "there is memory in every nervous cell and, indeed, in every organic element of the body" (*Physiology* 182). Gwendolen's dawning somatic awareness of past experience is not necessarily an indicator of pathology. Within Maudsley's framework, it can be regarded as a normative operation of consciousness, in which sensory stimulus awakens latent memory, as "nothing of which we have had experience can be absolutely forgotten" (*Physiology* 183), even if intentionally put aside. It is unspecified what "suppressed experience" acts upon Gwendolen's high-strung and superstitious nature. But we might hypothesize it is her forcibly suppressed "ghastly vision" of the woman and children she displaced, which to Gwendolen served as a universal emblem of the female condition. Or perhaps the strange psychic alliance of "exultation" and "dread" has roots in Gwendolen's paradoxical youthful experience of being enabled to play at predominance as a direct result of indulgences apologetically granted to make up for her despised stepfather's authority.

Beer and Wood have both addressed Eliot's appropriation of the term "dread," which had scientific and specifically evolutionary and pathological connotations. Beer asserts that Eliot "associates [it] with woman's experience and with enforced passivity," noting connections to hysteria, pregnancy, and maternity within the context of sexual selection (226–27). Wood observes that Maudsley linked fear and dread to morbid egoism and a less evolved state (146–47, 151). This passage, I suggest, demonstrates Eliot's more specific use of the term, which carries a moral valence. Gwendolen's dread—like Hetty Sorrel's, like Mrs. Transome's, even like Daniel's "dread" when he imagines himself a fallen woman's child—inheres in irredeemable, feminized and sexual wrongdoing that produces biological traces and carries economic consequences. Gwendolen chose to supplant Lydia Glasher for economic gain; now she may become pregnant with the son that will seal that disinheritance. Gwendolen's upbringing, with its unstable mixture of luxury and misery, privilege and subjugation, punctuated by her mother's unwelcome childbearing, has led her to this supposedly triumphant wedding. Marriage interpolates her into the system of biological and economic descent that has broken down her beloved mother. In Gwendolen's rising "dread," Eliot rewrites what had been derogatory terminology for women's allegedly less evolved mental physiology. Instead, "dread" here denotes a sophisticated though futile moral response to entrapment in a sex-gender system where chance predominates and women's agency is tightly constrained.

Gwendolen descends from sensitivity into pathology shortly after arrival at Ryelands, when she receives the Grandcourt diamonds with Lydia's note.

The jewels that give aristocratic wealth and privilege a tangible form, displayed upon women but passed down through the male line, catalyze her latent dread. When the packet of diamonds arrives, Gwendolen, unsuspecting of their connection to her predecessor, finds that "in this moment of confused feeling and creeping luxurious languor she was glad of this diversion—glad of such an event as having her own diamonds to try on" (358). What terrifies Gwendolen is the revelation that the diamonds are not, in fact, "her own." Her reaction to the discovery of Lydia's letter enclosed with the diamonds is "as if an adder had lain upon them" (358). Of course, this metaphor calls to mind monitory emblems of dangerous female desire for power: Eve in the garden, Shakespeare's Cleopatra and the adder. But more simply, it denotes a visceral fear response. Shaking, Gwendolen reads "the horrible words of the letter over and over again" (359) until "with a new spasm of terror" she flings it into the fire in hopes of concealing from Grandcourt her interactions with Lydia (359). This act proves futile, as Grandcourt learns the truth of Cardell Chase, and Lydia's words are seared in her own memory. When Grandcourt reenters the room, "the sight of him brought a new *nervous shock,* and Gwendolen screamed again and again with *hysterical* violence" (359; emphasis mine). In a phrase that calls back Lydia's incinerated but well-remembered letter, Gwendolen later tells Daniel that her "dreading to increase my wrongdoing and my remorse" at the usurpation of Lydia has been "like a writing of fire within me" (695). In Gwendolen's physical fear response and unwilling repetition of troubling experience, both immediately and then throughout the novel, modern readers recognize patterns typical of PTSD. Victorian readers would notice that hysteria and nervous shock are each named in this precipitating incident, with Gwendolen's initial and subsequent mental and physiological symptoms mingling both. The precipitating incident, however, accords with normative expectations for neither hysteria nor nervous shock at the time of the novel's writing. It is not a feminine biological life stage or a sudden bodily threat that triggers Gwendolen's pathology. Rather, she descends into nervous disorder upon recognizing, simultaneously, her economic harm to Lydia, and its necessary corollary in Gwendolen's own legal, physical, and emotional vulnerability to Grandcourt, who has shown no regard for her predecessor's well-being.

Gwendolen's subsequent disordered perceptions exaggerate past culpability while emphasizing present helplessness. During her brief marriage, Gwendolen's fixation on her wrongdoing grows (encouraged by Daniel), in tandem with awareness of her husband's malicious dominion over her person (including implied sexual violence) and finances. It is exacerbated by Lush's explication of the will, which shifts benefits to Lydia should Gwendolen fail to produce an heir. She perceives her present suffering in matrimony as proof of the enormity of her past sin. She briefly contemplates a petition for legal separation (newly possible under the Matrimonial Causes Act), but recognizes "she had absolutely nothing she could allege against him in judicious or judicial ears" (603). Gwendolen's misery focuses on her absence of control within marriage despite the presence of personal responsibility in her choice to marry, and perceiving her lack of independent agency, she fantasizes "some possible accident" (673) as her only means of release.

The accident that unexpectedly widows Gwendolen only deepens her simultaneous conviction of both culpability and powerlessness. Grandcourt progressively restricts her social circle and mobility first through yachting and finally, fatally, by isolating her on a small boat with only himself. Grandcourt's drowning, while accidental, arguably results from his own choice to take unnecessary risk, disregarding warnings of sailors who counsel against boating when changes of weather are anticipated (681). Gwendolen, despite being present for that conversation, fixates on her own culpability after the "severe physical shock" (687) of witnessing Grandcourt's accident and leaping into the ocean to join him: She tells Daniel, "I know only that I saw my wish outside me" (696). She explains her simultaneous experience of helplessness and blameworthiness within married life by saying, "I felt a hatred in me that was always working like an evil spirit—contriving things" (689–90). Gwendolen communicates self-alienation: in which the subject experiences her own will as an external destructive force. Her description resonates with modern accounts of PTSD in veterans, whose present reckless or antisocial impulses, disconnected from their conscious goals and values, can be linked to guilt and unprocessed trauma from past violent actions in wartime.[9] Gwendolen's "fragmentary" (691) initial account of the accident to Daniel and subsequent declaration that "things repeat themselves in me so" (770) likewise accord with modern PTSD symptomology.

Yet Gwendolen's response to overwhelming shock reflects the Victorian era's different priorities, which, as Matus argues, foregrounded individual responsibility. George Eliot, Matus suggests, is "less interested in Gwendolen's wounded psyche than in her potential guilt and responsibility for her own pain," as "Eliot's is less a 'wound culture' than a conscience culture" (*Shock* 156, 159). We see the character voice an extreme version of this ideology when Gwendolen tells her mother, "It is because I was always wicked that I am miserable now" (756). She experiences the memory disruptions we now associate with PTSD, but they center on internal self-blame rather than external

9. For an example, see van der Kolk's case study of "Tom" in *The Body Keeps the Score* (7–15).

threat. Following the accident, she recalls little beyond the scope of her own wrongdoing: "Poor Gwendolen's memory had been stunned, and all outside the lava-lit track of her troubled conscience, and her effort to get deliverance from it, lay for her in dim forgetfulness" (772). Memories of blameworthiness crowd out present-day perception: She finds herself "overmastered by those distasteful miserable memories which forced themselves on her as something more real and ample than any new material out of which she could mold her future" (787). In the midst of hysterical grief, she tells her mother, "I shall live. I mean to live. . . . I shall be better" (807), but we may reasonably be skeptical of her potential to develop forward motion. Attempting to recover agency in an unstable and insecure world, Gwendolen fixates on the one moment where she claimed power, her acceptance of Grandcourt's proposal, and its economic consequences for Lydia. Unable or unwilling to accurately perceive the constraints upon her agency in that moment of decision, Gwendolen further conflates her blameworthiness in marrying Grandcourt with her subsequent failure to save him from drowning. Her disordered perception directs the reader's focus along similar retrospective and judgmental tracks.

Eliot situates Gwendolen's increasingly fractured and unstable psyche within women's embodied experience of constrained agency and economic precarity. Victorian understandings of the physiological and psychological symptoms of nervous sensitivity, shock, and hysteria inform Eliot's representation. But in its focus on economic determinants, the novel revises scientific accounts ascribing women's instability to innate biological factors. Gwendolen's intense guilt over the choice she makes to survive within this system is rooted in a childhood injury—one that links her, empathetically and structurally, to Daniel.

SPOILED CHILDREN

Daniel is drawn to both Gwendolen and Mirah by more than his sense of chivalry. The commonality with these women that at once attracts and disconcerts Daniel can be found in lingering traces of the parallel childhood traumas all three "spoiled children" share. Daniel implicitly recognizes this bond when, after rescuing Mirah, he connects her search for lost family with his own questions about his mother (205–6). All three characters bear in adulthood the psychic traces of youthful experience that painfully illustrated the exploitive intersection of sexuality and economic power endemic to patriarchy. Each recognizes, in early adolescence, that traditional patriarchal marriage and inheritance systems require women's exchange of sexual availability or objectification for economic security; crucially, each connects this broad social pattern with a specific economic and emotional injury done to themselves through a parent's error. Their varied responses to injury ultimately bring Daniel and Mirah together, and isolate Gwendolen.

The most obvious implication of titling Book 1, focused on twenty-year-old Gwendolen, "The Spoiled Child" is to draw attention to her self-indulgence and immaturity. Doreen Thierauf also notes this title's linkage to Laycock's medical descriptions of hysteria (447). On further inspection, another meaning surfaces: Gwendolen is permanently blighted by her childhood. The phrase "spoiled child" similarly resonates with Daniel and Mirah. All three were raised apart from at least one natural parent and, in youth, felt their best interests unjustly compromised by the living arrangement. All three, as children and young adolescents, developed knowledge of the intersections between adult sexuality and its financial and emotional consequences that they experienced as shameful and, in confusion, both blamed on a parent and felt as a personal humiliation. All three, despite perceived injustices, were provided with material luxuries that made complaint difficult to justify. What, precisely, did they want for? The injuries were both socially unspeakable for children and difficult to quantify and define. After tracing these parallel childhood traumas with special attention to Eliot's mobilization of the medical language of psychic shock, I address their formative influence on the characters' adult worldview. The troubling associations among property, adult sexuality, and moral guilt that Gwendolen, Daniel, and Mirah learn in youth mold their adult attitudes toward interactions with the opposite sex and patriarchal models of domestic life, determining the trajectories of their relationships with one another.

Gwendolen's youthful trauma receives less explication than Daniel's or Mirah's, which may signal its unprocessed or diffuse nature. We do know several key facts about Gwendolen's childhood unhappiness. First, it is linked to her stepfather, Captain Davilow; second, her negative experiences with him have colored her memory of her biological father, who died in her infancy; and third, she developed in childhood and continued into young adulthood a capacity for sudden aggression, an unpredictable nervous constitution, and an intense drive to preserve her own interests to the exclusion of the valid claims of others. When twelve-year-old Gwendolen's mother shows her a picture of her father, the girl, "immediately thinking of the unlovable step-father," exclaims, "Why did you marry again, mamma? It would have been nicer if you had not." Gwendolen's mother blushes and cries "with a violence quite unusual in her" that "You have no feeling, child!" The girl, "who was fond of her mamma, was hurt and ashamed, and had never since dared to ask a question about her father" (24). This scene efficiently indicates that the stepfather's introduction into the household rapidly became a source of pain and guilt to mother and daughter. Each feels herself at once victim and unwilling victimizer of the other. The guilt is compounded by the fact that Gwendolen's half-sisters, toward whom Gwendolen and her mother are obliged to feel affection, owe their existence to the stepfather's resented presence. Further, the absent father, and hence Gwendolen's heritage, becomes a forbidden topic, because any mention of him conjures the excruciating question of what their family might have been had he lived to prevent the stepfather's incursion. The geographical rootlessness of her youthful lifestyle has a parallel in the emotional and cultural rootlessness of Gwendolen's shrouded family background and the disruption of the most immediate channels for her youthful affections, parents and siblings, that the unhappy second marriage entails.

While the details of Captain Davilow's injury to Gwendolen are up for debate, clues suggest it resonates with the novel's broad concern about problematic intersections between sexuality and control of property. Margaret Loewen Reimer has provocatively suggested that incest by the stepfather is the key to Gwendolen's troubled adult psyche. While I agree wholeheartedly with her contention that "in psychological terms, one sees Gwendolen 'acting out' her anger for the acts done to her, while desperately clinging to a sense of entitlement for what she has endured" (Reimer 39), I do not find convincing the textual evidence that those acts were necessarily incest. Further, reducing the trauma to a sexual or emotional element misses the crucial intersection between sexuality and property, and relatedly Gwendolen's developing awareness of the ways women harm one another through competition within patriarchal systems of marriage and inheritance.

Several aspects of Captain Davilow's negative impact on Gwendolen's life are certain: He controlled the family's lifestyle and his wife's access to money, and his intermittent presence in the household, though unwelcome to both Gwendolen and her mother, resulted in Gwendolen's acquiring four half-sisters. He made a habit of spiriting away his wife's jewelry and selling it, which remains a sore point for Mrs. Davilow (274–75). Upon her widowhood, she promptly establishes residence in an English country house, breaking the family's chain of foreign apartments, an action that "rather mysteriously to Gwendolen, appeared suddenly possible on the death of her step-father" (23). Since we know that even up through her unmarried young adulthood Gwendolen sleeps in a small bed in her mother's room, we can be certain that she would have developed an intimate knowledge of pregnancy and, if not childbirth itself, its aftereffects. Gwendolen describes her mother as the only person whose feelings she has ever much considered (450). Any fear or distaste young Gwendolen would have experienced watching her mother endure the discomfort, uncertainty, and danger that accompanied Victorian pregnancy would have been heightened by developing knowledge that a man they both despised was responsible for her mother's state. Moreover, Gwendolen, who has long considered herself "exceptional" (23), could hardly miss the impact four plain younger sisters have on Mrs. Davilow's ongoing ability to provide her with luxuries, and on her chances of making the splendid marriage that is the only socially appropriate outlet for her ambition. Unsurprisingly, as an unmarried young adult Gwendolen is torn by her conflicting awareness that marriage is "social promotion" and her personal view of it as "rather a dreary state, in which a woman could not do what she liked, had more children than were desirable, was consequently dull, and became irrevocably immersed in humdrum" (39). With marriage and domesticity as her only respectable aims, Gwendolen learns early to associate sexuality and family life with guilt, resentment, and loss of control over one's material circumstances. Moreover, she learns to regard the family unit as an amalgamation of competing claims in which weaker members' interests are inevitably sacrificed. This upbringing paves the way for Gwendolen's adult antipathy to sexuality and incapacity for forming affective bonds. It also determines her never to be the weaker party whose interests are pushed aside and heightens her terror when she perceives herself to be so in the marriage with Grandcourt.

Young Daniel likewise recognizes a guilty and shameful intersection of adult sexuality and control of property; like Gwendolen, he both blames a parental figure and reproaches himself for anger toward an indulgent guardian of whom he is genuinely fond. Sir Hugo Mallinger, who provides Daniel every luxury, including the stable home life Gwendolen lacks, has taught Daniel to call him "uncle." The boy's first instance of doubt—or more accurately, mistaken certainty—regarding their relationship occurs at age thirteen, just as adolescence encroaches. Daniel's idle inquiry, sparked by a history book, regarding the many "nephews" of popes and cardinals leads his tutor to explain the practice of referring to illegitimate children of great men by that term. Suddenly, the boy's connection to his "uncle" takes a troubling new shape. Although he immediately feels a "dread of utterance about any shame connected with [his] parents" (167), he finds that "a secret impression had come to him which had given him something like a new sense in relation to all the elements of his life" (168). This epiphany, described as a "shock" (168), takes on the language of haunting. When the possibility of illegitimacy is introduced, "Daniel felt the presence of a new guest, who seemed to come with an enigmatic veiled face, carrying dimly-conjectured, dreaded revela-

tions" (167). The notion of a veiled alien presence directing the psyche resonates with current formulations of trauma response.

Eliot subtly underscores the economic basis of Daniel's emotional pain by
metaphorically linking his presumed disinheritance, as an illegitimate son, to
the bodily harm done through modern capitalism. The boy's suffering is figured in terms that conjure industrial accidents, in which the carelessness of
the powerful grievously harms the innocent: Daniel "[feels] the injury done
to him as a maimed boy feels the crushed limb which for others is merely
reckoned into an average of accidents" (170). This simile recalls the "working of mines" (159) that further enriches the baronet. Unequal distribution
of wealth is the connecting thread between the victim of industrial accident
and Daniel as disinherited youth. Daniel suffers through an economic system
in which the basic needs of some lives (illegitimate children, laborers, even
hapless rail passengers) are sacrificed to concentrate wealth in the hands of
the few (the industrialist of railways, factories, or mines, the baronet who
inherits entailed lands). Daniel's pain is intensified by his love for Sir Hugo,
whom he imagines as the unthinking instrument of his harm. With the suddenness of accident, Daniel's suspicion of illegitimacy—described as a "revolu-
tionary shock" (172)—violently disrupts their relationship. Sir Hugo's personal
choice not to marry Daniel's mother, and impersonal laws of inheritance, are
presumed equally blameworthy, resulting in Daniel's emotional withdrawal
from Sir Hugo and more general adolescent disillusionment. Like Gwendolen's mother, Daniel's father figure is assumed to have made selfish choices
that harm the offspring, and like Gwendolen, Daniel is too absorbed in his
own sense of injury to consider the parent's limited set of choices within an
established economic game. In Daniel, Eliot draws a nuanced portrait of the
psychic violence that sexual double standards and classism visit on the next
generation, not only through illegitimacy, but also through primogeniture.

Daniel's pain cultivates his feminized inward turn, the reserve and empathy he simultaneously develops in adolescence. We are told Daniel's consciousness of unspeakable knowledge about his mother "set up in him a premature
reserve which helped to intensify his inward experience" (168). Inwardness,
in this novel, is associated with feminine experience, domesticity, and particularly unspoken feminine pain, such as Gwendolen's interiority, which
develops in dynamic relation to her marital misery. Markedly different from
Latimer's self-isolating sensitivity in the earlier novella, Daniel's vulnerable
inwardness is figured as in large part situational (not innate) and productive
of sympathy with, not revulsion from, others. His "sense of injury" generates a
"hatred of all injury" (178), and his desire to rescue takes the feminized forms
of nurture and moral guidance in his care for both Hans Meyrick and Mirah.

His feminized interiority and impulse to rescue the morally weak also define his relationship with Gwendolen, which Ann Cvetkovich has insightfully read as sadomasochistic.[10] As Cvetkovich suggests, while "Daniel's sympathy, the predominant sign of his interiority, is a function of his displaced social position," it "remains the response of a man projecting onto women his relations to the patriarchy, even when it looks like the work of a man who is sensitive enough to turn himself into a woman" (*Mixed Feelings* 153). Believing himself illegitimate, Daniel shares Gwendolen's sense of economic disadvantage within patriarchy, but as a man he seeks different forms of redress.

Like Gwendolen, Daniel acquires some of adulthood's uglier forms of knowledge too young, and like her, in early adolescence, he abruptly lashes out at a beloved parent. A month after his "revelation" (168), the musically talented Daniel is asked by Sir Hugo to sing for company. At the conclusion of the performance, his uncle summons him, after making "a smiling remark to his next neighbor" (168). Daniel seems to have hypothesized that his discarded mother was a musical actress, and suspects his uncle's unheard remark to the friend (perhaps in reality some expression of pride) was a comment regarding Daniel's vocal inheritance. Sir Hugo's query of "What do you say to being a great singer?" (169), teasing praise of Daniel's performance, is taken as an indication that he, like his mother, is the lower-class entertainment, to be enjoyed by Sir Hugo but not belonging to his aristocratic milieu. Daniel, blushing, declares that he would hate it and leaves the room, taking refuge in a window seat that offers a view of the beautiful estate he calls home. Daniel's "ardent clinging nature had appropriated it all with affection," and while he "knew a great deal about what it is to be a gentleman by inheritance," he never before "supposed that he could be shut out from such a lot, or have a very different part of the world from that of the uncle who had petted him" (169). Implicit in these musings is the sinking certainty—which Daniel doesn't dare articulate even inwardly—that if Sir Hugo had sufficient respect for his mother to marry her, the loved home of his boyhood would have passed to him. As an illegitimate child, he understands, he is entitled to nothing. Daniel identifies with the objectified mother his imagination conjures, silently taking her part against the supposed father whom he believes to have done them both a great wrong.

The key difference between this incident and Gwendolen's unthinking reproach of her mother is the reaction of the parent. Gwendolen and her mother, equally injured by the incident and conscious of its import, conspire in their subsequent silence. Sir Hugo, who in fact is neither Daniel's natural father nor his uncle, but his adoptive father and his mother's unsuccessful

---

10. See ch. 6, "The Inside Story: On Sympathy in *Daniel Deronda*," in *Mixed Feelings*.

admirer, fails to recognize the source of Daniel's anger. While aware of the general suppositions about Daniel's parentage, his pride in the boy makes him "pleased with that suspicion" (174), and nothing suggests he understands the motive of Daniel's uncharacteristic outburst or divines the depth of the rift opened between them. He attributes Daniel's being out of sorts to his expectation of impending departure for Eton. While confirmation that he is intended for a gentleman's education pacifies Daniel somewhat, the fissure of distrust widens with Sir Hugo's subsequent marriage to a respectable young lady, not the imagined opera-singer mother whom Daniel believes Sir Hugo tossed aside.

The disparity in Daniel's and Gwendolen's responses to youthful injury is ascribable not only to distinctions of innate temperament, but also to the difference in their interactions with the simultaneously blamed and loved parent. Gwendolen resents her mother's second marriage, but discerns that her mother is also an injured party, and recognizes not only was the individual man to blame, but also the legal and social system of patriarchal marriage. In adolescence, she sets out to redeem—or perhaps revenge—her own and her mother's wrongs by playing the system to win. In contrast with Gwendolen, whose response to a youthful sense of familial injury is to do all she can to insure she is never on the receiving end of it again, Daniel discovers "his mind ripened toward the idea of tolerance of error" (175), and finds himself drawn to people "in proportion to the possibility of his defending them, rescuing them, telling upon their lives with some sort of redeeming influence" (324). It is significant that Daniel, unlike Gwendolen, loves the father figure whom he believes to have caused both himself and his mother personal humiliation and financial hardship. He cannot disentangle his affection for Sir Hugo from his attitude toward patriarchal socioeconomic systems. Daniel identifies with the sexually objectified and legally hindered feminine position. Yet he seeks not only to champion people who are threatened, especially women, but also to direct them toward the path of conventional virtue, as he cannot do for his long-lost, presumably "fallen" mother. Upon rescuing Mirah when she attempts to drown herself in the Thames (a stereotypical fate for fallen women), he thinks, "Perhaps my mother was like this one" (191). Daniel strives to redeem for others what he cannot redeem for himself. While Gwendolen's selfhood has ossified into self-protective vanity, Daniel's has fragmented into intense yet diffuse sympathy. It is key to remember, however, that Daniel's desire to save is inseparable from an impulse to control, which shores up his shaky position within patriarchy: As Marlene Tromp argues, "asserting the authority of this [patrilineal] law with Gwendolen assures his place within a system that threatens to exclude him as a bastard" (228).

Daniel's valuation of lineage is, ironically, modeled and encouraged by his upbringing. He is raised in a grand home that embodies English aristocratic history from the campaigns of William the Conqueror through each epoch of fashion, architecture, and politics, up to the current one in which his so-called uncle is a Whig in Parliament. Under the dumb gaze of a gallery of portraits of Mallinger "descendants, direct and collateral, females of the male line, males of the female" (165), young Daniel implicitly learns to valorize the heritage and personal, biological connection to recorded history that he himself lacks. However disappointing to feminist readers, Daniel's inability to empathize with his actual birth mother, who aggressively rejected the heritage Daniel longingly seeks, and his preference for a chest of historical documents affirming legitimate patrilineal descent, is a predictable result of his upbringing. The type of Jewish identity Daniel embraces affirms the individual's connection to a lengthy history of culture and nation-building through recorded familial descent within a patriarchal social framework.

Daniel's bride is perhaps the one developed character in the book who consistently and uncritically embraces her place within this historicized system of descent. Mirah Cohen Lapidoth, whose lifestyle, family structure, and even name change when her father kidnaps her away from her mother and brother at age six, suffers a more profound childhood disruption of her sense of unified self than do either Gwendolen or Daniel. Yet unlike them, Mirah never forms a strong emotional bond with the parent whom she perceives has done her injury; pity is her strongest emotion for her father (217). She harbors vague but positive memories of her mother and previous home life. While living with her father, Mirah neatly divides her identity into an authentic-feeling private self, cohering around memories of religion and domesticity, and a false but protective public shell, which, whether onstage or off, is acting without emotional investment.

As her mother's singing of Hebrew hymns is one of the few memories that remains clear, Mirah seeks knowledge of the faith practice her father ignores. Since her childhood and adolescence have been defined by hardships of gothic proportion, such as being kidnapped and later threatened with sexual slavery, one might expect Mirah to be more psychically damaged than Gwendolen upon entering adulthood. The contrary is true. Mirah experiences a psychic break only when she finds herself cast out into the public sphere without a domestic haven. After travelling to London alone to elude her father's nefarious plan, Mirah maintains her fragile composure until "blinded and bewildered by the sudden shock" (221) of discovery that her childhood home has been torn down, she attempts suicide in the Thames. But as soon as Daniel settles her in a safe and traditionally feminine home environment with the

Meyricks, she becomes stable and content. The fact Mirah can recount her childhood trauma to Mrs. Meyrick in an unbroken narrative, without any indication of shame, suggests she has come to terms with it in a way Gwendolen and Daniel have not. She can articulate the experience as a closed narrative that does not threaten her present sense of self.

Gwendolen, by contrast, cannot differentiate between the source of her youthful anger, guilt, and anxiety, the domestic relationships she has seen her mother model, and the only available outlet for her own ambition. She is left without a path forward into adulthood or a culturally legible goal within the narrative structure. Unlike Mirah, who mourns a lost domestic angel and seeks to replicate the home life her mother provided, Gwendolen has no defined sense either of what she has lost or of what future role she might embrace. Both temperament and personal history make Gwendolen uniquely ill-suited to the wifely role that is the only culturally commendable narrative available. Daniel, Mirah, and Gwendolen have all been injured by patriarchal family relationships gone awry, but Daniel and Mirah harbor no essential quarrel with patriarchy per se, only with the misuse of patriarchal authority. Gwendolen does not consciously question the validity of traditional family structures, and indeed "would at once have marked herself off from any sort of theoretically or practically reforming women by satirising them" (53), but she cannot imagine integrating herself into the patriarchal family without risking her own interests and stable identity.

Daniel Deronda closes with a socially stabilizing union between an ambitious, politically minded gentleman and a spiritual, domestically inclined lady, whose complementary virtues should satisfy bourgeois sensibilities. Its transgressive and morally ambiguous female protagonist finds her space in the text, and the story's imagined world, reduced; Gwendolen's dissatisfaction is not allowed to intrude upon the novel's conclusion. *No Name* similarly contains its ethically equivocal protagonist, not by cordoning her off, but instead by erasing her rebellious interiority with a well-timed fever, and returning her to consciousness ready to "sacrifice" "her old perversity and her old pride" and be guided in "a new and nobler life" (737) by her conventional sister, new brother-in-law, and a conveniently appearing suitor. The unease readers feel at the mental and physical disintegration of these once independent and physically vital female protagonists differs from the kind of loss modern readers might register at the defeat of the brilliant schemer Lucy Audley or the relegation of the intellectual Dorothea Brooke to a supporting role of reformist politician's wife. Lucy and Dorothea make a series of choices that lead to their respective fates, which, however disappointing to the twenty-first-century reader, align with the governing logic and dominant values of their imagined worlds. Contrastingly, Magdalen and Gwendolen are chastened by chance events just as surely as they are by patriarchal social mores.

Magdalen Vanstone and Gwendolen Harleth inhabit novelistic worlds where feminine interiority is particularly vulnerable to the sudden shocks and ambient anxieties of modern life: not because of any features inherent to female physiology, but rather due to legal structures and cultural conventions leaving ladies, more so than gentlemen, prey to the economic vicissitudes of developing industrial capitalism. The novels present their female protagonists not as pathological by nature, but instead as possessing abundant nerve force and sensitivity that make them uniquely reactive to tensions they encounter and accidents that befall them. Both novels dramatize the psychic and bodily strain of being obliged to act and take moral responsibility for actions within circumstances of constrained agency. They document impediments to stable and empathetic community relations within a world where social mores and legislation have not kept pace with emergent technology and financial systems. Ladies like Magdalen and Gwendolen, of course, were hardly the only or indeed the primary victims of such accidents of modernity. In my final chapter, I examine the equal or greater stressors encountered by ambitious working-class men within industrial capitalism of the mid-to-late Victorian era.

⟨∿⟩

CHAPTER 5

Charles Dickens, Thomas Hardy, and the "Self-Unmade" Man

G reat Expectations and *Jude the Obscure* both feature recognizable elements of the traditional bildungsroman in its English iteration: an orphaned, ambitious young man seeking to rise in the world, formal and social education, a true love and a false, mentor figures, a transition from rural to urban. Yet these novels stubbornly, indeed spectacularly, deny their protagonists the mature social integration we would expect to crown their efforts. Both entail repetition without progression: Pip fails to gain insight from his experiences, and Jude learns from books and social interactions without any opportunity to profit from his knowledge. Pip and Jude exemplify the limits and malformations of Victorian individuality. While the marriage plot increasingly fell short of women's lived experience of growth toward maturity, *Great Expectations* and *Jude the Obscure* evidence the shortcomings of the male ambition plot as a narrative of men's lives under industrial capitalism.

The divergence of these novels from the bildungsroman trajectory they reference has already been noted, of course. In his influential reading, Peter Brooks observes that "whereas the *Bildungsroman* seems to imply progress, a leading forth, and developmental change, Pip's story . . . becomes more and more as it nears its end the working through of past history, an attempted return to the origin as the motivation of all the rest" (134). Foundational as well as more recent readings emphasize the influence of Pip's weak character (in formal or moral senses) on the novel's atypical contours: The protagonist's vacillation, regret, or tendency to be overwhelmed by what is external gives his narrative its shape.[1] *Jude*'s narrative peculiarities have been identified not only as marks of difference but as flaws, notably incoherence of theme and form. Frank Giordano affirms that while the bildungsroman "stresses development into a full, harmonious personality," culminating in the hero's engagement in "an organic, progressive society" (582), *Jude*'s social critique lies in its rendition of "an inevitable and intolerable conflict between the developing individual and the society he has outstripped intellectually, emotionally, and morally" (589). Modern criticism of *Jude the Obscure* often connects the novel's formal experimentation and its radical reimagining of human experience (either how humans experience the world through our senses, or how we find or refuse meaning in our social interactions).[2] *Great Expectations* and *Jude the Obscure* both engage the English bildungsroman tradition in order to subvert its primary goal: the meaningful social integration of the protagonist, solidifying his choice of the "right" values and priorities. Their formal divergences from generic standards follow from this key refusal.

My phrase "self-unmade man" seeks to capture the psychic risk inherent in Victorian socioeconomic mobility. It is inspired by the account a character in Dickens's earlier *Bleak House* gives of his biography. In the midst of shifting class relations attendant on industrialization, George Rouncewell and his brother Robert, sons of an upper servant to Sir Leicester Dedlock, have taken markedly different paths. Both reject the humble stability offered by a life spent, like those of their ancestors, in service to the Dedlocks. Robert enters business and becomes a manufacturing magnate, while George enlists as a dragoon, fails to advance, and bounces between odd jobs after leaving the military until he reaches an unremarkable, financially lean middle age. As

---

1. Emphasis on Pip's weakness (as protagonist or within the novel's imagined world) unifies otherwise disparate interpretations. See Julian Moynahan, "The Hero's Guilt: The Case of *Great Expectations*" (*Essays in Criticism* 1960); Curt Hartog, "The Rape of Miss Havisham" (*Studies in the Novel* 1982); Beth Herst, *The Dickens Hero: Selfhood and Alienation in the Dickens World* (1990); Alex Woloch, *The One vs. the Many: Minor Characters and the Space of the Protagonist in the Novel* (2003); and Aleksandar Stević, *Falling Short: The Bildungsroman and the Crisis of Self-Fashioning* (2020).

2. More recent readings also emphasize the interdependency of the novel's formal experimentation, its biting social critique, and its undermining of assumptions regarding character. Regenia Gagnier calls its murder-suicide conclusion "a parody of the [realist Victorian] novel form's organic closure" that "may be seen as Hardy's rejection of the conventional novel as a realistic form of modern society" (124). See also Norman Prentiss, "The Tortured Form of Jude the Obscure" (1995); Aaron Matz, "Terminal Satire and *Jude the Obscure*" (2006); Kay Young, *Imagining Minds: The Neuro-Aesthetics of Austen, Eliot, and Hardy* (2010); and Claire Jarvis, *Exquisite Masochism: Marriage, Sex, and the Novel Form* (2016).

George tells it when reunited with his mother, instead of "rising to be prosperous and famous" like his brother, he has lived a life "roving, unsettled, not self-made like him, but self-unmade—all my earlier advantages thrown away, all my little learning unlearnt, nothing picked up but what unfitted me for most things that I could think of" (782). George has stayed away from home out of an ashamed sense that his impetuous grasp for adventure and accomplishment has in fact produced the reverse of what he sought. He lives a life made monotonous by economic lack and social irrelevance. George Rouncewell is a minor character in *Bleak House,* but seven years later, in *Great Expectations* (1860–1861), Dickens gives fuller attention to the problem of self-unmaking catalyzed by ambition, allowing Pip to tell this story at length. Thirty-five years subsequent, Thomas Hardy's *Jude the Obscure* (1895) engages the same theme with bitter vehemence. Regenia Gagnier has argued that authentic Victorian working-class narratives do not document the self-reflective individualism that characterizes the literary subject (27–28). What *Great Expectations* and *Jude the Obscure* attempt to do, I suggest, is place working-class male experience in dialogue with the individualistic social and professional ambition that we might call the defining characteristic of both nineteenth-century bourgeois masculinity and the Victorian realist novel.

At the apex of mid-Victorian prosperity and at the century's anxiety-ridden close, Dickens and Hardy ask the same question: What becomes of a working-class youth who catches the spirit of opportunity and advancement that animates industrial capitalism, but cannot actualize it? The repeated failures of their protagonists, which produce repetitive rather than progressive narration, are failures of ambition, either of the protagonist to regulate and direct it productively, or of the society to accommodate the impulse to self-betterment it has inspired. The bildungsroman tells the story of an individual who is exemplary because he is typical of his age and culture; the fates of Pip and Jude sound an alarm about the state of Victorian masculinity. Both novels harness the familiar bildungsroman form to call into question its core assumption: that through the right process of formal and informal education, a young man can situate his unique talents and opinions within a coherent social whole.

THE NERVOUS HERO

In addition to their structural variance from the expected narrative arc, *Great Expectations* and *Jude the Obscure* are, in their depiction of emotion, more aligned with the sensation genre than with realist nineteenth-century novels of self-development.[3] Rapid emotional transitions and extreme psychological states, hallmarks of sensation fiction, were also characteristic of nervous dysfunction in Victorian medical parlance. Dickens's and Hardy's novels of self-unmaking mobilize medical theories to guide characterization and narrative structure. Pip and Jude display what was commonly termed "the nervous temperament," sensitivity to external stimuli connected to modernity and urbanity. This chapter traces how the traditional bildungsroman turns back on itself when male ambition, its driving energy, is pathologized through linkage to nervous dysfunction. Pip and Jude both covet a psychically damaged woman (Estella and by proxy her creator Miss Havisham, Sue Bridehead), and each suffers nervous breakdown when his working-class origins impede his desire for high culture. Their psychic and somatic sensitivity and related collapse suggest symptomology of neurasthenia, a disorder understood as gender-neutral and often coded male. The intellectual history of neurasthenia is intimately bound to nineteenth-century glorification of masculine ambition and its material rewards. The cultural and scientific history of neurasthenia constructed the male body as a medium that passively registered the disruptive economic, technological, and social changes and pressures of its day as the modern man worked to get ahead.[4]

Victorian scientific context throws into relief the sharp critique of socioeconomic systems inherent in how these protagonists fail and how their stories repeat. Reading *Great Expectations* as a record of the nervous temperament in a modern world reveals Pip's overwhelming ambition and persistent self-sabotage as more than symptoms of individual pathology or moral failure. Similarly, considering Jude's fixation on Christminster learning and tortured devotion to Sue in relation to his neurasthenic constitution uncovers a meaningful unity in seemingly disparate aspects of his suffering. The weaknesses of these protagonists can be understood as widespread hazards of Victorian masculinity: Pip and Jude embody failed ambition.

The neurasthenic protagonist was an effective tool for social critique because however severe his debility, he remained within the orbit of cultural and medical normalcy; indeed, his illness typified modern trends. In 1833, thirty-six years before neurasthenia was formally codified, its symptomology and causation were already sufficiently well-known to be played for laughs at the Drury Lane Theatre. In William Bayle Bernard's farce *The Nervous Man and the Man of Nerve*, the leading man, "the head of a large establishment

---

3. See Richard Nemesvari, *Thomas Hardy, Sensationalism, and the Melodramatic Mode*, especially his discussion of *Jude the Obscure*'s "employment of excess, whether physical, emotional, or psychological," "to create sensationalist tragedy" (181).

4. See Oppenheim, ch. 5, "Manly Nerves," in *Shattered Nerves*.

with many clerks under him" (11), claims to be so exhausted by his responsibilities that the slightest noise unsettles his "shattered system" (9). He tells his physician, "I owe my unhappy state to the moral atmosphere of London" (11). He is equally upset by the dampness of his newspaper and the frightening crime stories it contains, which confirm his fear that everyone is out to swindle him (8–9). The play invites laughter at these anxieties, but it takes them seriously: The plot ultimately turns on a con man, "the man of nerve," who impersonates the protagonist to appropriate his country estate. *The Nervous Man and the Man of Nerve* links capitalist achievement and urbanity with moral and bodily danger, even and especially for men who live industrious, blameless lives.[5] Indeed, doctors would insist sufferers like Bernard's hapless hero were on a continuum with healthy men. In an 1878–1879 lecture series entitled "Nervous Exhaustion, or Neurasthenia, in Its Bodily and Mental Relations," physician J. S. Jewell explained that neurasthenia was essentially an intensification of ordinary fatigue, with the key difference that the neurasthenic's bodily resources were not adequately replenished by regular rest (451–52). Summing up contemporaneous scientific knowledge, Jewell suggests all sensation, motion, cognition, and reflex action causes "waste or wear" to the nervous pathways (451). He regards neurasthenia as "simply the carrying of a natural, healthy process, to an unnatural or unhealthy degree" (452). This ailment was not ascribed to constitutional pathology or to unwise or immoral behavior, but rather to everyday processes of social and economic participation. The neurasthenic served as a warning to the ordinary man striving for success, and an indictment to the society that taxed him to the breaking point. In a soberer literary medium than farce, the nervous protagonist expresses the human cost of modern achievement.

Reading protagonists like Pip and Jude through masculine forms of nervous dysfunction helps make sense of their intense physical and emotional responses to economic hardships. Although diagnosed across socioeconomic levels, neurasthenia and nervous exhaustion were most connected to struggles for ascension associated with the professional classes. Particularly, neurasthenia correlated with new models of masculinity in industrialized society; the neurologists who studied and treated it emphasized what historian F. G. Gosling terms "the social origins of stress" (17). The aspiring Victorian gentleman had a vexed relationship with work. Historian John Tosh explains work "held deeply contradictory associations," both "pride in climbing the ladder

---

5. In his linkage of nervous debility and urban business activity, Bernard's character Aspen is more suggestive of the movement toward neurasthenia than of the older diagnostic category for male nervous dysfunction, hypochondriasis, a typically aristocratic complaint and unconnected to the sufferer's work life. See Oppenheim 141–43.

of success, and acquiring the esteem of his peers" and "resentment of the time and toil required, fear of failure at the impersonal hands of the market, and revulsion from the morals of the business world" (34). As the medical record demonstrates, ambition and the exertions it inspired were believed to trigger nervous collapse in men lacking adequate reserves of vigor. In *Great Expectations* and *Jude the Obscure*, Dickens and Hardy intensify the psychic pressures and socioeconomic challenges faced by their ambitious protagonists by situating these characters with distinctly genteel aspirations in working-class origins.

By applying Victorian theories of nervous sensibility to characters born near the bottom of the socioeconomic scale, these novels implicitly challenge negative stereotypes of working-class men. As Vivyan Adair has observed, sociological analyses reveal how the bodies of the poor are constructed as discordant and abject by Western society (1657–60). Drawing both from theoretical knowledge and personal experience of poverty, Adair argues that under industrial capitalism, "the bodies of the poor are produced as sites of moral and intellectual lack and of chaos, pathology, promiscuity, illogic and sloth, juxtaposed always against the order, progress, control and decency of the bodies of allegedly 'deserving citizens'" (1663). As Victoria ascended the throne, such negative constructions of the poor intensified in England, where Malthusian philosophy and working-class social agitation (such as Peterloo and Chartism) fueled bourgeois fears about the loss of social control to purportedly atavistic masses (Young 50–51). The representation of a working-class protagonist as neurasthenic implicitly resists this stigma. Neurasthenics were generally viewed by physicians as refined, sensitive people who registered an acquired social pathology rather than expressed an inherent individual pathology. Neurasthenia was understood as the unfortunate by-product of ambition considered normative and even admirable within a capitalist system. By presenting their protagonists as nervous, these novels, especially *Jude the Obscure*, work against bourgeois stigmatization of working-class men as brutish and lazy. These protagonists are animated by the same desire for accomplishment and inclusion bourgeois Victorian society celebrated, yet they remain trapped in painful economic stasis.

Replacing an ambitious hero with a nervous hero, whose aspirations receive a bodily and psychic check from socioeconomic forces, *Great Expectations* and *Jude the Obscure* produce narratives whose circularity questions the value (in Pip's case) or the possibility (in Jude's) of socioeconomic mobility. It is crucial to my argument that both Pip and Jude are truly working-class men by birth, not, like John Halifax or Oliver Twist, hereditary gentlemen in disguise. The traditional bildungsroman belongs to the ambitious middle-class hero, whose merit allows him to rise. When the hero of a Victorian novel aspires to be a gentleman, he is not only seeking material wealth and social influence, but engaging in a Smilesian process of self-improvement with moral and, potentially, reformist political implications.[6] As Arlene Young contends, "middle class identity is both sustained and defined by the myth of progress embodied in the nineteenth-century bourgeois novel. This progress is typically highly personal and individualistic, involving a process of coming to understand the self" (46). By casting working-class men in this role, Dickens and Hardy appear to challenge bourgeois hegemony on upward mobility. However, their protagonists, as nervous sufferers, are ultimately undone (in a literal, embodied sense of the term) by the very ambition that seems to mark them out as worthy of advancement. Pip and Jude take differing attitudes toward the work social ascension entails, with Pip attempting to efface it entirely and Jude embracing its performance as a demonstration of virtue. Yet the end result is similar: mental and physical breakdown for the protagonist, and accordingly, a narrative that repeats and stalls rather than achieving progression. In their psychic and somatic collapse, Pip and Jude illustrate the overwhelming pressure of masculine competition and its destructive, in modern parlance traumatizing, consequences. Dickens and Hardy implicitly criticize not only the contemporary society that discourages ambitious working-class men, but also the bildungsroman form that excludes them from its narrative arc. Despite parallel trajectories, the contrasting fates of early-to-mid-century Pip, who lives in bourgeois respectability, and fin de siècle Jude, who dies in poverty, shame, and despair, illustrate related cultural shifts.

"LIFE AT HIGH-PRESSURE": NEURASTHENIA AND MODERN AMBITION

In the mid-to-late Victorian era, British, European, and American medical communities sought a comprehensive understanding of nervous exhaustion to connect disparate symptoms that straddled the mind/body divide and seemed increasingly to plague modern life. The term "neurasthenia" was coined in the US, with etiology of the disorder linked to the fast-paced US culture and, secondarily, the temperate North American climate, but British, French, and German physicians rapidly co-opted the terminology to describe

---

6. See Robin Gilmour, ch. 1, "The Idea of a Gentleman" in *The Idea of the Gentleman in the Victorian Novel*.

the ills engendered by their nations' socioeconomic pressures.[7] When in 1869 American physician George Beard first attached the term "neurasthenia" to a cluster of psychological and somatic symptoms related to disruption or depletion of nerve force, he was not so much introducing a new disorder as providing diagnostic criteria for commonly reported medical problems (Chatel and Peele 1639). In an 1880 essay extending earlier work, Beard presents a list of over eighty known symptoms ranging from the physical (pain in the back or feet, "abnormal dryness of skin") to the psychological ("fear of open places or of closed places," "deficient mental control," "hopelessness") and including symptoms of an ambiguously mental or bodily nature ("a feeling of profound exhaustion unaccompanied by positive pain," "special ideosyncrasies in regard to food") (7–8). Far-flung though these symptoms may seem, Beard offers a straightforward explanation of their etiology: "Nervousness is nervelessness—a lack of nerve force" (5). Attentive to the potential for misdiagnosis given his long list of possible symptoms, Beard separates nervousness from psychological states and bodily injuries that produce similar effects but have different causation (1–5, 15). Nervousness, in Beard's understanding, is a potentially recoverable depletion of mental and bodily energy caused by emotional, intellectual, or physical overtaxing of natural reserves (10). Beard employs metaphors of an overdrawn bank account (9) and depleted battery (10) to illustrate the concept, stipulating that as a rich man can spend more without bankruptcy, so an individual with greater natural reserves of nerve force can undergo greater exertions and stressors without breakdown (9–10). In sum, Beard declares, "nervousness is a physical and not a mental state, and its phenomena do not come from emotional excess or excitability or from organic disease but from nervous debility and irritability" (17). He identifies the ailment as a functional disorder that originates from somatic problems, but cannot be localized within a particular lesion or injury perceptible by his contemporary science. Two key points to take from Beard are his positioning of nervousness as liminal between the mental and the physical and his implication that virtually any individual has the potential both to fall prey to, and recover from, nervous exhaustion. The popularity of this diagnostic category with physicians and their respectable middle-class clientele may be linked to its synthesis of bodily causes and psychic effects: It provided a nonstigmatizing rubric under which to treat psychological symptoms.

---

7. Edward Shorter traces the migration of American terminologies and treatments to British, French, and German spas and nerve clinics in his chapter entitled "Nerves" in *A History of Psychiatry*. F. G. Gosling offers a comprehensive account of the disease within the US in *Before Freud: Neurasthenia and the American Medical Community, 1870–1910*.

Neurasthenia or nervous exhaustion (Beard and others used these terms interchangeably) was a gender-neutral diagnosis that cast no aspersions on the sufferer's character. If anything, it was likelier to be coded masculine, and ascribed to the stressors modern commerce, politics, and intellectual application inflicted upon modern urban men. It typically afflicted men in the prime of life: their peak period of economic exertion (Oppenheim 144–45). While the imprecision of Victorian nervous diagnoses makes it difficult to draw a clear dividing line, the emerging diagnosis of neurasthenia and the more amorphous "nervous exhaustion" may be differentiated from another typically male nervous disorder, the older hypochondriasis or popularly, hypochondria. Hypochondria was associated more with elites (as opposed to middle-class strivers) and typified by intense anxieties focused on bodily illness; it was generally treated as constitutional rather than triggered by any discrete event.[8] Neurasthenia, in contrast, was understood as being brought about by an external event and/or ongoing socioeconomic behaviors and environmental stimuli, and therefore associated with more positive outcomes when lifestyle changes were possible.

Neurasthenia was regarded as a risk for self-harm but not as a precursor to inevitable loss of reason: As late as 1899, Thomas Allbutt, MD, Regius Professor at the University of Cambridge, warned that "neurasthenia patients are apt to be suicidal," yet stipulated, "although I have to indicate the dangers of insanity in neurasthenia, the transition is not one of ordinary anticipation" (140). His prognosis for the neurasthenic is more optimistic than for the hysteric, hypochondriac, or sufferer of insane delusions, as the neurasthenic has a "mind . . . open to argument, and his heart to hope" (155). British physician Thomas Stretch Dowse, in his tome on nerve exhaustion published in 1880 and in its fourth edition by 1894, presents a typical example of nervous prostration as a "strong, athletic, active man, with nerves like iron bands, the head of a great business firm, a man of great capacity and business powers, regular in his habits," who fails badly in an effort to expand his company's trade, suffering a severe reversal of fortune, and as a result finds himself physically weak, unable to sleep well, exercise, or focus mentally (27). Not only his bodily constitution but his entire character, Dowse explains, is changed: It is now "remarkable only for its feebleness, irresolution, indecision, hesitancy, vacillation, doubt, dread, and capriciousness" (28). Dowse echoes Beard and other practitioners when he asserts that "professional men . . . seem to be more prone to these attacks of brain exhaustion than others" (53), and ascribes the

---

8. On hypochondria, see Jane Wood, ch. 2, "Nervous Sensibility and Ideals of Manliness," especially 59–63, in *Passion and Pathology in Victorian Fiction.*

contemporary spike in nervous disorder to "life at high-pressure [which] is the prominent feature of the nineteenth century" (51). Such an etiology continues the eighteenth-century thread of interpreting nervous disorder as a pathological response to overstimulation, but shifts it from an aristocratic affliction of overindulgence to a bourgeois plight of overexertion. Despite its association with conventionally masculine public-sphere ambition, neurasthenia, Oppenheim observes, "brought men perilously close to the feminine condition" by "reducing its male victims to passivity, removing them from business activities and public affairs, rendering them utterly indecisive" (141). Ironically, this disorder associated with striving urban professional men often sent its victims to the country for treatments whose cardinal points were complete mental and physical rest in a domestic environment. Neurasthenia's effect was to confuse gendered categories or convert one extreme into another. Whereas Victorian women's nervous diagnoses were often read as commentary on the sufferer's faulty sexual or family life, male nervous disorders signaled the sufferer's incapacity for economic participation.

Ambition—economic, social, or educational—is the key factor differentiating neurasthenia/nervous exhaustion from other male nervous complaints and their literary representation. Victorian understandings of nervous ailments as functional disorders rather than organic diseases made it difficult to scientifically justify firmly gender-segregated diagnoses, but gendered associations persisted nonetheless (Wood 62–63). Jane Wood observes that "in spite of the rapid developments in neurological science, the taint of effeminacy which attached to all forms of male nervous disorder was extraordinarily difficult to eradicate" (67). In neurasthenia, however, the male sufferer was not inherently or consistently effeminate by Victorian cultural standards; rather, his excessive masculine striving in combination with nervous susceptibility led to collapse in feminized passivity.

This subtly distinguishes a protagonist like Pip or Jude from one like George Eliot's Latimer in *The Lifted Veil*, who better aligns with hypochondria. Latimer, who develops a limited but real ability to read minds and inwardly see distant events and places, exceeds the boundaries of realist representation, even as his symptomology demonstrates grounding in physiological theories of the author's day. His ambiguous "power" or "disease" (12) is not so much extrasensory as it is an intensification of the normative interactions of senses and brain processing stimuli. Wood insightfully observes how "Latimer's diseased perception is described in language which draws attention to its slippage from, or its superfluity in relation to, an implied norm" (93). He perceives things that are potentially available to his conscious knowledge, but not immediately at hand. This ability is portrayed as an outgrowth of Latimer's innate sensitivity, which connects with his pointed lack of ambition and vitality: especially in comparison to his father, "a firm, unbending, intensely orderly man, in root and stem a banker, but with a flourishing graft of the active landholder, aspiring to county influence" (5), and his athletic brother, who "would probably have stood for the borough at the next election" (28) if not killed by a chance fall from his horse. From childhood onward, Latimer possesses "the poet's sensibility without his voice" (7). He is troubled by intense awareness of the negative emotions of others, especially as directed at him, and his "nervous fatigue" (30) entails both these social causes and profoundly negative self-assessments of his physical appearance and health. Notably, Latimer is born to wealth and ease, as aligns with eighteenth- and early-nineteenth-century representations of hypochondria as a disorder of the elite. His is a narrative of social endurance and economic stability, in which his only changes in geographical location (sojourn in and return from Geneva) and social status (marriage to Bertha) are substantially engineered by his father's wishes.[9] It is in no sense a bildungsroman. Pip and Jude, in contrast, lack Latimer's financial resources and social connections, but have what initially appear to be the great advantages of ambition and bodily vitality, which allow geographical, social, and potentially even economic mobility, situating their stories within the bildungsroman genre even as their working-class origins make its traditional progression impossible.

When ambition becomes a site of conflict instead of a source of forward momentum, the bildungsroman changes. The rise of neurasthenia demonstrates how in the literary era of what Peter Brooks termed "the ambitious hero" (39), ambition itself was a vexed question. Brooks suggests "a defining characteristic of the modern novel (as of bourgeois society) is that it takes aspiration, getting ahead, seriously, rather than simply as the object of satire" (39). Yet according to Victorian physicians, modern economic and social opportunities brought with them modern psychological and physiological dangers. They believed "the frantic pace of life devoted to the relentless pursuit and display of affluence, without adequate time for mental repose and physical relaxation, drained nerve force faster than countless men and women could replenish it" (Oppenheim 101). It is telling that one of the most memorable Victorian novels featuring an ambitious hero, Dickens's *Great Expectations,* presents ambition as deeply problematic: not simply as a character trait to be moderated or chastised within the imagined world of story, but as a faulty narrative motor, insufficient to power the novel to satisfactory closure.

---

9. Significantly, the path of Latimer's "foreign" (42) wandering after his split from Bertha is unspecified and all but excised from narrative discourse, reduced to two sentences.

Despite their melodramatic events, *Great Expectations* and *Jude the Obscure* produce an odd sense of stasis: as if opposing forces have canceled the possibility of forward progress. Both are characterized by repetitions: Pip's rejection of father figures (Joe and Magwitch), Jude's multiple, abortive efforts to start over in a new city, and both men's tireless pursuit of a damaged and capricious love object. Nonetheless it is the novels' conclusions that are most productive of this sense that meaningful transformation is unattainable. As *Great Expectations* draws to its ambivalent close, Pip is still unmarried yet entranced with Estella, his expectations in all senses unrealized. Biddy and Joe remain the emotional center of hearth and home, whom Pip admires but with whom he, as the ever-aspiring gentleman, cannot fully identify. The bleaker conclusion of *Jude the Obscure* similarly leaves its protagonist very much where he started: Sue, his love, has remarried her husband, Jude has remarried his wife, Jude and Sue's union has been brutally effaced by the deaths of their children, Jude remains reverent of a Christminster that has no use for him, and most important, the socioeconomic systems that he and Sue challenged remain undisturbed. Pip lives chastened, and Jude dies embittered, but neither protagonist has fulfilled or renounced the desires that set the story in motion.

These bildungsroman have closed in the sense that the protagonist's youth has ended: for Pip, in unremarkable middle-aged bachelorhood, and for Jude, in weary and lonely death. But the texts have not fulfilled the task Moretti identifies as the primary goal of the traditional English bildungsroman; they have not "establishe[d] a classification different from the initial one but nonetheless perfectly clear and stable" (7). The sense of stasis these novels produce results from the irresolution of their endings: The protagonist has not successfully integrated into society, nor has the author, in his protagonist's choices, solidified a definitive set of values. The disequilibrium D. A. Miller posits as the impetus of narration remains in place. We may understand this irresolution through each protagonist's vexed relation to work. Nancy Armstrong has recently argued that whereas traditional bildungsroman protagonists acquire narrative value and achieve resolution by transcending their need to work for pay, twenty-first-century bildungsroman protagonists can display only limited development because technologies already enable bourgeois subjects to opt out of productive labor ("Why" 2091–93). Pip and especially Jude may be regarded as inhabiting a midpoint in the financial and technological transitions that transform the bourgeois subject's relationship to productive labor.

The readerly dissatisfaction their endings produce attains new significance when considered in relation to the pathological nature of the ambition that drives each protagonist toward his conclusion. To Victorian audiences, characters like Pip and Jude would be recognizable as sufferers of what was variously termed "nervousness," "nervous exhaustion," and "neurasthenia." Both are physically strong, intellectually able men who at key points break down, in body and mind, in the face of blocked ambitions and frustrated desires, overwhelmed by their own futile efforts. Reading these novels through neurasthenia enables us better to see them as meditations on the cost of modern ambition, and reading them together allows us to trace a progression in ideas about masculinity and social mobility as early-to-mid-Victorian optimism gave way to late-Victorian political and cultural crisis. Unease about the consequences of ambition and the effects of social mobility is registered in each novel's inability to satisfactorily place its protagonist. The close of *Great Expectations*, which Dickens is known to have wrestled with, cannot situate Pip: It is unclear whether he will marry or separate from Estella and whether he will remain in England or return to his merchant's post abroad. His class identity is also ambiguous; he is genteel, but not a leisured gentleman, and his renewed ties to working-class Joe seem incompatible with future union with a lady of Estella's rank. Thirty-five years later, Thomas Hardy conveys no such uncertainty about the fate of *his* ambitious working-class hero; society has no place for the aspirations of the protagonist or the swelling ranks of men like him. Jude dies alienated both from his working-class origins and from the intellectual and professional realms to which he aspires, abandoned by the one woman who shared his vision of a more equitable society. Neurasthenia, the disease culturally linked to blocked ambition and capitalist overexertion, provides imaginative language for the implosion of the male ambition plot as it seeks to accommodate aspirants drawn from the working classes.

The symptomology of neurasthenia represents a Victorian medical and cultural model of thwarted ambition. Male neurasthenia's central characteristic is the collapse of an excessive performance of the most revered masculine qualities into an assemblage of the most reviled traits coded feminine. The assertive, decisive, intellectually and physically powerful man is reduced to irritability, fickleness, and fearfulness. As Beard's and Dowse's perspectives indicate, the nineteenth-century medical community blamed its contemporary economic environment for placing unprecedented pressure on masculine achievement. Victorian readers of Dickens and Hardy would recognize in Pip and Jude both broad personality types and specific symptoms associated with "nervousness," and could read their stories within the framework of cultural and medical debates about consequences of modern ambition. In both *Great Expectations* and *Jude the Obscure*, the protagonist's lacking self-will and tainted desires hobble his progress toward meaningful social integration.

"THE OPPRESSIVE STRENGTH OF HIS AFFECTION":
PATHOLOGIZED DESIRES

Limited agency and pathologized desire are interrelated problems for Pip and Jude. In place of self-directed assertion, these protagonists are motivated by desires they cannot rationalize or explain, attractions to women and to urban environments that prove damaged and corrupting. A comparison with an earlier Dickens hero is illustrative: At ten, David Copperfield takes stock of his bleak future as a factory hand for his cold-hearted stepfather and decides to better himself. He avers, "I had no intention of passing many more weary days there. No. I had resolved to run away" (170) and seek aid from his one remaining blood relation, his aunt Betsey Trotwood. While David does not know "how this desperate idea came into [his] brain," he finds that before long it "hardened into a purpose than which I have never entertained a more determined purpose in my life" (170–71). David's goal, releasing himself from drudgery through application to a potentially sympathetic relative, is reasonable and moderate, and his execution in carrying the plan out is logical: He seeks information about his aunt's whereabouts from a mutual acquaintance and borrows the modest sum he needs to convey himself there. Whatever moral and practical errors David makes throughout his life, he continues to display this capacity for identifying an attainable and socially acceptable object of desire (career, romantic interest) and taking the necessary steps to secure it. Even his ill-starred first marriage to Dora Spenlow results from a thoroughly conventional, superficially practical choice of love object: his employer's daughter. David becomes progressively more socially connected as he strives to attain his desires; both Pip and Jude, by contrast, inadvertently alienate themselves.

Attenuated self-will is both a trademark symptom of nervous collapse and an impediment to the bildungsroman protagonist's progress toward mature social integration. Before outlining the repetitive, stalling narratives that result from Pip's and Jude's thwarted ambitions, I will first explore the nature of those desires and their objects. Dickens and Hardy portray these men's concrete objects of desire—the women they love and the cities that contain their aspirations—as inherently problematic, in ways that typify dangers of modernity. Pip and Jude do not, like David, form deliberate intentions and decisively act; rather, they are drawn through the narrative by intense, unregulated desires. Jude, for example, is undone by "the oppressive strength of his affection for Sue" (177) as much as the contrariety of Sue herself. Both protagonists are dominated by desires that exceed conscious control.

The most powerful driving force of *Great Expectations*, Pip's love for Estella, functions as if it were an external force overriding his conscious will. Pip's fusion of erotic and economic desire, centered on efforts to win Estella, consistently defies the narrator-protagonist's own powers of explanation. Pip claims, "I loved her simply because I found her irresistible," "against reason, against promise, against peace, against hope, against happiness, against all discouragement that could be" (232). Reason and the "discouragement" of wise friends' advice should be tools of the bildungsroman protagonist's upward climb; promise and hope motivate him, and peace and happiness crown his successful labors. Pip's attraction to Estella is the force that negates these standard bildungsroman elements and indeed, renders them irrelevant. Estella is simply "irresistible," a force that draws the protagonist's consciousness forward through life, and through the text, without necessitating explanation. Throughout much of *Great Expectations*, the vacuum of Pip's selfhood is filled with desire for Estella and the world she emblematizes.

Estella's attraction lies in the way she exposes the constructed nature of privilege and permeability of class boundaries. Pip is cognizant that Estella's coquettish drawing-room persona is a performance learned from Miss Havisham's tutelage. More important, he knows from the outset that her class identity, to which he aspires, is likewise manufactured. Long before Pip learns Estella is the natural daughter of an impoverished, unmarried criminal couple (therefore born lower on the class scale than Pip himself), he is aware that she is adopted, rather than descended from the genteel Havisham line. Moreover, Estella's adoptive mother is herself from a family of relatively recent upper-class vintage; her father made his fortune trading beer brewed on-site at Satis House. That the feminized leisure of Miss Havisham and Estella originates in male commercial enterprise is underscored for young Pip when he explores the empty brewery casks upon his first visit. Given her unique circumstances, Estella's poised hauteur has a different resonance from that of an heiress of old aristocratic heritage, for instance, *Jane Eyre*'s Blanche Ingram. Without legitimate upper-class biological descent, living isolated with an eccentric invalid in the darkened, rotting wreck of a grand house, Estella may have as much cause to be "ashamed of home" (125) as does Pip, who admits it. The "self-possessed" (56) Estella maintains impressive composure in the face of circumstances that could as easily be uncomfortable for her as for the child she calls the "common labouring-boy" and treats with "disdain" (60). That Pip senses this potential for Estella's embarrassment is evidenced in his protective resistance to telling Mrs. Joe and Pumblechook about her home life.[10] Estel-

---

10. Young Pip "felt convinced that Miss Havisham too would not be understood" and felt "there would be something coarse and treacherous in my dragging her as she really was (to say

la's enduring attraction, which Pip claims is inexplicable, inheres in how she demonstrates that economic mobility and confident performance of upper-class identity are attainable for an individual of low origins with a socially abnormal domestic life.

Pip connects Estella, shamefully and inevitably, with economic striving. Upon reuniting with grown Estella returned from France, he reflects,

> Truly it was impossible to dissociate her presence from all those wretched hankerings after money and gentility that had disturbed my boyhood—from those ill-regulated aspirations that had first made me ashamed of home and Joe—from all those visions that had raised her face in the glowing fire, struck it out of the iron on the anvil, extracted it from the darkness of night to look in at the wooden window of the forge and flit away. In a word, it was impossible for me to separate her, in the past or in the present, from the innermost life of my life. (235–36)

The inseparability of desire for Estella from Pip's broader ambition is noted elsewhere (247, 272, 364), by both Pip and Herbert, but it finds its clearest articulation here. Pip associates not only "money and gentility" with Estella, but his own desire for them. The phrase "ill-regulated aspirations" suggests the excessive ambition Victorian doctors believed instigated nervous exhaustion, and also implies a properly scaled and disciplined ambition could be a productive force. Significantly, the language of this passage fuses the leisured, wealthy Estella with Pip's physical labor at the forge. Not only does her face haunt him in the "glowing fire," it is "struck . . . out of the iron on the anvil," it is "extracted" as from raw materials in a factory—Estella herself is produced through manual labor. Of course, the same might be said of any fine lady whose leisure is underwritten by bodily hardship of the working classes. But Pip is acutely conscious of Estella's entanglement in his own manual labor and economic ambition. Moreover, he imaginatively places Estella at the window of Joe's forge, subtly suggesting an awareness that she is not in fact so fully removed from the "common" and "coarse" (60) way of life she has openly scorned. When Pip as narrator envisions her as she "flits away" from the forge, he may imply recognition of the shame Estella would feel were she cognizant of her true antecedents: Magwitch and Molly. Perhaps Estella is the only fine young lady Pip as narrator even bothers to describe, let alone loves, because

---

nothing of Miss Estella) before the contemplation of Mrs. Joe" (66). During his later apprenticeship he adds, "That shrinking from having Miss Havisham and Estella discussed, which had come upon me in the beginning, grew much more potent as time went on" (96).

she is the one who, in her very person, makes class ascension a visible reality to him.

Jude Fawley's romantic interests are more fully drawn characters than Estella, and therefore impossible to reduce to aspects of the protagonist's psyche. Arabella Donn, the wife happenstance foists upon him, and Sue Bridehead, his lover and intellectual companion, are developed individuals, distinct from one another and from Jude's public-sphere goal of achievement through religion and learning. Jude appears more assertive and capable than does Pip, yet he, too, is portrayed as overly susceptible to social forces and indeed hypersensitive to physical environment. Like Pip, Jude gives in to desires that run contrary to his conscious intention. Equally unreasoning as Pip's devotion to Estella, Jude's fixation on Christminster is "more nearly related to the emotional side of him than to the intellectual" (77). The fact that his aunt's photograph of his pretty cousin Sue, resident in the chosen city, "formed a quickening ingredient in his latent intent" (78) of going there underscores the conflation of erotic desire and socioeconomic aspiration.

Unlike Pip's desire for Estella, which aligns with his ambition for class ascension, Jude's erotic desires always undercut his socioeconomic ones. Jill Ehnenn quite credibly reads his relationship behavior within the historical frame of "erotolepsy," "a term coined by Hardy to denote a more reckless and intense form of sexual desire than erotomania," which exceeds the state-regulated compulsory reproductive heterosexuality of marriage that Hardy critiques (160). Jude cannot moderate and direct his erotic desires. In an emblematic early scene, both his literal momentum and his professional ambitions are interrupted when, walking home from his stonemason's work and contemplating his future as a bishop, he finds himself transfixed by Arabella's fleshly appeal. In their first conversation, "the unvoiced call of woman to man, which was uttered very distinctly by Arabella's personality, held Jude to the spot against his intention—almost against his will, and in a way new to his experience" (40). Arabella's attraction is universalized: It is not her specific physicality any more than her unique psyche that appeals to Jude. Rather, she awakens new awareness of sexuality, which the narrator figures as a realm of female agency and male passivity: "the unvoiced call of woman to man." Jude is arrested in place by a desire represented as at odds with his conscious goals and almost outside of his selfhood. He soon turns from dutiful study of ancient Greek to afternoons courting Arabella, "as if materially, a compelling arm of extraordinary muscular power seized hold of him" (44), despite realizing she is "quite antipathetic to that side of him which had been occupied with literary study and the magnificent Christminster dream" (41). Jude swings wildly between ascetic scholarship in the service of economic ambition and sensual indulgence that will financially hobble him. He fails entirely at self-regulation.

The women Jude Fawley longs for are clearly and self-consciously products of their historical moment, unlike Estella, who seamlessly performs a timeless simulacrum of aristocratic identity. Different though they are, Arabella and Sue are both explicitly associated with modernity and the city. Arabella, despite rural birth, is linked to the mass production, modern commerce, and female consumerism of the late-Victorian urban milieu. Her work as a barmaid enmeshes her in the production of entertainment and facilitates her mobility across the globe. Reflecting bitterly on how easily his new wife has been influenced and molded by town life, Jude observes that she belongs to the class of women with "an instinct toward artificiality in their very blood" (59). Her fake hair, purchased love philter, and "optional dimples" (291) position Arabella as at once consumer and purveyor of feminine attractions, an active and eager participant in her own commercial transformation and sale. Whereas Arabella is associated with material and economic changes of modernity, Sue, in contrast, demonstrates emotional and intellectual aspects of rapidly shifting fin de siècle urban life. She displays stereotypical markers of what would come to be termed the "New Woman": intellectual attainment, principled rejection of traditional religion, physical activity, and unconventional attitudes about sexuality. She disdains those whose "philosophy only recognizes [male/female] relations based on animal desire" (167). Elizabeth Langland identifies Jude's connection with Sue as indicative of his rejection of rigid, class-bound constructions of masculinity typical of the late-Victorian period. On first meeting Sue in Christminster, Jude finds her "a revelation of a woman" (102), explicitly associating her "pitch of niceness" (90) with her London experiences. Both women Jude desires are, in their various ways, products of the modern city, women who would not have been possible in an earlier era.

Hardy's characterization is informed by thorough an acquaintance with psychology and neurology developed through extensive reading (including, notably, Henry Maudsley) and social connections with professionals.[11] Among the overwhelmingly negative reviews that Hardy's final novel met with, one positive assessment came from physician and human sexuality researcher Havelock Ellis, an established Hardy admirer, who, in an essay first published in *The Savoy* in 1896, called *Jude* "the greatest novel written in England for many years" (15). By the time Ellis's essay appeared, critics had bitterly attacked *Jude* on the grounds of its indecency, its hostility toward marriage and religion, its pessimism and focus on failure, and the pathology of its char-

---

11. See Keen, ch. 1, "Psychological Influences on Hardy," in *Thomas Hardy's Brains*.

acters, especially Sue Bridehead (Wright 180–99). Countering the last charge, Ellis alleges that readers calling Sue "neurotic" should recognize that "many a charming 'urban miss' of their own acquaintance would deserve the name at least as well" (28). He continues, "in representing Jude and Sue as belonging to a family of failing stock," Hardy does not "bring before us a mere monstrosity, a pathological 'case,'" but instead shows "the channels of least resistance along which the forces of life most impetuously rush" (28–29). Ellis's language calls up the concept of nerve force, an organic vitality that the cultural environment and material conditions can direct productively or check disastrously. He implies that mutilating socioeconomic forces bear much blame for the wreck of Jude and Sue's unconventional union.

Sue's despairing moods and extreme actions follow directly from social constraints or condemnations that grate against her deeply held values and intellectual positions, often in ways that materially affect her liberty and livelihood. When word spreads through Aldbrickham that Jude and Sue have been secretly married after living together unmarried, the local men cease to lift their hats to her as she runs her errands, and "the neighbouring artizans' wives looked straight along the pavement when they encountered her" (299). Jude and Sue's "temperaments were precisely of a kind to suffer under this atmosphere" (299), and social condemnation is worsened by its economic consequence: Jude begins to have difficulty finding work. Sue discerns the origins of her emotional state, declaring to Jude through her tears, "I am much depressed by the way they look at me here" (299). Sue is at this point pregnant, but neither she, Jude, nor the narrator ascribes her dark emotional excess to uniquely feminine physiology. Negative affect is produced through the interplay of cultural and economic injustices: not only Sue's social alienation that results from sexual double standards, but also the impact of these mores on Jude's employment, which leads to their poverty. Sue experiences disapproving looks almost as a bodily assault, but she is not irrational in doing so: She correctly understands their economic impact on the family when she tells Jude, "I wish we could both follow an occupation in which personal circumstances don't count. . . . I am as disqualified for teaching as you are for ecclesiastical art" (306–7). Hardy suggests it is not his protagonists' nervous energy that is pathological, but rather the socioeconomic structures that misdirect and deform it.

All three of Jude's attractions—to Arabella, Sue, and Christminster—are described in similar language, and have similarly wasting effects. These parallels invite the reader to question whether Jude's desire for Christminster, which he sees as a new Jerusalem, is fundamentally different from, let alone more admirable than, his erotic desire for either woman. In his boyhood, Jude is "so romantically attached to Christminster that, like a young lover alluding to his mistress, he felt bashful at mentioning its name" (24). As when pursuing a love interest, the isolated Jude studying alone in Christminster discovers "his desire absorbed him, and left no part of him to weigh its practicability" (87). Here the desire under discussion is for education, not sexual or romantic gratification. Later, Sue will declare "Christminster is a sort of fixed vision with him, which . . . he'll never be cured of believing in" (313), equating his devotion to illness. Jude himself concedes that despite resounding disappointment, Christminster remains "the centre of the universe to me, because of my early dream" (320). This fidelity to the love object's illusory virtues in the face of its less admirable realities resonates not only with Jude's changeless dedication to Sue but also with his earlier self-delusion regarding Arabella's proven limitations: "His idea of her was the thing of most consequence, not Arabella herself" (57). Jude finally recognizes his aspiration for Christminster inclusion as a mere "infatuation" (329). His self-destructive attraction to the learned city mirrors even as it competes with his attraction to women.

For both Pip and Jude, a city becomes the locus of pathologized desires. Although Dickens's London, capital of government, finance, and society, differs markedly from Hardy's Christminster, center of scholarship and faith, both literally contain the protagonist's objects of desire and figuratively represent his struggle to place himself within a meaningful community. As James Donald argues, "*the city* provides an imagery for the way we represent ourselves as actors in the theatre of the world, and for what it feels like to act out that drama of the self on that stage" (96). Pip and Jude strive to fashion new identities as they move from rural to urban locations; for both men, social acceptance in the desired city as the partner of the desired woman would presumably signify class ascension and emotional fulfillment. But neither Pip nor Jude can socioeconomically establish himself within an urban space. As *Great Expectations* and *Jude the Obscure* draw to a close, both men are financially indigent, psychologically tormented, and physically exhausted in their urban lodgings. Pip withdraws to the country, and Jude dies under the shadow of university walls that exclude him. The bildungsroman traditionally associates the city with possibility and transformation, but these novels echo Victorian mental science in imagining urbanity as hazardous to coherent selfhood: London and Christminster are spaces of decay and exclusion.

Great Expectations presents London as inseparable from Pip's newfound fortune, and his troubling first impressions of it signal the flawed foundations of his youthful dreams. Upon arrival, Pip is both intimidated and disappointed by London, "scared by the immensity" and conceding "some faint doubts whether it was not rather ugly, crooked, narrow, and dirty" (163). His introductory walk takes him first to Smithfield cattle market, "all asmear with filth and fat and blood and foam" (165), and then to Newgate Prison, where the condemned are hanged. The slaughter of animals and men, exposed as cruel and revolting but nonetheless integral frameworks of society, dominate Pip's initial impressions of both the urban center and his own class ascension. His new home at Barnard's Inn is "the dingiest collection of shabby buildings ever squeezed together in a rank corner" (173). While Pip's tone is sardonic as he imagines "the gradual suicide of the present occupants and their unholy interment under the gravel," his surprised disappointment at "this realisation of the first of my great expectations" is genuine (173). Pip's first urban home is beset by "dry rot and wet rot and all the silent rots that rot in neglected roof and cellar" (173), exhibiting a "dusty decay" (173) as pervasive as that of Miss Havisham's mansion. Pip's comparison to "a flat burying-ground" (173) recalls the scene in which he first encounters his benefactor Magwitch. Wemmick's supposition that "the retirement [of Barnard's Inn] reminds you of the country" (173) is funny as much for the way it is right as for the way it is wrong: Pip's first London experiences echo rather than supersede his youthful, provincial memories of mortality, criminality, and shabbiness, even as the city overwhelms him with its material and social unfamiliarity. It is a space of repetition rather than transformation. Many interactions that take place in London duplicate Pip's boyhood disappointments and errors: tormented courtship of an imperious Estella, implicit competition with Herbert Pocket, rejections of Joe and Magwitch as working-class father figures.

Similarly, Jude's initial encounter with Christminster replays childhood feelings of exclusion and alienation and consciousness of decay. Despite his impression of being "encircled as it were with the breath and sentiment of the venerable city," Jude finds the colleges exude an "extinct air . . . accentuated by the rottenness of the stones" (79). The evening of his arrival, he becomes "impressed with the isolation of his own personality, as with a self-spectre, the sensation being that of one who walked, but could not make himself seen or heard" (79). The city Jude envisioned as a center for exchange of ideas shuts down his own facility for communication. His isolation intensifies as he studies in solitude, feeling cut off intellectually from his fellow stonemasons and socioeconomically from the scholars whose "conversation . . . seemed oftentimes, owing to his long and persistent preparation for this place, to be peculiarly akin to his own thoughts" (86). He experiences radical self-division in which psychic life becomes divorced from socioeconomic milieu. Without social recognition of the value of his contributions (through manual labor or intellectual work), Jude is unable to actualize his potential and harmonize his physical, social, and mental experience.

Pip's and Jude's failures as bildungsroman protagonists are underscored by the fact that neither successfully makes the transition from rural to urban space. In Hardy's fin de siècle novel, peripatetic physical movement between cities replaces the temporary but real socioeconomic ascension Pip experiences in London, and the misplaced optimism of Dickens's protagonist gives way to the rapidly embittered idealism of Hardy's. In 1861, writing with conscious retrospection about the origins of social reforms and democratizing movements associated with the Victorian age, Dickens allows Pip to imagine possibility for progression upon his arrival in London, despite material and social evidence of stasis and decay.[12] By the 1890s, Hardy's final novel undercuts such hopes in the protagonist's first walk through Christminster, and quashes them altogether little over a hundred pages into the book with Jude's summary rejection by Biblioll College, subsequent barroom blasphemy, and humiliated retreat to the country.

Seeking inclusion, Pip and Jude find in urban spaces romantic disappointment, failed socioeconomic ambition, and related alienation. Both fall prey to desires they cannot regulate, including erotic desires for women who embody key cultural movements. The traits that make each woman problematic as a romantic partner also mark her as characteristic of either mid- or late-Victorian trends: Estella's pretense of effortless luxury that masks the reality of recent economic ascension, Arabella's commercial adaptability and self-marketing, Sue's intellectual refinement and affective sensitivity. In each case, erotic desire fails to facilitate social connections. Pip's longing for Estella is both unrequited and isolating; Jude's romantic relationships result in social opprobrium and personal despair. In both novels, male protagonists who cannot moderate and direct their desires pursue love interests whose shortcomings represent the perceived hazards of modern urbanity: emotional vacancy and ambiguous class status (Estella), self-serving materialism (Arabella), and hypersensitivity to social judgment (Sue).

SOCIAL DISLOCATION AND ABSENT SELF-WILL

The repetitive narratives generated by these pathologized objects of desire demonstrate what happens to the novel of self-development when the protag-

---

12. Robin Gilmour elucidates the historical timeline of *Great Expectations* in connection to Victorian reformist impulses (105–48). Gilmour uses textual clues to date Pip's birth to approximately the turn of the nineteenth century, making Pip a representative character (127–28), and relates his aspirations toward gentility to broader civilizing and democratizing impulses of the early Victorian era (129–39).

onist's self-will is lacking: The same mistakes recur and the goal looms unattainable on the horizon. *Great Expectations* and *Jude the Obscure* represent these behavior patterns and emotional states, medically ascribed to biological phenomena, as generated through socioeconomic structures of modern industrial capitalism. These novels reveal how material lack and economic instability produce psychic and somatic damage, preventing the individual from developing a healthy sense of self in relation to community.

Socially oriented psychoanalytic theory, such as Kelly Oliver's, helps define the narrative and social consequences of the absent self-will that Victorian medicine ascribed to depleted nerve force. Oliver contends that all subjectivity formation requires a responsive external witness (*Witnessing* 88). She further argues that beyond such familial or community interactions, individuals whose society fails to provide them with positive images of themselves experience debilitating negative affects, which in turn "become interpreted as signs of inferiority or weakness rather than symptoms of oppression" (*Colonization* xxii). We might productively consider Pip and Jude, as socially devalued working-class Victorian orphans, through this interpretive lens. The overwhelmingly negative social messages Pip and Jude receive prevent them from maintaining a healthy self-image that would support constructive action. Their diminished sense of self, which produces symptomology Victorians ascribed to depleted nerve force, originates in economic lack, not only as working-class children but as orphans, dependent upon uncertain charity for basic needs.

Pip and Jude are made to feel intensely undeserving of relatives' scant material resources; growing into adulthood, these boys fixate on grandiose socioeconomic goals that, if achieved, would seem retroactively to justify the trouble their existence has caused. Relatedly, each in adulthood exhibits a marked lack of agency at key moments when his ability to attain goals is threatened or foreclosed. As a result of weak self-will, Pip's and Jude's stories are not progressive but circular, returning the protagonist to his origins without social integration and leaving the reader with a discomfiting sense the novel's key questions remain unsettled. Both protagonists account for their actions in ways that ascribe their motives to external forces; at times, they resist forward momentum altogether. Superficially, they have the standard bildungsroman protagonist's goals: winning a love interest and attaining socioeconomic advancement. But they markedly lack agency in defining and directing those aspirations. The limited progress of Dickens's conclusion, in relation to the total negation of Hardy's, correlates with the early-to-mid Victorian period's greater psychiatric optimism and confidence in British masculinity.

The weak self-will Pip and Jude display in adulthood originates in the sense of superfluity each develops in childhood. As grown narrator reflecting on his youth, Pip satirically remarks, "I was always treated as if I had insisted on being born, in opposition to the dictates of reason, religion, and morality, and against the dissuading arguments of my best friends" (23). Similarly evincing a sense that he is somehow at fault simply for taking the material resources he requires, young Jude identifies with the crows he is hired to shoo away from a farmer's crops. He finds "his heart grew sympathetic to the birds' thwarted desires. They, like himself, seemed to be living in a world which did not want them" (15). After being dismissed in shame from his job as a result of showing pity for hungry birds, Jude "[feels] more than ever his existence to be an undemanded one" (18). Both boys develop their key ambitions in direct relation to their acute sense that they do not inherently deserve resources and social care. They believe extraordinary public and socioeconomic achievement is needed to justify their existence. Pip, who from early childhood is hired out as an odd-jobs boy and contributes to family earnings (43), develops aspirations to gentility only after he sees his sister respond with excitement to Miss Havisham's summons for him, declaring, "This boy's fortune may be made by his going to Miss Havisham's" (52). Jude fixes his attention on Christminster shortly after Farmer Troutham's beating; he wonders if that city is "a spot in which, without fear of farmers, or hindrance, or ridicule, he could watch and wait, and set himself to some mighty undertaking like the men of old of whom he had heard?" (25). Christminster attracts Jude's attention not only because of his love for learning, but more simply because the university is visible from a nearby hill and has been praised by a favorite schoolmaster. The ambitions that come to define each protagonist's identity are grafted by chance interactions into an affectively impoverished psyche; ambitions do not develop organically out of inclinations and talents of a socially nourished consciousness. For each boy, the ambition thus generated seems the only feasible path to meaningful social participation, in fact, the only way to justify the space he takes up.

These aspirations are, of course, markedly out of step with each protagonist's socioeconomic milieu, and as Pip and Jude progress toward maturity, their stories demonstrate the unevenness produced by such a radical disconnect. While it can hardly be called a sanguine novel, *Great Expectations,* set in the first half of the nineteenth century, reflects upon the recent memory of the capitalist, imperialist optimism that found expression in the Crystal Palace, and closes with the protagonist's moderated and qualified class ascension, a partial achievement of his goal.[13] *Jude the Obscure,* in contrast, emerges out of

---

13. In "Seeing the Invisible: The *Bildungsroman* and the Narration of New Regime of Accumulation" in *Working Fictions,* Carolyn Lesjak situates *Great Expectations* within broad-

a less stable historical moment: one characterized by British anxiety over control of imperial possessions and even England's own borders, by agitation for workers' and women's rights, and by growing scientific doubts about locating and ameliorating biological causes of psychic dysfunction. In Hardy's bleak novel, narrative repetitions wear down the protagonist. Jude's final nervous collapse results in wholesale dissolution, reflecting the exhaustion not only of the protagonist, but of the author's faith in realist representation and social possibility.

The differing outcomes of Pip's and Jude's nervous breakdowns demonstrate complex cultural and intellectual changes, particularly intensification of the pressures of masculinity. Neurasthenia was codified during a transformative period: As Oppenheim explains, "the late 1840s until the end of the 1870s formed a transitional phase in British attitudes toward manliness, when the free expression of male emotions and the ready vibration of masculine nerves were neither discredited nor applauded" (147). In the period when Dickens related Pip's accesses of emotion and dramatic breakdown, such displays were ambivalently coded in terms of both gender and ethics. Not a full generation later, when Hardy published *Jude the Obscure,* cultural and scientific shifts, including the ascent of muscular Christianity, caused the same symptomology to be read in a more conclusive and less accepting way: as an indication of failed self-regulation and potentially as an ominous marker of genetic unfitness (Oppenheim 147–49). By 1886, prominent psychiatrist Henry Maudsley, once a firm believer that experience shapes personality and mental well-being, was arguing that moral character, like intellectual capacity, depends on heredity ("Heredity" 649). However, even as he insisted on inborn predispositions, Maudsley exhorted that the madman and genius alike display "an organic variation, which in the one case is physiological or evolutional, in the other pathological and degenerative" (656). The pressure, then, lay on the individual, whose self-control must prove that his originality indicates progress rather than atavism. As Amy Milne-Smith has shown, the 1880s brought increasing anxiety that chronic neurasthenia, not in itself considered a loss of reason, might finally descend into the dreaded diagnosis of lunacy for increasingly overworked men (165–66). The contrast between Pip's nervous breakdown and Jude's, and relatedly their divergent narrative outcomes, do not reflect substantially different etiologies of nervous disease between the mid-Victorian era and the fin de siècle. Instead they show a change in thinking about men's responsibility to control and direct their bodies and minds. The late-Victorian and Edwardian man had less leeway in expressing emotion than his immediate predecessors did; he was subjected to greater economic

---

scale Victorian economic development, particularly as connected to the practical workings of empire.

competition, and expected to prove his fitness for survival through stoicism and material success.

Writing before these cultural constraints ossified, Dickens portrays a nervous hero whose sensitivity signals both vulnerability and adaptability. *Great Expectations* provides an apt illustration of the narrative usefulness of nervous collapse as a means to plausibly reconstruct and reorder a character's psyche within the traditional realist novel we associate with the early-to-mid-Victorian period: As Miriam Bailin suggests, the sickroom scene "serves as a kind of forcing ground of the self" (5), and for Dickens's characters particularly, "illness . . . is the *sine qua non* both of restored or reconstructed identity, and of narrative structure and closure" (79). It is noteworthy, however, that unlike other Dickensian delirium suffers such as Esther Summerson (infectious disease) or Eugene Wrayburn (narrowly surviving attempted murder), Pip's illness pointedly emerges out of, and amplifies, inherent tendencies in his physiology and character. The nervous Pip has always been a fragmented psyche. *Great Expectations* is a novel in which events are portrayed as happening to, rather than because of, its narrator-protagonist. The pause created by Pip's nervous exhaustion slows narrative momentum and facilitates reevaluation of past actions, providing believable justification for changed priorities, and resolving a central conflict: Pip's simultaneous love for Joe and shame over the humble origins Joe represents. This climatic illness emerges seamlessly out of tendencies that have defined Pip's character throughout. His disorientation and extreme passivity in his sickbed are no more than the intensification of his usual psychic state and narrative style.

From early on Pip as narrator has drawn our attention to the nervous oversensitivity of Pip as character, particularly in connection to his intense awareness of class position and guilty aspiration to wealth. Reflecting on the strange intermingling of opulence and decay, and of working class and leisure class, that characterizes his singing of the blacksmith's "Old Clem" with Miss Havisham and Estella, Pip asks, "What could I become with these surroundings? How could my character fail to be influenced by them? Is it to be wondered at if my thoughts were dazed, as my eyes were, when I came out into the natural light from the misty yellow rooms?" (96). The confusing and overwhelming effect of bizarre physical surroundings mingles with that of conflicted human interactions. Such rhetorical questions, like Pip's private tears upon parting from Joe, Biddy, and his sister (159) and his paralyzing but unspecified emotional response (225) following Joe's exit in London, may strike the modern reader as wheedling narratorial pleas for understanding, excuses for self-serving behavior. Yet to a Victorian reader attuned to vicissitudes of manly nerves, such sensitivity, particularly when entangled with ambition, places Pip within the orbit of the nervous temperament. When such an aspiring man meets with a significant financial or social setback, as Dowse's case study indicates, entire collapse may result.

Pip's descent into nervous illness begins when Magwitch's self-revelation exposes the physical toil and grasping ambition facilitating Pip's veneer of refined ease. Carolyn Lesjak's incisive reading interprets Pip's horrified confrontation with his benefactor as the response of an imperial leadership class forced to acknowledge the impoverished labor that enables its leisure (97). Without challenging the validity of this analogy, my analysis focuses on Pip as a realistically imagined embodied consciousness navigating the inescapable relation between his own ambition and the work that sustains it. Revolted by Magwitch's ungenteel expressions of affection, Pip is put over the edge not by any recital of crimes, but rather by Magwitch's narration of the industrious manual labor that produced the wealth they share and the goal-directed ambition that fueled it. As the reality of his relationship to the convict Magwitch sinks in, Pip registers his astonishment somatically; he feels "the room [begin] to surge and turn," noting a sensation of "suffocating" (319). When Magwitch avers that "I lived rough, that you should live smooth; I worked hard, that you should be above work" (319), Pip's response is shockingly extreme: "The abhorrence in which I held the man, the dread I had of him, the repugnance with which I shrank from him, could not have been exceeded if he had been some terrible beast" (320). Pip's reaction dehumanizes Magwitch, reducing him to an object of loathing while at the same time figuring him as a source of profound threat (although it is Magwitch, not Pip, whose life is in danger). Despite the recurrence of criminality, emblematic of Pip's moral guilt, throughout the novel, it is not Magwitch's status as criminal, but instead his status as ambitious manual laborer, that repels his adopted son. When Magwitch points to Pip's jeweled ring as an emblem of his own successful labor, Pip "recoil[s] from his touch as if he had been a snake" (320). Pip's horror of Magwitch as a benefactor springs from the same well as his shame of Joe. Both father figures take pride in skillful manual labor, and through their affection entangle Pip in their working-class identities: as producers and actors in the world, rather than contemplative individuals focused on achieving and articulating self-development. Magwitch's labor invalidates Pip's self-image as a gentleman, recalling the worthlessness and dread he experienced as a working-class orphan. The economic nature of Pip's core psychic conflict and related physiological symptoms is illustrated in the shattering effect Magwitch's revelation of their financial tie has on Pip's self-identity and health.

Magwitch's reappearance strikes at the core of Pip's anxiety, which Dickens figures as a physiological, not only a psychological, response. On the morn-

ing after Magwitch's appearance, Pip finds himself "greatly dejected and dis-
tressed, but in an incoherent wholesale sort of way" (329). The shock impedes
his capacity for logical thought and even his sense of individual identity; he
finds that "as to forming any plan for the future, I could as soon have formed
an elephant," and can only reflect upon "how miserable I was, but hardly knew
why, or how long I had been so, or on what day of the week I made the reflection, or even who I was that made it" (329). He moves about his flat "in a sort
of dream or sleep-waking" (329), seemingly bereft of volition. Here for the
first time Pip's nervous temperament descends into clear symptomology of
nervous exhaustion. Dowse identifies "indifference, unconcern, and insensi-
bility towards his belongings and surroundings" as typical masculine symptoms of nervous exhaustion (28). The cultural and medical pervasiveness of
this interpretation is indicated by Dowse's assertion that "I hold, and so does
everybody else I should think, that the defect of will-power is one of the most
prominent, if not the most characteristic, signs of neurasthenia" (29). While
the term "neurasthenia" was not coined until eight years after *Great Expectations* was published, the phenomena it codified were certainly then an established subject of medical concern.

In Pip, desire for material wealth and its attendant social standing is
divorced entirely from the process of working toward those goals. The result
is a fractured, radically diminished sense of self and the poisoning of emotional bonds. Tellingly, absence of independent will—key to symptomology of
neurasthenia, the disorder culturally tied to misfires of masculine ambition—
manifests in deeply self-destructive ways as the novel builds toward crisis.
Walking into Orlick's trap, Pip seems pointedly bereft of individual agency,
even of a clear sense of selfhood. Immediately prior to his receipt of the anonymous letter that draws him to the limekiln, Pip learns of his friend Herbert's
impending departure for Egypt, and observes, "I felt as if my last anchor were
loosening its hold" (416), figuring himself as a boat adrift in a current. Blaming hurry for his lack of deliberate cognition, Pip finds that having read the
letter several times, "its injunction to me to be secret got mechanically into
my mind" (419), and discovers he is "yielding to it in the same mechanical way" (419). Rushing off to the ill-advised private meeting with an anonymous stranger, Pip reflects, "I really had not been myself since the receipt
of the letter" (419). Later, setting out across the marshes for the rendezvous
that nearly costs his life, Pip acknowledges misgivings but is strangely incapable of acting on them: "Having come there against my inclination, I went
on against it" (421). Rather than prompting decisive character development,
the crisis confirms Pip in his pattern of surrender to social pressures outside
his own psyche. Unable to claim cohesive, independent selfhood, Pip, like

men described in case studies of severe nervous exhaustion, is at the mercy of external forces that invade and overwhelm his fragile consciousness.

Following Magwitch's self-revelation, Pip moves from one disaster to another, body and mind weakening at each turn: first Miss Havisham's burning after their final interview, then his own near-death at Orlick's hands, finally Magwitch's capture, conviction, and death. At each stage his mental control diminishes, he becomes less socially grounded, and he is subject to regressive memories and engages in repetitive actions devoid of meaningful volition. As the facade of gentility falls violently away, Pip suffers increasing confusion between external world and internal psyche, which inflects his narration. Events transpire that appear to Pip to externalize, as physical threat or material loss, his anger toward others or his personal guilt: Miss Havisham's accident, Orlick's attack, the forfeit of the fortune he feels conflicted to possess, and the death of the benefactor of whom he was ashamed. With the final blow of Magwitch's death, Pip suffers intense physical illness and total loss of motivation, collapsing "with a heavy head and aching limbs, and no purpose, and no power" (461). Beset by failure in the masculine public sphere, Pip suffers both a literal overdrawn bank account and the metaphorical one of nervous exhaustion. In alignment with contemporary framing of psychic trauma, he experiences dissociation among his self-identity, actions, and sense of temporality. Past events impinge on his consciousness, replaying their sensations and motivating repetitive, self-injuring actions that slowly wear away his capacity for forming and carrying out logical intentions. Alone after Herbert's departure, Pip in a state almost of sleepwalking engages in actions that attempt to save the dead Magwitch and Miss Havisham: seeking a boat, lighting a lamp in anticipation of Magwitch's return, and fearing Miss Havisham is burning within his own fire. Among these muddled actions and visions, the unwelcome sensory memory of the "vapour of the lime-kiln would come between me and them, disordering them all" (461). Then Pip recovers enough consciousness to perceive that he is being arrested for debt.[14]

The dissolution of Pip's personality through this total collapse enables him to build an arguably better character, but the new beginning thus achieved is predicated on repetition. It is Joe who draws Pip back from this void, as Pip realizes that all the figures by his bedside "sooner or later . . . settle down into the likeness of Joe" and recognizes "the dear old home-voice" that responds to his call (463). Pip's affirmation that he has and accepts a home with Joe might be said to mark moral and psychological growth. It entails awareness of his

---

14. In *Shock, Memory, and the Unconscious in Victorian Fiction*, Matus identifies the final delirium Pip calls "fever" (462) as "brain fever," an ambiguously physical/mental nineteenth-century diagnosis (5–6).

error in casting off the kindness of this father figure in favor of vain ambitions, but it also returns Pip to the point where his story began, and is therefore a circling back rather than a progression. After a period during which Pip, weak and attended by Joe, "fancied I was little Pip again" (466), the protagonist, denied the easy answer of a marriage to Biddy, sells his possessions to pay debts and again sets out into the world to make his fortune, this time at a merchant's post abroad.

It can hardly be said that *Great Expectations* resolves—Pip's desire for Estella hovers unrealized and unrenounced on the novel's final page. But the total breakdown of Pip's personality occasioned by nervous collapse facilitates working through one of the novel's key conflicts: Pip's intense aversion to labor that prevents him from realizing his ambition in an integrated way. The novel's penultimate chapter closes with a paragraph on Pip's pride in his work at Clarriker's, which is aligned with his friendship with Herbert and "constant correspondence with Biddy and Joe": "We were not in a grand way of business, but we had a good name, and worked hard for our profits, and did very well" (480). The reformed character Pip develops through his nervous breakdown results in a new, more moderate, thoroughly capitalist ambition: grounded in the individual's gratification in his labor and supported by meaningful connections both to middle-class peers and community of origin. Armstrong reminds us of the unsteady alliance Pip's employment entails: "subjecting the emotional attachments of village life to the risks of venture capitalism" ("Why" 2095). Crucially, the work Pip finally accepts as integral to his identity is urban intellectual labor connected to mercantile empire-building, not the rural, community-focused manual labor of blacksmithing alongside Joe. Matthew Taft argues that Pip's ascension into this imperial merchant post "replaces the fixed hierarchy of traditional British society with the restricted mobility of nineteenth-century capitalism," pushing *Great Expectations* beyond the stable conservative resolution Moretti associates with traditional English bildungsroman (1971). This outcome, presented with authorial approbation, highlights British self-identity increasingly contingent upon global economic engagement and domination moving into the second half of the nineteenth century.

Great Expectations declines to envision the mature results of Pip's reformulated aspirations, calling into question whether he can achieve social integration through marriage and publicly endorsed success. Thirty-five years later, *Jude the Obscure* issues a more conclusive negative to the question of working men's social mobility. Hardy figures Jude's nervous breakdown not as an opportunity to rebuild but as simply and profoundly destructive, marking the confusion of the protagonist's moral system and underscoring the futility of his ambition. Unlike Pip, who as narrator represents his failed ambitions as unique individual experience, Jude regards his thwarted dreams as determined by his historical moment, and the narrator supports his response. Homeless with a family to feed in Christminster, Jude reflects on his failed efforts at class ascension, declaring, "I was, perhaps, after all, a mere paltry victim to the spirit of mental and social restlessness, that makes so many unhappy in these days!" (327). This hard-won insight linking his individual weakness to broader social forces makes Jude an effective mouthpiece for Hardy's social critique, but it does not enable him, within the storyworld, to better navigate the socioeconomic forces that wear down his body and embitter his psyche. Jude's fatal collapse is presented as the inevitable result of overwhelming forces of socioeconomic negation; his final illness brings him back to his point of origin depleted, without any social support to repair a psyche devastated by grief and disappointment.

Jude's final bodily collapse, which correlates with the wreck of his goals and dissolution of his values, is represented as the likeliest end result for a working-class man of his temperament and gifts in fin de siècle Britain. Hardy indicates from the outset his protagonist is destined to suffer: Jude's intense empathy for other creatures, including nonhuman animals, ill-suits him for an inherently competitive world.[15] In the second chapter, the narrator reflects, "though Farmer Troutham had just hurt him [in the beating], he was a boy who could not himself bear to hurt anything. . . . This weakness of character, as it may be called, suggested that he was the sort of man who was born to ache a good deal before the fall of the curtain upon his unnecessary life should signify that all was well with him again" (17). While the passage has an evident religious valence in connecting Jude with Christ's disciples, it also suggests the nervous temperament. The terms are ambiguously psychic and somatic: "weakness" (as opposed to the simply moral "fault" or "flaw"), and "ache" (as opposed to the more strictly emotional "sorrow"). Qualities of character that unfit Jude for late-Victorian masculine aggression are not only mental but embodied. As a growing boy, Jude reflects, "All around you there seemed to be something glaring, garish, rattling, and the noises and glares hit upon the little cell called your life, and shook it, and scorched it" (18). The result of this observation is young Jude's overt rejection of the role of bildungsroman protagonist: "If he could only prevent himself growing up! He did not want to be a man" (18). Like little Pip in the graveyard, who only recognizes his own identity as "the small bundle of shivers growing afraid of it all" (4), Jude as a child defines himself through his sense of threat from overwhelming external

---

15. Suzanne Keen connects Jude's intense empathy for nonhuman animals both to Hardy's boyhood experiences and his reading of Darwin, which confirmed his sense of family relation (*Thomas Hardy's Brains* 200–203).

stimuli. Notably, although Jude passes his entire childhood in the country, Hardy's language in the above passage resonates with the clatter of modern, mechanized cities: "glaring" and "garish" like lights of urban shops; "rattling" like carriages, locomotives, and factories; a life "shook" and "scorched" like a body caught in machinery. Late-Victorian formulations of psychic injury identified technological innovations such as the railway as central to the imaginative language of shock, even if not literally the source of harm to an individual sufferer.[16] The novel's opening connects its protagonist's sensitivity, indeed over-receptiveness, to social and material stimuli to his highly refined moral sense. This ambiguously psychic and somatic sensitivity not only dooms Jude to suffering, but checks his forward momentum. His receptiveness to environment at once poises him to absorb the spirit of intellectual progress and unfits him for the fierce economic competition that accompanies it.

As his protagonist grows into adulthood, Hardy figures nervous tension as a gender-neutral pressure of modern life, particularly destructive to men due to social constraints of masculinity. As Oppenheim observes, such constraints intensified in the last decades of the nineteenth century, when escalating threats to British political and military dominance made intense self-control the order of the day in the economic as well as military arena (149–51). Patience waned for the sensitivity of the nervous temperament. With Jude's example, Hardy demonstrates how forcing an innately responsive and expressive temperament into the stoic mold exacerbates the harm of life's setbacks. After the initial disappointment of his scholarly aspirations, compounded by a humiliating drunken visit to Sue, the near-penniless Jude retreats to Marygreen and suffers a breakdown intensified by standards of manliness. Following a night of broken slumber in a rural hayrick near his home village, Jude "awoke . . . as if he had awakened in hell. It *was* hell—'the hell of conscious failure,' both in ambition and in love" (124). He meets with these decisive negatives to professional and erotic desires less than a third of the way through the novel. There is no narrative path forward, so he must move backward, toward the disdained town of his childhood and regression into helplessness. The narrator observes, "If he had been a woman he must have screamed under the nervous tension which he was now undergoing. But that relief being denied to his virility, he clenched his teeth in misery, bringing lines about his mouth like those of Laocoon, and corrugations between

---

16. Charcot noted that men who became ill with nervous symptoms following sudden life-threatening fright sometimes described sensations and sights similar to machinery and specifically a locomotive, even when the source of their fright had nothing to do with trains. George Drinka connects this phenomenon with the fact "many of the traumas from which [Charcot's] patients suffered were caused by civilization and its new machines" (114).

his brows" (124). The inward turn required by masculinity intensifies Jude's suffering. His contorted visage signifies not only grief but the distortion of his psyche as strong emotion, denied a social outlet, turns back on itself. Hardy's reference to Laocoon—crushed by serpents for attempting to block the Trojan Horse from entering Sparta—connects Jude's inner strife to heroic but futile efforts against impossible external pressures. The class boundaries persisting in late-Victorian society prevent Jude from rising through academic channels by his able intellect; working-class men were still denied entry to the most prestigious universities even as the middle classes began to gain admittance.[17] At the same time, lingering cultural constraints of separate spheres gender ideology fatally complicate his unconventional bond with Sue. Masculinity dictates strict self-restraint, and these intolerable pressures of professional and romantic failure disorder his psyche through resultant social isolation.

All of Jude's subsequent attempts to begin again (new city, new occupation, renewed relationship) repeat on a greater scale this initial failure and resultant collapse. Gagnier suggests that the novel's anxious preoccupation with seeking employment parallels the thematic concern of much authentic working-class Victorian autobiography (108). Yet Jude's geographical circuit is as much about failed self-actualization as it is about subsistence. Norman Prentiss observes, "although the novel covers so much physical territory, the characters never escape each other, and they never escape embarrassing reminders of their past failures" (179). The broad structure of *Jude* follows these socially claustrophobic repetitions, tracing the brief development and slow dissolution of the protagonist's ambitions for intellectual, social, and financial betterment. Each section of the text bears the name of its locale, foregrounding the relation between the individual and his socioeconomic and material environment. Jude's fortunes steadily ebb after an initial grasp at fulfillment: "At Marygreen" chronicles bucolic beginnings as he learns his stonemason's trade, "At Christminster" places him aspirant to ecclesiastical learning, "At Melchester" documents the unraveling of his reduced, lower-middle-class ambitions to become a curate, "At Shaston" his return to stonemasonry, "At Albrickham and Elsewhere" his reduction to threadbare itinerant laboring. Finally, "At Christminster Again" returns Jude to the site of his grandest dreams penniless, homeless, and incapable of supporting his family. Each new desire—for a woman, a job, a form of community inclusion—is positioned as a substitute for that one early, encompassing desire that cannot be satisfied, the impossible

---

17. Patricia Ingham observes that in selecting Christminster (based on Oxford) as the focus of his ambition, "Jude chooses to attack a virtually impregnable bastion of the upper classes" (170).

ambition. As the novel approaches its horrific climax, Sue in Christminster reflects upon "the strange operation of a simple-minded man's ruling passion" that "led Jude, who loved her and the children so tenderly, to place them here in this depressing purlieu, because he was still haunted by his dream" (332). Jude's ambition for Christminster learning is figured as something divorced from his personality and conscious cognition, even as it directs his behavior. His unfulfilled aspiration repeats destructively, dominating his consciousness, like the memory of a traumatic event. It interferes with his ability to perceive and process social information. Jude is haunted by unattainable ambition, driven by the unwilled return of a failure that cannot be assimilated. His story circles the Christminster dream thematically and geographically, never taking its protagonist—or the reader—inside the ancient walls of the colleges, which are the dominant absence of the narrative.

Following the children's deaths and Sue's resultant return to her husband Phillotson, Jude displays physical decline, emotional despair, and decreasing self-control as he confronts the totality of his failure. The late-Victorian physician Allbutt observed that "bodily, mental, or emotional strain may produce neurasthenia with the suddenness of a traumatic case" (150). We might connect Allbutt's theory of traumatic onset of neurasthenia to Jude's final crisis. With the children gone, Jude's last remaining hope is destroyed: the dream his son might achieve the Christminster education he did not.[18] When Sue parts from Jude, she makes explicit the total wreck of Jude's ambitions, perversely framing it as an indicator of his spiritual virtue: "Your generous devotion to me is unparalleled, Jude! Your worldly failure, if you have failed, is to your credit rather than to your blame. Remember that the best and greatest among mankind are those who do themselves no worldly good. Every successful man is more or less a selfish man. The devoted fail . . . 'Charity seeketh not her own'" (361). This speech, made at their children's graves, is Sue's final communication with Jude before returning to Marygreen, except for her brief farewell (362). In her reactionary embrace of Christian dogma no less than her earlier progressive, antireligious intellectual phase, Sue is out of step with late-Victorian mores. By the 1890s, Oppenheim argues, British masculinity was governed by "a secular creed that took a man's success or failure as an accurate index of his private worth and judged worth in terms of economic value, not moral worthiness" (151). Although Sue's phrase "worldly failure" most obviously pertains to Jude's ambitions for education and professional advancement (the economic value Oppenheim references), by making this

---

18. See Jude's observation of "meekly ignorant parents, who had known no college in their youth" (323) attending their sons' Christminster ceremonies on Remembrance Day and related encouragement to his own son (330).

pronouncement at the gravesite, Sue inadvertently enfolds their family tragedy within Jude's wrecked aspirations. On her departure the following day, Jude "had no heart to go to his work" (363) and instead wanders through the cold damp, courting illness, possessed by the thought of her absence. When we next see him, receiving an unexpected visit from his ex-wife, his self-control is rapidly diminishing.

Sue's tragic transformation, destructive though it is, is a masterwork of self-restraint, whereas Jude's parallel downfall is characterized by diminished will and impulse control. By the time of this novel's composition, debates among physiologists and psychiatrists regarding automatism had transformed educated Britons' understanding of free will, enmeshing what was once a philosophical or religious question in measurable material phenomena of nervous system and brain function (Smith, *Free Will* 17–18). Prentiss argues that while many of the novel's repetitions appear coincidental, the most destructive returns—Jude's and Sue's remarriages to their first spouses—result from the character's choice (190). I concur with respect to Sue, but I suggest a more ambivalent reading of Jude's intentionality. Sue's determination to return to Phillotson is "the one thing on earth on which she was firm" (360) following her children's deaths. Jude, in contrast, is devoid of any goal after the tragedy; it is in fact Sue who presents him with the idea to remarry his first wife, referencing the permanence of the Christian marriage sacrament (360). Arabella readily picks up this refrain, literally showing up on Jude's doorstep, pleading for shelter after a quarrel with her father. Her predictable wiles are of far less interest than what Jude's submission demonstrates about his flagging self-regulation and decreased agency. His feeble resistance to taking her in, and to hearing her news of Sue's remarriage, are soon overcome. He later, in "misery and depression . . . walked to well-nigh every spot he had visited with Sue," then "turned into a public-house, for the first time during many months" (373). In its combination of frustrated aspirations and drunken self-destruction, this sojourn echoes and amplifies Jude's first Christminster disappointment, following his rejection by Biblioll college, which occasions his first major breakdown.

Jude's capacity for conscious self-direction is already worn away when he finds Arabella waiting in the pub and allows her to get him drunk, repeating all the while, "I don't care what happens to me" (375). The narrator makes clear that Arabella carefully remains sober (375). Her relative sobriety and Jude's drunkenness is key to understanding Jude's diminished agency in this reunion. Following 1870s physiological debates about the operation of the will, medical historian Roger Smith argues, the concept of automatic reflex action—absent of conscious intention—was extended "to ever larger domains of human life—to instincts, habit, and character, to drunkenness, hysteria and madness" and located in the brain rather than merely the spinal cord (*Free Will* 19). In this scientific context, Jude's already sensitive nervous system, overtaxed by emotional strain, physical exhaustion, and bad weather, might be understood as already depleted in agency; his ex-wife's liquor then reduces him to a state of automatic action. When Arabella conducts Jude, so inebriated he can scarcely walk, to her father's home, he assents saying, "Anything—anywhere . . . What the devil does it matter to me?" (375). In much the same state of intoxication and apathy, Jude allows Arabella to bring him before the parson a few days later. In combined socioeconomic failure and personal grief, under physically taxing conditions, Jude succumbs to the trademark symptom of neurasthenia, an absence of individual will. Oppenheim documents how "overwork," in combination with "intense professional or personal disappointment, grief or bereavement, and any form of powerful shock" were typical and interrelated causative factors in Victorian etiologies, with bereavement often dealing the final blow (155). Jude's final error, his remarriage to Arabella, occurs after the grief-stricken collapse of his ability to mold and carry out his own intentions.

Jude's decline differs little from Pip's in causation and symptomology. Both emerge through a combination of disappointed love, socioeconomic failure, and bereavement, and both are characterized by bodily decline, emotional depression, and most crucially an absence of independent will and coherent self-identity. Whereas Pip's downward arc into nervous collapse is meticulously documented through his self-assessing retrospective narration, Jude's final spiral is treated almost as an afterthought. It is sketched loosely in comparison to the vivid chronicling of each phase of Jude and Sue's evolving relationship and every vicissitude of Jude's thwarted professional aspirations. Following his remarriage, we are told merely that Jude "had done a few days' work during the two or three months since the event, but his health had been indifferent, and it was now more precarious" (384). His emotional life during this period is absent from the narrative; his physiological state receives sparse description. Beyond coughing and general malaise, his ailments are undefined; they appear to merge elements of the infectious and constitutional, the psychic and somatic. Jude's carelessness of his bodily well-being following the shock of Sue's departure has exposed him to environmental stressors: fatigue, inclement weather, cold. His final deliberate act is an unannounced and fruitless visit to remarried Sue, undertaken in a chill rain that signifies "almost certain death" to any "sick man" (387). He later admits that suicide was his deliberate goal in this journey (391). In his nihilism and bodily wasting following Sue's rejection, we see in sharp relief the key likeness between the once able, aspiring father and his stunted son, Little Father Time, who exemplifies "the coming universal will not to live" (337), possessing all Jude's vulnerability without his intense empathy. Jude's lonely death in a garret room is a foregone conclusion. The markedly different fates of Pip and Jude reflect not only differences of characters' temperament and authors' ideological investments. In the 1860s, the expanding empire appeared, to many Victorians, a plausible outlet for surplus men with aspirations of class ascension; by the 1890s, confidence in the imperial project was faltering, although its policies were stubbornly maintained. Jude's repeated failures and related psychic and bodily dissolution indicate a cultural moment that could not productively channel the economic and intellectual desires it ignited in a changing class of working men.

Men like Pip and Jude test the boundaries of the traditional British bildungsroman. The gaps in their stories, and their returns to people, locations, and situations without psychological or economic progression, underscore how few Victorian men's lives fit within its expected arc of gratified ambition and social integration. Not only the failures of their aspirations, but the irregularities of narration those frustrated dreams produce, implicitly critique the ambitious hero's status as a representative figure of modernity in the nineteenth century. Pip and Jude reveal that the self-reflective individualism characteristic of the ambitious hero is not, in itself, sufficient to produce narrative resolution. Without a socioeconomic groove in which the protagonist's desires can run, his attempts to formulate a meaningful identity inevitably meet resistance. The scant opportunity for advancement available to even the most intellectually acute and motivated Victorian working-class men provides partial explanation for the fractured narratives that result when Dickens and Hardy represent these lives. Pip's and Jude's stories, particularly when read through the lens of nervous sensitivity, suggest the broader vulnerability of embodied masculine consciousness under the intense competition of industrial capitalism.

Victorian men who suffered nervous collapse understood their bodies and minds to have succumbed not only to a specific setback or tragedy, but to diffuse yet concrete environmental stressors endemic to modern struggles for economic ascendency. The disorder's familiarity in popular as well as scientific culture highlights fissures at the core of aspirational middle-class masculinity. Economic participation was the defining practice of masculine identity under separate spheres ideology, but ambitions of socioeconomic advancement carried the risk of feminizing nervous dysfunction. When the bildungsroman protagonist is a nervous hero rather than simply an ambitious one, the depleted agency typical of his disorder disrupts narrative progression and resolution. Male neurasthenia, the ailment of modern striving gone awry, was culturally correlated with vacillation, uncertainty, and self-doubt in an era when confident, steady self-will was the mark of manhood. The neurasthenic protagonist's psychic life revealed masculine self-assertion as always in danger of collapsing into feminized submission in a complex and threatening world.

Expanding Our Frame

One of the central goals of this study has been to recover the cultural and medical prehistory of insidious trauma: forms of psychic injury owing to diffuse and interrelated social, material, and economic influences. The novels under discussion certainly do include, as plot points, violent and even catastrophic forms of harm: notably, rape, hanging, shipwreck and drowning, railway disaster, and varied forms of serious or fatal accident. But crucially, they place these events offstage, and instead focus on the psychic consequences of physical violence, and even more so on the ambiguously mental and somatic pain that emerges from more subtle and ongoing threats their socially marginalized protagonists encounter. We are asked to attend to Jude Fawley's isolation as privileged scholars pass him without notice on Christminster streets, to Lucy Snowe's pained awareness of her social liminality as genteel-poor spinster, to Lady Ana's shifting feelings of shame and guilt as she privately contemplates the stigma her family could face if her experience of sexual violence were revealed. Even as they include elements of the catastrophic, these novels focus on harm done by an accumulation of stressors, most of which are difficult to define, culturally unspeakable, or both. Materially based Victorian medical theories of nervous disorder provided novelists language for communicating these experiences and logic for understanding their effects on formation of the psyche. Victorian researchers and physicians were sometimes wrong on the mechanics of brain and nervous system function, and their work, necessarily, problematically imbricated in its era's patriarchal and Eurocentric biases. But nascent Victorian mental science, in its close attention to interplay between social and somatic stressors, offers salient connections to diffuse and less obvious forms of mental harm we are called to attend in the twenty-first century.

At this writing, parts of the world have begun medically and economically to recover from a pandemic that claimed approximately three million lives in one year's time. In other regions and communities, where vaccination rates lag, medical resources are less available, or more pathogenic variants dominate, the suffering continues unabated. As the novel coronavirus (COVID-19) pandemic began to unfold in early 2020, researchers predicted a "second wave" comprised of PTSD, citing as precipitating factors the effects of uncertainty upon families of the mortally ill, and of isolation and chronic stress upon health care workers (Dutheil et al. 1). One-fourth of survivors of SARS, a similar virus whose prevalence in the world population was much lower, experienced PTSD (Dutheil et al. 2), suggesting the scope of the problem we face.

Initial research begins to substantiate these expectations. Studies of health care workers in the early months of 2020 in hard-hit regions of China, Italy, and Greece identify significant numbers of medical personnel meeting provisional PTSD diagnosis criteria (from 9 percent to almost 40 percent), or displaying elevated levels of depression and anxiety.[1] Patients who survive severe COVID-19 may also demonstrate PTSD-like symptoms. While it is difficult to clinically distinguish neurocognitive deficits caused by neurologic complications of disease from those caused by PTSD, contracting COVID-19 unquestionably leads to known traumatogenic situations: for example, near-death experiences and intubation (Kaseda and Levine 1499–1501). Of course, one need not be a health care worker or COVID-19 patient to experience psychologically damaging stressors and awareness of risk, which differently affect individuals according to personal and cultural history and relative structural privilege.

---

1. See Xueyuan Li et al., "The Prevalence and Risk Factors of PTSD Symptoms among Medical Assistance Workers during the COVID-19 Pandemic," *Journal of Psychosomatic Research*, vol. 139, October 2020, pp. 1–7; Xingyue Song et al., "Mental Health Status of Medical Staff in Emergency Departments during the T Coronavirus Disease 2019 Epidemic in China," *Brain, Behavior, and Immunity*, vol. 88, 2020, pp. 60–65; Marta Bassi et al., "The Relationship between Post-Traumatic Stress and Positive Mental Health Symptoms among Health Workers during COVID-19 Pandemic in Lombardy, Italy," *Journal of Affective Disorders*, vol. 280, June 2021, pp. 1–6; Apostolos Blekas et al., "COVID-19: PTSD Symptoms in Greek Health Care Professionals," *Psychological Trauma: Theory, Research, Practice, and Policy*, vol. 12, no. 7, July 2020, pp. 812–19.

Despite declarations that "We're all in this together," the lived experience of pandemic anxiety for a front-line grocery bagger and a quarantined executive teleworking while caring for children would be materially different. Further, people of Asian descent living in majority-white countries, particularly Asian Americans, are subject to hostility ranging from verbal abuse to lethal violence, as the virus's recorded origins in Wuhan, China, have been politically weaponized to intensify established racism and xenophobia. Moreover, preliminary clinical perspectives indicate groups with preexisting personal or familial trauma history, including children of Holocaust survivors and refugees, may experience greater sensitivity to pandemic stressors for both psychological and practical reasons.[2] Conversely, some veterans with PTSD have found temporary relief from hyperarousal symptoms and justification for preexisting social avoidance strategies in pandemic lockdowns and social distancing (Sciarrino et al. S70). Relief in avoiding triggering or otherwise harmful stimuli is not restricted to clinical PTSD cases. In a March 2021 essay for *The Nation* titled "I Am Not Ready to Reenter White Society," Elie Mystal reflects on a similar sense of reprieve he felt as a Black American in home quarantine: "One of the principal benefits of the pandemic is how I've been able to exclude racism and whiteness generally from my day-to-day life," evading daily microaggressions and ever-present risks of mundane activities like driving to the store. Critical examination on a societal level of what aspects of "normalcy" we wish to recover, and which we cannot continue to accept as normal, may prove one constructive outcome of this worldwide trauma. As vaccinations enable a gradual return to typical social and economic behavior and institutional functioning, the effects of COVID-19 will linger for years, with widespread yet differentially felt material and psychological impact.

One effect may be a change in the way we define psychic trauma, both colloquially and clinically. Recent psychological research suggests the COVID-19 pandemic necessitates revising standard models of PTSD causation and symptomology. A study of five English-speaking countries conducted in late 2020, led by Victoria M. E. Bridgland of Dr. Melanie Takarangi's Forensic and Clinical Cognition Lab, finds that dominant PTSD models, including DSM-V diagnostic criteria, fail to capture emerging pandemic conditions. Current PTSD models "attribute traumatic stress reactions to past, and largely direct,

2. See Amit Shrira and Irit Felsen, "Parental PTSD and Psychological Reactions during the COVID-19 Pandemic among Offspring of Holocaust Survivors," *Psychological Trauma: Theory, Research, Practice, and Policy,* 1 March 2021; Sandra Mattar and Linda A. Piwowarczyk, "COVID-19 and U.S.-Based Refugee Populations: Commentary," *Psychological Trauma: Theory, Research, Practice, and Policy,* vol. 12, no. S1, 2020, pp. S228–S229; and Jan Ilhan Kizilhan and Michael Noll-Hussong, "Psychological Impact of COVID-19 on a Refugee Camp in Iraq," *Psychiatry and Clinical Neurosciences,* vol. 74, 2020, pp. 659–60.

exposure to certain life-threatening events" (Bridgland et al 1). Bridgland and her colleagues find "people's traumatic stress reactions to the COVID-19 pandemic may relate more to: the future than the past; indirect (e.g., via media coverage) than direct (e.g., contact with the virus) exposure; and stressful events (e.g., unemployment, isolation, non-sudden illness/death) that do not meet Criterion A (i.e., actual or threatened death, injury or sexual violation)" (1–2). Quantitative data correlating COVID-19-era PTSD-like symptomology with expected future events, indirect trauma exposure, and perception of ongoing threat supported the researchers' broader hypothesis that "*direct exposure to a past event that threatens death, injury, or sexual violation, is not the only circumstance capable of precipitating PTSD-like symptoms*" (Bridgland et al. 7). The concept that anticipated, mediated, or diffuse harm can be a significant stressor has been acknowledged in prior twenty-first-century research, but COVID-19 pandemic conditions give greater scope and urgency to such claims. The catastrophic trauma model—dominant in Caruth's theory as well as the DSM-V—is apt for the COVID-19 ICU survivor, but it fails to encompass nuances of psychological harm experienced by many others subjected to prolonged uncertainty, constant threat and worry, and deprivation from accustomed social contact and physical touch, often while frantically navigating unfamiliar technology in lockdown. In these circumstances, panic can hit with immediacy but time feels oddly stagnant. Memory has long been a central concern of trauma studies, but COVID-19 requires us to rethink the temporality of trauma.

COVID-19 emerged against a background of newfound public attention to insidious, structurally produced forms of psychic harm that are difficult to pinpoint, quantify, and articulate. As the #MeToo and #BlackLivesMatter movements call all citizens to recognize the prevalence of sexual and racially motivated violence, they have simultaneously drawn attention to pervasive and toxic effects of microaggressions, and constant awareness of danger, that permeate daily experience for members of marginalized or historically excluded groups. Black Lives Matter and Me Too (pioneered, respectively, by Patrisse Khan-Cullors, Alicia Garza, and Opal Tometi, and by Tarana Burke) found their impetus in activist responses to discrete instances of overwhelming violence, which would fit DSM-V criteria for precipitating events of PTSD if witnessed or directly experienced: for example, the murder of Tamir Rice. But related public discourse has drawn attention to subtler ways people of color, women, and LGBTQI+ people are denied full human value, and to the means by which unconscious bias can erupt into physical violence. In her searing 2019 memoir *Know My Name,* Chanel Miller, unwillingly catapulted to fame as Emily Doe during Brock Turner's 2016 sexual assault trial, pointedly situates her life-altering direct experience of violence amidst a broader backdrop of misogynist threat, such as facing daily street harassment while walking to her graduate class or sheltering in a locked room while incel Elliot Rodger shot up her college town in 2013. As awareness builds regarding how insidious threats of sexual or white supremacist violence shape lived experience, popular psychology responds. Recent books by therapist Resmaa Menakem (*My Grandmother's Hands: Racialized Trauma and the Pathway to Mending Our Hearts and Bodies,* 2017) and law professor and mindfulness practitioner Rhonda V. Magee (*The Inner Work of Racial Justice: Healing Ourselves and Transforming Our Communities through Mindfulness,* 2019) incorporate principles of mind–body connection as they guide the general reader through reflection on concepts including structural racism, implicit bias, and microaggressions. Both present racial justice work as inseparable from self-awareness of our hardwired physiological reactions, connected to trauma response, and our conscious intervention in related patterns of thought. Magee defines "trauma" broadly to include "a vast spectrum, from stress to post-traumatic stress disorder" (44). She suggests, "Mindfulness can help you become more trauma-sensitive and more trauma-resilient. It may help you recognize when you or others are touching upon or reacting to latent trauma, and help you respond with appropriate acts of care and compassion" (45). Voices like Menakem's and Magee's call the general public to attend to unprocessed trauma as a political as well as interpersonal problem.

While the twenty-four-hour news cycle focuses predominantly on extreme violence and, with regard to COVID-19, on staggering numbers of deaths and hospitalizations, we also acknowledge the quieter pain of the colleague, neighbor, student, or friend who finds herself under similar threat but cannot pinpoint a single, overwhelming instance of harm. Circumstances like these are the emotional and narrative center of gravity in the novels that compose my study. These fictions do include major events of loss or threat "experienced too soon, too unexpectedly, to be fully known" (Caruth, *Unclaimed Experience* 4), which therefore return and repeat, calling out for witness even as they resist interpretation. But in these texts discrete precipitating events, which may be understood as conventionally traumatic, give narrative momentum to exploration of more subtle and diffuse forms of harm that are current or prospective rather than retrospective, and fail to align with any culturally grieveable category. Lucy Snowe's past loss of family and fortune drives her halting progress through the storyworld, and is unspeakable in Caruth's original sense: Lucy perceives both the devastating loss, and her survival in its wake, as too cosmically unjust to accept through articulation. But Lucy's narration adheres to subtler forms of injustice or pain in the present-day storyworld, which are structural in causation: mundane, wearying tasks and casual social insults that her socioeconomically degraded position obliges her to tolerate. And the emotional heft of her story is found less in the memory of long-dead family, than in the fear of future loss: through either rejection (as in Dr. John's unequal return of her love) or through another death (as ultimately transpires with M. Paul). *Villette*'s narrative gaps and repetitions align with patterns of retrospective narration of catastrophic trauma, but the novel's focus on diffuse present-day stressors and anticipated harm show both its grounding in nineteenth-century models of psychic injury, and its relevance to contemporary conversations in trauma studies.

In drawing our attention to more subtle forms of psychic injury, Victorian fiction that centers the traumatized and transgressive heroine or the self-unmade man changes narrative form. The marriage plot distills lifelong values into a single consequential choice. The traditional bildungsroman privileges a goal-directed consciousness that is or strives to be unitary, and develops in dynamic and increasingly nourished relation to its social environment. In either mode, conflicts promote protagonist growth and enable solidification of coherent social values by prompting action and choice. In contrast, the protagonists I have discussed either lack meaningful choices, or discover that opportunities to act and choose bring only regret or incomprehension, returning them to their starting point psychologically, and perhaps physically and socioeconomically as well. In contrast with the maturing bourgeois mores of Jane Eyre or David Copperfield, which are openly shared with readers, the socially marginal positions and culturally unacceptable emotions of the protagonists I have discussed necessitate that their stories proceed with gaps, elusions, and cross-talk. The lens of trauma studies, with an expanded frame acknowledging insidious trauma, brings into sharper focus the critiques of modern life embedded in these Victorian narratives of loss. As we move through a twenty-first-century world where crisis has come to feel mundane, both omnipresent and inarticulable, these stories of characters seeking a meaningful path forward through a field of diffuse threat may strike contemporary readers as oddly familiar.

WORKS CITED

Abbey, Susan E., and Paul E. Garfinkel. "Neurasthenia and Chronic Fatigue Syndrome: The Role of Culture in the Making of Diagnosis." *The American Journal of Psychiatry,* vol. 148, no. 12, 1991, pp. 1638–46.

Adair, Vivyan. "The Classed Body in the Sociological Imagination." *Sociology Compass,* vol. 2, no. 5, 2008, pp. 1655–71.

Ahern, Stephen. *Affected Sensibilities: Romantic Excess and the Genealogy of the Novel 1680–1810.* AMS Press, 2007.

Allbutt, Thomas Clifford. "Neurasthenia." *A System of Medicine,* edited by Thomas Clifford Allbutt, MacMillan and Co., Ltd., 1896–1899, pp. 134–61.

Allen, Emily. "Gender and Sensation." *A Companion to Sensation Fiction,* edited by Pamela K. Gilbert, Wiley-Blackwell, 2011, pp. 401–13.

Anderson, Amanda. *Tainted Souls, Painted Faces: The Rhetoric of Fallenness in Victorian Culture.* Cornell University Press, 1993.

Archimedes, Sondra M. *Gendered Pathologies: The Female Body and Biomedical Discourse in the Nineteenth-Century English Novel.* Routledge, 2005.

Armstrong, Nancy. *Desire and Domestic Fiction: A Political History of the Novel.* Oxford University Press, 1987.

———. "Why the Bildungsroman No Longer Works." *Textual Practice,* vol. 34, no. 12, 2020, pp. 2091–111.

Bailin, Miriam. *The Sickroom in Victorian Fiction: The Art of Being Ill.* Cambridge University Press, 1994.

Baker, William. *The George Eliot–George Henry Lewes Library: An Annotated Catalogue of Their Books at Dr. Williams Library, London.* Garland Publishing, 1977.

Balfour, Ian. "Torso: (The) Sublime Sex, Beautiful Bodies, and the Matter of the Text." *Eighteenth-Century Studies,* vol. 39, no. 3, 2006, pp. 323–36.

Barker, Juliet. *Charlotte Brontë: A Life in Letters.* 1997. The Overlook Press, 2002.

Beard, George Miller. "Nature and Definition of Nervousness." 1881. *American Nervousness; Its Causes and Consequences, a Supplement to Nervous Exhaustion (Neurasthenia),* Arno Press, 1972.

Beer, Gillian. *Darwin's Plots: Evolutionary Narrative in Darwin, George Eliot, and Nineteenth Century Fiction.* 1983. ARK Paperbacks, 1985.

Benjamin, Walter. *Illuminations: Essays and Reflections.* 1955. Translated by Harry Zohn, Schocken Books, 2007.

Berlant, Lauren. *Cruel Optimism.* Duke University Press, 2011.

Bernard, William Bayle. *The Nervous Man and the Man of Nerve: A Farce in Two Acts.* 1833. Samuel French, 1857.

Bérubé, Michael. *The Secret Life of Stories: From Don Quixote to Harry Potter, How Understanding Intellectual Disability Transforms the Way We Read.* New York University Press, 2016.

Booth, Michael. *English Melodrama.* Herbert Jenkins, 1965.

Bostick, Theodora. "The Press and the Launching of the Women's Suffrage Movement, 1866–1867." *Victorian Periodicals Review,* vol. 13, no. 4, Winter 1980, pp. 125–31.

Boynton, Eric, and Peter Capretto, editors. *Trauma and Transcendence: Suffering and the Limits of Theory.* Fordham University Press, 2018.

Brave Heart, Maria Yellow Horse, et al. "*Iwankapiya* American Indian Pilot Clinical Trial: Historical Trauma and Group Interpersonal Psychotherapy." *American Psychological Association,* vol. 57, no. 2, 2020, pp. 184–96.

Brewer, Elizabeth. "Coming Out Mad, Coming Out Disabled." *Literature of Madness: Disability Studies and Mental Health,* edited by Elizabeth J. Donaldson, Palgrave Macmillan, 2018, pp. 11–30.

Bridgland, Victoria M. E., et al. "Why the COVID-19 Pandemic Is a Traumatic Stressor." *PLoS ONE,* vol. 16, no. 1, 2021, pp. 1–15.

Brodie, Benjamin Collins. "Local Nervous Affections." *Three Hundred Years of Psychiatry: 1535–1860,* edited by Richard Hunter and Ida Macalpine, Oxford University Press, 1963, pp. 861–64.

———. *Psychological Inquiries: In a Series of Essays, Intended to Illustrate the Mutual Relations of the Physical Organization and the Mental Faculties,* Longman, Brown, and Green, 1854.

Brontë, Charlotte. *Villette.* 1853. Oxford University Press, 2008.

Brooks, Peter. *Reading for the Plot.* Vintage, 1985.

Brown, Laura. "Not Outside the Range: One Feminist Perspective on Psychic Trauma." *Trauma: Explorations in Memory,* edited by Cathy Caruth, Johns Hopkins University Press, 1995, pp. 100–112.

Brumberg, Joan Jacobs. *Fasting Girls: The History of Anorexia Nervosa.* 1988. Vintage Books, 2000.

Burg, B. R. "'Women and Children First': Popular Mythology and Disaster at Sea, 1840–1860." *Journal of American Culture,* vol. 20, no. 4, 1997, pp. 1–9.

Butler, Judith. *Bodies That Matter: On the Discursive Limits of "Sex."* Routledge, 1993.

Carlson, Susan. "The Impact of Clinical Depression on Charlotte Brontë's *Villette.*" *Brontë Studies,* vol. 45, no. 1, 2020, pp. 13–25.

Carpenter, William Benjamin. "The Power of the Will over Mental Action" from *Principles of Mental Physiology.* 1874. *Embodied Selves: An Anthology of Psychological Texts,* edited by Jenny Bourne Taylor and Sally Shuttleworth, Oxford University Press, 1998, pp. 95–101.

Carroll, Siobhan. "'Play you Must': *Villette* and the Nineteenth-Century Board Game." *Nineteenth-Century Conteexts,* vol. 39, no. 1, 2017, pp. 33–47.

Carter, Robert Brudenell. "On the Pathology and Treatment of Hysteria." *Three Hundred Years of Psychiatry: 1535–1860,* edited by Richard Hunter and Ida Macalpine, Oxford University Press, 1963, pp. 1002–03.

Caruth, Cathy. *Literature in the Ashes of History,* Johns Hopkins University Press, 2013.

———. *Trauma: Explorations in Memory.* Edited with introductions, Johns Hopkins University Press, 1995.

———. *Unclaimed Experience: Trauma, Narrative, and History,* Johns Hopkins University Press, 1996.

Celeste, Mark. "Metonymic Chains: Shipwreck, Slavery, and Networks in *Villette.*" *Victorian Review: An Interdisciplinary Journal of Victorian Studies,* vol. 42, no. 2, 2016, pp. 343–60.

Charcot, J. M. *Lectures on the Diseases of the Nervous System.* Translated by George Siegerson, The New Sydenham Society, 1877.

Charuvastra, Anthony, and Marylene Cloitre. "Social Bonds and Posttraumatic Stress Disorder." *Annual Review of Psychology,* vol. 59, no. 1, 2008, pp. 301–28.

Chatel, John C., and Roger Peel. "A Centennial Review of Neurasthenia." *The American Journal of Psychiatry,* vol. 126, no. 10, 1970, pp. 1404–13.

[Chorley, H.F.] *"No Name." The Athenaeum,* Iss. 1836, (Jan 3, 1863), pp. 10–11.

Clarke, Edwin, and L. S. Jacyna. *Nineteenth-Century Origins of Neuroscientific Concepts.* University of California Press, 1987.

Cohen, Margaret. *The Novel and the Sea.* Princeton University Press, 2010.

Cohn, Elisha. *Still Life: Suspended Development in the Victorian Novel.* Oxford University Press, 2016.

Collins, Wilkie. *No Name.* 1862. Oxford University Press, 1999.

Combe, George. *The Constitution of Man Considered in Relation to External Objects.* 1847. Edited by John Van Wyhe, Thoemmes Continuum, 2004.

Corbett, Mary Jean. *Family Likeness: Sex, Marriage, and Incest from Jane Austen to Virginia Woolf.* Cornell University Press, 2008.

Cvetkovich, Ann. *An Archive of Feelings: Trauma, Sexuality, and Lesbian Public Cultures.* Duke University Press, 2003.

———. *Mixed Feelings: Feminism, Mass Culture, and Victorian Sensationalism.* Rutgers University Press, 1992.

Dale, Peter Allan. *In Pursuit of a Scientific Culture: Science, Art, and Society in the Victorian Age.* The University of Wisconsin Press, 1989.

Daly, Nicholas. *Literature, Technology, and Modernity, 1860–2000.* Cambridge University Press, 2004.

———. *Sensation and Modernity in the 1860s.* Cambridge University Press, 2009.

Dames, Nicholas. *Amnesiac Selves: Nostalgia, Forgetting, and British Fiction, 1810–1870,* Oxford University Press, 2001.

———. *The Physiology of the Novel: Reading, Neural Science, and the Form of Victorian Fiction.* Oxford University Press, 2007.

Davis, Lennard. "Who Put the *the* in *the Novel?* Identity Politics and Disability in Novel Studies." *Novel: A Forum on Fiction,* vol. 31, no. 3, 1998, pp. 317–34.

Dickens, Charles. *Bleak House.* 1853. Oxford University Press, 1996.

———. *David Copperfield*. 1850. Penguin Books, 1996.

———. *Great Expectations*. 1861. Penguin Books, 2003.

———. *The Letters of Charles Dickens*. Edited by Graham Story et al., Clarendon Press, 1993.

Dodson, Thomas, and J. Gale Beck. "Posttraumatic Stress Disorder Symptoms and Attitudes about Social Support: Does Shame Matter?" *Journal of Anxiety Disorders,* vol. 47, 2017, pp. 106–13.

Donald, James. *Imagining the Modern City*. University of Minnesota Press, 1999.

Dowse, Thomas Stretch. *On Brain and Nerve Exhaustion (Neurasthenia), and on the Nervous Sequelae of Influenza*. 1880. Balliere, Tindall, and Cox, 1894.

Drinka, George. *The Birth of Neurosis: Myth, Malady, and the Victorians*. Simon and Schuster, 1984.

Duncan, Ian. "The Bildungsroman, the Romantic Nation, and the Marriage Plot." *Replotting Marriage in Nineteenth-Century British Literature,* edited by Jill Galvan and Elsie Michie, The Ohio State University Press, 2018, pp. 15–34.

Dutheil, Frédéric, et al. "PTSD as the Second Tsunami of the SARS-Cov-2 Pandemic." *Psychological Medicine,* April 24, 2020, pp. 1–2.

Ehnenn, Jill. "Reorienting the *Bildungsroman*: Progress Narratives, Queerness, and Disability in *The History of Sir Richard Calmady* and *Jude the Obscure*." *Journal of Literary & Cultural Disability Studies,* vol. 11, no. 2, 2017, pp. 151–68.

Eliot, George. *Daniel Deronda*. 1876. Penguin, 1995.

———. *The Lifted Veil*. 1859. Oxford University Press, 1999.

———. *The Mill on the Floss*. 1860. Penguin Books, 1985.

Ellis, Havelock. "Concerning *Jude the Obscure*." 1896. The Ulysses Bookshop, 1931.

Ellis, Markman. *The Politics of Sensibility: Race, Gender, and Commerce in the Sentimental Novel*. Cambridge University Press, 1996.

Erichsen, John Erik. *On Concussion of the Spine: Nervous Shock and Other Obscure Injuries to the Nervous System in Their Clinical and Medico-Legal Aspects*. W. Wood & Co., 1886.

Faflak, Joel, and Julia M. Wright. Introduction. *Nervous Reactions: Victorian Recollections of Romanticism,* State University of New York Press, 2004.

Feldman, Ezra Dan. "Weird Weather: Nonhuman Narration and Unmoored Feelings in Charlotte Brontë's *Villette*." *Victorians: A Journal of Culture and* Literature, vol. 130, 2016, pp. 78–99.

Ferguson, Frances. *Solitude and the Sublime: Romanticism and the Aesthetics of Individuation*. Routledge, 1992.

Foucault, Michel. *The History of Sexuality: An Introduction. Vol 1*. 1978. Vintage Books, 1990.

Frawley, Maria. *Invalidism and Identity in Nineteenth-Century Britain*. University of Chicago Press, 2004.

Freedgood, Elaine. *Victorian Writing about Risk: Imagining a Safe England in a Dangerous World*. Cambridge University Press, 2000.

———. *Worlds Enough: The Invention of Realism in the Victorian Novel*. Princeton University Press, 2019.

Freeman, Barbara Claire. *The Feminine Sublime: Gender and Excess in Women's Fiction*. University of California Press, 1995.

Frewen, Paul, and Ruth Lanius. *Healing the Traumatized Self: Consciousness, Neuroscience, Treatment*. W. W. Norton & Co., 2015.

Fyfe, Paul. "Illustrating the Accident: Railways and the Catastrophic Picturesque in the *Illustrated London News*." *Victorian Periodicals Review,* vol. 46, no. 1, Spring 2013, pp. 61–91.

Gagnier, Regenia. *Subjectivities: A History of Self-Representation in Britain, 1832–1920.* Oxford University Press, 1991.

Galea, Sandro, et al. "Social Context and the Psychobiology of Posttraumatic Stress." *Annals of the New York Academy of Sciences,* vol. 1071, 2016, pp. 231–41.

Gibson, Anna. "Charlotte Brontë's First Person." *Narrative,* vol. 25, no. 2, 2017, pp. 203–26.

Gilbert, Pamela K. *Victorian Skin.* Cornell University Press, 2019.

———. "Feminism and the Canon: Recovery and Reconsideration of Popular Novelists." *Antifeminism and the Victorian Novel: Rereading Nineteenth-Century Women Writers.* Edited by Tamara Wagner. Cambria Press, 2009, pp. 19–33.

Gilbert, Sandra, and Susan Gubar. *The Madwoman in the Attic: The Woman Writer and the Nineteenth Century Literary Imagination.* 1979. Yale University Press, 2000.

Gilmour, Robin. *The Idea of the Gentleman in the Victorian Novel.* George Allen & Unwin, 1981.

Giordano, Frank. "*Jude the Obscure* and the *Bildungsroman.*" *Studies in the Novel,* vol. 4, no. 4, 1972, pp. 580–91.

Gosling, F. G. *Before Freud: Neurasthenia and the American Medical Community, 1870–1910.* University of Illinois Press, 1987.

Hall, John Charles. *Medical Evidence in Railway Accidents.* Longmans, 1868.

"Railway Pathology: Case of Harris 'Versus' the Midland Railway Company." *The British Medical Journal,* vol. 2, no. 780, December 11, 1875, pp. 728–30.

Hall, J. Marshall. *Memoirs on the Nervous System.* Sherwood, Gilbert, & Piper, 1837. Electronic access via Wellcome Library.

Hardy, Thomas. *Jude the Obscure.* 1895. Penguin Books, 1998.

Harrington, Ralph. "The Railway Accident: Trains, Trauma, and Technological Crises in Nineteenth-Century Britain." *Traumatic Pasts: History, Psychiatry, and Trauma in the Modern Age, 1870–1930,* edited by Mark S. Micale and Paul Lerner, Cambridge University Press, 2001.

Henry, Nancy. *Women, Literature, and Finance in Victorian Britain: Cultures of Investment.* Palgrave Macmillan, 2018.

Herman, Judith Lewis. *Trauma and Recovery: The Aftermath of Violence from Domestic Abuse to Political Terror.* Basic Books, 1992.

Hingston, Kylee-Anne. "'Skins to Jump Into': The Slipperiness of the Body and Identity in Wilkie Collins's *No Name.*" *Victorian Literature and Culture,* vol. 40, no. 1 2012, pp. 117–35.

Horsley, Victor. "Traumatic Neurasthenia." *A System of Medicine by Many Writers,* edited by Thomas Clifford Allbutt, Macmillan & Co., 1899, pp. 164–76.

Horwitz, Allan V. *PTSD: A Short History.* Johns Hopkins University Press, 2018.

Hughes, Winifred. *The Maniac in the Cellar: Sensation Novels of the 1860s.* Princeton University Press, 1980.

Iantaffi, Alex. *Gender Trauma: Healing Cultural, Social, and Historical Gendered Trauma.* Jessica Kingsley Publishers, 2021.

Ingham, Patricia. *The Language of Gender and Class: Transformation in the Victorian Novel.* Routledge, 1996.

Itzkowitz, David C. "Fair Enterprise or Extravagant Speculation: Investment, Speculation, and Gambling in Victorian England." *Victorian Studies,* 2002 Autumn, vol. 45, no. 1, pp. 121–47.

Jacobus, Mary. *Reading Woman: Essays in Feminist Criticism.* Columbia University Press, 1986.

Jewell, J. S. "Nervous Exhaustion, or Neurasthenia, in Its Bodily and Mental Relations." 1878–1879. *Journal of Mental and Nervous Disease,* vol. 6, no. 3, 1879, pp. 449–60.

Jolly, Emily. "All in the Wrong, or, the Tamer Tamed: A Story without a Moral." *Blackwood's Edinburgh Magazine*, vol. 92, no. 566, December 1862, pp. 671–95.

———. "My First and Last Novel." *Blackwood's Edinburgh Magazine*, vol. 84, no. 513, July 1858, pp. 101–10.

———. *A Wife's Story. Household Words*, vol. 1, 1 September–22 September 1855, pp. 97–105, 123–30, 149–55, 180–86.

———. *Witch-Hampton Hall: Five Scenes in the Life of Its Last Lady. Blackwood's Edinburgh Magazine*, vol. 95, no. 579, February 1864, pp. 185–215.

Kaplan, Fred. *Sacred Tears: Sentimentality in Victorian Literature*. Princeton University Press, 1987.

Kaseda, Erin T., and Andrew J. Levine. "Post-Traumatic Stress Disorder: A Differential Diagnostic Consideration for COVID-19 Survivors." *The Clinical Neuropsychologist*, vol. 34, no. 7–8, 2020, pp. 1498–514.

Keen, Suzanne. *Empathy and the Novel*. Oxford University Press, 2007.

———. *Thomas Hardy's Brains: Psychology, Neurology, and Hardy's Imagination*. The Ohio State University Press, 2014.

Kennard, Jean. *Victims of Convention*. Archon Books, 1978.

Kiely, Robert. *The Romantic Novel in England*. Harvard University Press, 1972.

Kilgour, Maggie. *The Rise of the Gothic Novel*. Routledge, 1995.

Kreilkamp, Ivan. *Voice and the Victorian Storyteller*. Cambridge University Press, 2005.

Kucich, John. *Repression in Victorian Fiction*. University of California Press, 1987.

LaCapra, Dominick. *Writing History, Writing Trauma*. The Johns Hopkins University Press, 2001.

The Lancet. The Influence of Railway Travelling on Public Health. Robert Hardwick, 1862.

Langland, Elizabeth. "Becoming a Man in *Jude the Obscure*." *The Sense of Sex: Feminist Perspectives on Hardy*, edited by Margaret Higonnet, University of Illinois Press, 1993, pp. 32–48.

Laub, Dori, "Bearing Witness, or the Vicissitudes of Listening." *Testimony: Crises of Witnessing in Literature, Psychoanalysis, and History*. Edited by Dori Laub and Shoshanna Felman. Routledge, 1992, pp. 57–74.

Lawrence, Karen. "The Cypher: Disclosure and Reticence in *Villette*." *Nineteenth-Century Literature*, vol. 42, no. 4, 1988, pp. 448–66.

Laycock, Thomas. *An Treatise on the Nervous Diseases of Women; Comprising an Inquiry into the Nature, Causes, and Treatment of Spinal and Hysterical Disorders*. Longman, Orme, Brown, Green, and Longmans, 1840. Electronic access via Wellcome Library.

Lesjak, Carolyn. *Working Fictions: A Genealogy of the Victorian Novel*. Duke University Press, 2006.

Lewes, George Henry. "Psychological Principles" from *Problems of Life and Mind*. 1874–79. *Embodied Selves: An Anthology of Psychological Texts*, edited by Jenny Bourne Taylor and Sally Shuttleworth, Oxford University Press, 1998, pp. 89–91.

Lewis, Alexandra. "Being Human: De-Gendering Mental Anxiety; or Hysteria, Hypochondriasis, and Traumatic Memory in Charlotte Brontë's *Villette*." *The Brontës and the Idea of the Human: Science, Ethics, and the Victorian Imagination*, edited by Alexandra Lewis, Cambridge University Press, 2019, pp. 84–106.

Leys, Ruth. *Trauma: A Genealogy*. University of Chicago Press, 2000.

Lincoln, Margarette. "Shipwreck Narratives of the Eighteenth and Early Nineteenth Century: Indicators of Culture and Identity." *British Journal for Eighteenth-Century Studies*, vol. 20, 1997, pp. 155–72.

Logan, Peter Melville. *Nerves and Narratives: A Cultural History of Hysteria in Nineteenth-Century British Prose*. University of California Press, 1997.

Magee, Rhonda V. *The Inner Work of Racial Justice: Healing Ourselves and Transforming Our Communities through Mindfulness*. TarcherPerigree, 2019.

Maier, Sara E. "Portraits of the Girl-Child: Female *Bildungsroman* in Victorian Fiction." *Literature Compass*, vol. 4, no. 1, 2007, pp. 317–35.

Malane, Rachel. *Sex in Mind: The Gendered Brain in Nineteenth-Century Literature and Mental Sciences*. Peter Lang, 2005.

Mandel, Naomi. *Disappear Here: Violence after Generation X*. The Ohio State University Press, 2015.

Marcus, Sharon. *Between Women: Friendship, Desire, and Marriage in Victorian England*. Princeton University Press, 2007.

Martin, Daniel. "Wilkie Collins and Risk." *A Companion to Sensation Fiction*, edited by Pamela K. Gilbert, Wiley-Blackwell, 2011, pp. 184–95.

Matus, Jill. *Shock, Memory, and the Unconscious in Victorian Fiction*. Cambridge University Press, 2009.

———. "Trauma, Memory and Railway Disaster: The Dickensian Connection." *Victorian Studies*, vol. 43, no. 3, 2001, pp. 413–36.

Maudsley, Henry. *Body and Mind*. MacMillan and Co., 1870.

———. "Heredity in Health and Disease." *Fortnightly Review*, May 1886, pp. 648–59.

———. *The Physiology and Pathology of the Mind*. D. Appleton and Company, 1867.

Menakem, Resmaa. *My Grandmother's Hands: Racialized Trauma and the Pathway to Mending Our Hearts and Bodies*. Central Recovery Press, 2017.

Micale, Mark S. *Approaching Hysteria: Disease and Its Interpretations*, Princeton University Press, 1995.

Michie, Elsie. *The Vulgar Question of Money: Heiresses, Materialism, and the Novel of Manners*. The Johns Hopkins University Press, 2011.

Miller, D. A. *Narrative and Its Discontents: Problems of Closure in the Traditional Novel*. Princeton University Press, 1981.

Milne-Smith, Amy. "Work and Madness: Overworked Men and Fears of Degeneration, 1860s–1910s." *Journal of Victorian Culture*, vol. 24, no. 2, 2019, pp. 159–78.

Moglen, Helene. *Charlotte Brontë: The Self Conceived*. 1976. The University of Wisconsin Press, 1984.

———. *The Trauma of Gender: A Feminist Theory of the English Novel*. University of California Press, 2001.

Moretti, Franco. *The Way of the World: The Bildungsroman and European Culture*. 1987. Verso, 2000.

Mumm, Susan. "'Not Worse Than Other Girls': Convent-Based Rehabilitation of Fallen Women in Victorian Britain." *Journal of Social History*, vol. 23, no. 3, 1996, pp. 527–46.

Mystal, Elie. "I Am Not Ready to Reenter White Society." *The Nation*, 23 March 2021, https://www.thenation.com/article/society/after-covid-racism/.

Nead, Lynda. "Fallen Women and Foundlings: Rethinking Victorian Sexuality." *History Workshop Journal*, no. 82, 2016, pp. 177–87.

———. *Myths of Sexuality: Representations of Women in Victorian Britain*. Basil Blackwell Ltd., 1988.

Nemesvari, Richard. *Thomas Hardy, Sensationalism, and the Melodramatic Mode.* Palgrave Macmillan, 2011.

Newton, Judith Louder. *Women, Power, and Subversion: Social Strategies in British Fiction 1778–1860.* The University of Georgia Press, 1981.

"No Name." Masson, David (ed.). *The Reader,* Vol. 1, Iss. 1, (Jan 3, 1863), pp: 14–15.

[Oliphant, Margaret.] "Novels." Blackwood, John (ed.). *Blackwood's Edinburgh Magazine,* vol. 94, iss. 574, Aug 1863: pp. 168–83.

Oliver, Kelly. *The Colonization of Psychic Space: A Psychoanalytic Theory of Social Oppression.* University of Minnesota Press, 2004.

———. *Witnessing: Beyond Recognition.* University of Minnesota Press, 2001.

Oppenheim, Janet. *Shattered Nerves: Doctors, Patients, and Depression in Victorian England.* Oxford University Press, 1991.

Otis, Laura. *Banned Emotions: How Metaphors Can Shape What People Feel.* Oxford University Press, 2019.

Parkins, Wendy. *Mobility and Modernity in Women's Novels, 1850s–1930s.* Palgrave Macmillan, 2009.

Perry, Ruth. *Novel Relations: The Transformation of Kinship in English Literature and Culture 1748–1818.* Cambridge University Press, 2004.

Peschier, Diana. *Lost Souls: Women, Religion and Mental Illness in the Victorian Asylum.* Bloomsbury, 2020.

Prentiss, Norman D. "The Tortured Form of Jude the Obscure." *Colby Quarterly,* vol. 31, no. 3, 1995, pp. 179–93.

Price, Margaret. *Mad at School: Rhetorics of Mental Disability and Academic Life.* University of Michigan Press, 2011.

Prichard, James Cowles. *A Treatise on Insanity and Other Disorders Affecting the Mind.* Three Hundred Years of Psychiatry: 1535–1860, edited by Richard Hunter and Ida Macalpine, Oxford University Press, 1963, pp. 836–42.

Puar, Jasbir. *The Right to Maim: Debility/Capacity/Disability.* Duke University Press, 2017.

Punter, David. *The Literature of Terror: A History of Gothic Fictions from 1765 to the Present Day.* Longman, 1980.

Reimer, Margaret Loewen. "The Spoiled Child: What Happened to Gwendolen Harleth?" *The Cambridge Quarterly,* vol. 36, no. 1, 2007, pp. 33–50.

Robinson, A. Mary F. (Mme. Duclaux). "Neurasthenia." 1888.

Sadowsky, Jonathan. *The Empire of Depression: A New History.* Polity Press, 2021.

Schaffer, Talia. *Romance's Rival: Familiar Marriage in Victorian Fiction.* Oxford University Press, 2016.

———. "Why Lucy Doesn't Care: Migration and Emotional Labor in *Villette.*" *Novel,* vol. 52, no. 1, 2019, pp. 84–106.

———. "Victorian Feminist Criticism: Recovery Work and the Care Community." *Victorian Literature and Culture,* vol. 47, no. 1, pp. 63–91.

Sciarrino, Nicole A., et. al. "When Chaos Is the Norm: How Some Veterans with PTSD Are Continuing to Engage in Trauma-Focused Treatments during the COVID-19 Pandemic." *Psychological Trauma: Theory, Research, Practice, and Policy,* vol. 12, no. S1, 2020, S69–S70.

Sedgwick, Eve Kosofsky. *The Coherence of Gothic Conventions.* Methuen, 1986.

Shanley, Mary Lyndon. *Feminism, Marriage, and the Law in Victorian England, 1850–1895.* Princeton University Press, 1989.

Shorter, Edward. *A History of Psychiatry: From the Era of the Asylum to the Age of Prozac.* John Wiley and Sons, Inc., 1997.

Showalter, Elaine. *The Female Malady: Women, Madness, and English Culture, 1830–1980.* Pantheon Books, 1985.

Shuttleworth, Sally. *Charlotte Brontë and Victorian Psychology.* Cambridge University Press, 1996.

Silver, Brenda. "The Reflecting Reader in *Villette.*" *The Voyage In: Fictions of Female Development,* edited by Elizabeth Abel et al., University Press of New England, 1983, 90–111.

Smith, Roger. *Free Will and the Human Sciences in Britain, 1870–1910.* Pickering and Chatto, 2013.

———. *Inhibition: History and Meaning in the Sciences of Mind and Brain.* University of California Press, 1992.

Stevens, Jennifer S., and Tanja Jovanovic. "Role of Social Cognition in Post-Traumatic Stress Disorder: A Review and Meta-Analysis. *Genes, Brain, and Behavior,* September 2019, pp. 1–10.

Stević, Aleksandar. *Falling Short: The Bildungsroman and the Crisis of Self-Fashioning.* University of Virginia Press, 2020.

Stiles, Anne. "Victorian Literature and Neuroscience." *Literature Compass,* vol. 15, no. 2, 2018, pp. 1–8.

———. *Popular Fiction and Brain Science in the Late Nineteenth Century.* Cambridge University Press, 2012.

Swann, Mandy. "'The Destroying Angel of Tempest': The Sea in Villette." *Brontë Studies,* vol. 38, no. 2, 2013, pp. 145–56.

Taft, Matthew. "The Work of Love: *Great Expectations* and the English Bildungsroman." *Textual Practice,* vol. 34, no. 12, 2020, pp. 1969–88.

Taylor, Jenny Bourne. "Representing Illegitimacy in Victorian Culture." *Victorian Identities: Social and Cultural Formations in Nineteenth-Century Literature,* edited by Ruth Robbins and Julian Wolfreys, St. Martin's Press Inc., 1996, pp. 119–42.

Taylor, Jenny Bourne, and Sally Shuttleworth, editors. *Embodied Selves: An Anthology of Psychological Texts 1830–1890.* Clarendon Press, 1998.

Thierauf, Doreen. "Tending to Old Stories: *Daniel Deronda* and Hysteria, Revisited." *Victorian Literature and Culture,* vol. 46, 2018, pp. 443–65.

Tosh, John. *A Man's Place: Masculinity and the Middle-Class Home in Victorian England.* 1999. Yale University Press, 2007.

Tromp, Marlene. *The Private Rod: Marital Violence, Sensation, and the Law in Victorian Britain.* University of Virginia Press, 2000.

van der Kolk, Bessel. *The Body Keeps the Score: Brain, Mind, and Body in the Healing of Trauma.* Penguin, 2014.

van Wyhe, John. *Phrenology and the Origins of Victorian Scientific Naturalism.* Ashgate, 2004.

Vrettos, Athena. "From Neurosis to Narrative: The Private Life of Nerves in *Villette* and *Daniel Deronda.*" *Victorian Studies,* vol. 33, no. 4, 1990, pp. 551–79.

Wagner, Tamara. *Financial Speculation in Victorian Fiction.* The Ohio State University Press, 2010.

Williams, Anne. *Art of Darkness: A Poetics of Gothic.* University of Chicago Press, 1995.

Williams, Bernard. *Shame and Necessity.* University of California Press, 1993.

Woloch, Alex. "*Daniel Deronda:* Late Form, or after *Middlemarch.*" *A Companion to George Eliot,* edited by Amanda Anderson and Harry E. Shaw, Wiley Blackwell, 2013, pp. 166–77.

Wood, Jane. *Passion and Pathology in Victorian Fiction*. Oxford University Press, 2001.

"Wreck of the Birkenhead Troop Ship." *The Yorkshire Gazette* (York, England), issue 1721, Saturday 10 Apr. 1852, p. 3. *British Library Newspapers, Part IV: 1732–1950*. Accessed 29 Jan. 2019.

Wright, T. R. *Hardy and His Reviewers*. Palgrave Macmillan, 2003.

Yehuda, Rachel, and Linda Bierer. "The Relevance of Epigenetics to PTSD: Implications for the DSM-V. *Journal of Traumatic Stress*, vol. 22, no. 5, October 2009, pp. 427–34.

Young, Arlene. *Culture, Class and Gender in the Victorian Novel: Gentlemen, Gents, and Working Women*. Palgrave Macmillan, 1999.

INDEX

Brumberg, Joan Jacobs, 11

Burg, B. R., 71

Butler, Judith, 77

Capretto, Peter, 20

Carpenter, William Benjamin, 36–37

Carter, Robert Brudenell, 90

Caruth, Cathy, 25–29, 53, 74n17, 204–205

Charcot, Jean-Martin, 37, 194n16

Caste (Jolly), 87

chronic fatigue syndrome, 2

city life: Bildungsroman and, 180–84; nervous disorder and, 30–31, 166–67, 171–72, 184

Collins, Wilkie, 125; *The New Magdalen,* 106n15; *No Name,* 10, 18–19, 106n15, 118–20, 122–24, 129–37, 161–62; *The Woman in White,* 34–35, 45, 134

Combe, George, 60–61

Commemoration, 25, 26. *See also* memory

Cohen, Margaret, 70, 73

Cohn, Elisha, 58n8, 64n14, 73

Companies Acts (1856 and 1852), 119

COVID-19, 19, 20, 202–205

Cvetkovich, Ann, 26, 28, 51, 80, 121, 123n2, 135, 158

Dale, Peter Allan, 36

Daly, Nicholas, 119–21, 124–25, 128, 129n3

Dames, Nicholas, 59n10–11, 60, 63n14, 64, 66, 140

Daniel Deronda (Eliot), 10, 18, 118–20, 122–25, 129, 137–62

Darwin, Charles: influence on Thomas Hardy, 193n15, influence on psychiatry, 37–39

David Copperfield (Dickens), 7, 42, 99, 105–06, 176, 206

Davis, Lennard, 15

debility, 15–16

Dickens, Charles, 82, 85, 87n1; *Bleak House,* 106n15, 115, 164–5; *David Copperfield,* 7, 42, 99, 105–06, 176, 206; *Great Expectations,* 4, 7, 18–19, 163–66, 168, 173–79, 182–92, 199–200; *Oliver Twist,* 42, 168

disability: as field of scholarly study, 14–15; in relation to nervous disorder, 30–31

divorce, 119, 121

Divorce Law (1857), 121. *See also* Matrimonial Causes Act

Donald, James, 182

Dowse, Thomas Stretch, 171–72, 175, 189–90

dreams, 25–26, 34, 45–46, 67, 72–75, 76, 113, 148, 190

Dutheil, Frédéric, 20

East Lynne (Wood), 133–34

Ehnenn, Jill, 7, 179

Ellis, Havelock, 180–81

Ellis, Markman, 92

Eliot, George: *Adam Bede,* 99, 106n15, 142; *Daniel Deronda,* 10, 18, 118–120, 122–25, 129, 137–162; "The Lifted Veil," 144, 172–3; *Middlemarch,* 83, 117, 142; *The Mill on the Floss,* 142

emotion, 3–4, 32, 46, 70–71, 84, 95–96, 116, 121–22, 135, 160, 165–66, 173, 196, 205–6; regulation and dysregulation of, 33, 35, 44, 69, 86, 90–92, 96–97, 112–13, 142–45, 167, 170, 181, 187–89, 194–95; and traumatic experience, 13, 17–18, 21–22, 24, 38–40, 53, 74–76, 80, 127–28, 131, 134, 148–49, 153–55, 157, 196

epigenetics, 23

Erichsen, John Erik, 38–39

erotic desire, 18, 143, 177, 179, 181–82, 184, 194. *See also* "fallen women," sexuality

exercise, as medical treatment, 29, 33n1

"fallen women," 85, 99–110, 114–17, 150, 159. *See also* illegitimacy, rape, sexuality

Felman, Shoshanna, 25

femininity, 8, 87–89, 97, 121, 180; contradictory directives of, 43, 49; as irrationality and emotionality, 4, 32, 84; and nurture, 98; and self-denial, 45; as weakness or limitation, 91–92, 94, 106–7, 132, 162. *See also* "fallen women," feminization, gender, hysteria

feminization: through illegitimacy, 157, 159; through nervous sensitivity or disorder, 9, 172, 175

Ferguson, Frances, 94n10

Foucault, Michel, 44n5, 51

Frawley, Maria, 30